# Fogg of War

## Book II

# *Assault on Carillon*

# *1758*

### Rolland A. Miner

**ISBN #978-1-4303-0181-3**

*This book is dedicated to*
*Eleanor Murray and Harrison Bird.*
*Thanks for everything.  Sorry it took so long.*

A great many people have contributed over the years to the experiences that made it possible for me to write this series of books.  Two people, in particular, contributed to the writing of this particular book.

First and foremost is my wife and best friend, Gigi L. Miner, who encouraged me to actually write it instead of just thinking about it.  She kept me on task, corrected my atrocious spelling and grammar plus did the final editing and formatting.  All this while working on her own books and projects.

Secondly, I would like to thank my friend, Tom Nesbitt, who lent his years of 18th century military study to this endeavor. Some of Tom's experience comes from being an 18th century living history enthusiast for thirty-five years, working as a researcher on projects like the National Park Service's Military Road from Ft. Edward to Lake George Project, and working for the NYS Parks at Crown Point, NY on special events and interpretation.  Tom is presently the Secretary for the NYS French and Indian War 250th Anniversary Commission.  Two other items made Tom a good source for my project. He grew up in the region between Fort Edward and Lake George and has thirty plus years experience as a licensed surveyor.  His geographical knowledge of the area both today and in the 18th century was invaluable.

# Prolog

It was July of 1803 and all of the gossip in the coffee-houses was about the Corsican and his thrashing of the Austrians in Italy. Everywhere one goes in the Holborn district, no in all of London, it is the topic of conversation. As the gentleman walked along Gate Street back toward his rooms next door to the Ship Tavern, he heard words of the French on every lip, in between the solicitations of the hawkers. When he reached the corner where Turnstile and Gate meet, he stopped for a moment in front of The Ship, thinking he might drop in to hear some more of the latest but decided against it. He would be going back there this evening for refreshment and conviviality. Living next door to The Ship was a good place for the son of a woman whose husband had passed away just two months before his birth.

The mid-afternoon light, filtering through the drapes, which covered the windows of the second floor flat, was barely enough to illuminate the room. It was a study-sitting room with shelves that covered the three walls without windows. The shelves were overly full of books and portfolios covering a multitude of subjects. There were books on alchemy, astrology, chemical science, botany, engineering, works of great authors and a great many books on law. There were books written in English, French, German, Latin, Greek and Arabic. At first glance, one would have supposed that this library belonged to a solicitor but, a closer examination would have proved different. Here was a library that would have caused many a scholar, nay many a school of the military arts, to turn green with envy. The shelves were full of the works of all of the well-known and not so well known authors of military treatises. Here one could find Sun Tzu sitting next to Vegetius, Ceaser and Sulla, all in the Latin section of the shelves. In with the works written in French were Vaubin, Saxe and Frederick the Great. The English section included Bland, Stevenson, Fawcett and others. Poor Machiavelli sat off all by himself, the only Italian in the whole library.

The entire library was arranged, strangely enough, by language not by subject. It was this scheme that made the library appear unorganized. Obviously, its owner had not arranged it for the convenience of browsers or borrowers. In two corners of the room were rolled up maps and military engineering drawings from all over the civilized and not so civilized parts of the world. It would seem, from a much more scrutinizing search of the shelves, that the occupant of these rooms was not a solicitor but a student of military history. The room itself had an air of restfulness and quiet in spite of the majority of the subject matter in the library's contents. The only sounds were coming from a John Harrison clock on the mantel of the fireplace and the muffled sounds from the busy street below.

The tranquility of the room, and indeed the rooms, is broken by the chirp of an over weight tortoise shell cat who had been asleep in one of the two wing back chairs, which occupied either side of the fireplace. Her keen hearing heard the turning of the key in the lock on the door to the rooms and was her signal to vacate the chair and stroll to the hallway to greet the human who shares her rooms and should be bringing home her milk. After all, it had been quite some time, at least a couple of human hours, since she had heard the familiar sound of the dairymaid as she had stopped in the street below and had conversed with the elderly female human who cleaned and managed the rooms that she, the cat, shared with her human companion.

The man who entered the flat was dressed modestly in the fashion of the times, not garishly like some tended to do. His suit was dark gray wool, neatly brushed with the waistcoat matching the suit. Upon his head, he wore one of the plug-type hats so popular these days. He carried in his hands a growler, the prize the cat was looking for, a black thorn walking stick with a brass ferule and shoe cap, and a copy of the London Chronicle. He was of normal height and build with dark sandy colored hair. Nothing about him made him stand out from any of the hundreds of other gentlemen in London who would appear to be close to his age, except perhaps his eyes, which were grey and looked much older than the man. If asked, one would guess him to be in his late thirties, maybe even early forties. He threw his cloak, which he was carrying over his arm, and hat and gloves onto a chair that sat in the hallway. The walking stick went into a rack by the door amid the other dozen that filled it.

Addressing the cat, who is beside herself with anticipation, "Well, Puss, are you glad to see me or would it be just the milk you're glad to see?"

This comment brought forth another chirp and a great deal of leg rubbing on the part of Puss, just to convince him that she was glad to see him until he poured the milk in her dish. After ten years, she knew that when he made that "pssssss" sound he was trying to communicate with her. Poor humans, they did not feel her moods as

2

she felt theirs. He removed the cover from the growler and poured half the contents into a good-sized bowl, which sat on the floor for Puss. As he did, he mused to himself that he had lived with this cat for ten years and had never thought of a better name than Puss.

After having taken care of the cat, the man went into his library and opened one of the drapes to allow in a bit more sunlight. Having done this, he plopped himself into the chair whose back was to the window and picked up the newspaper. The letter that he had stuck into the paper on the way up the stairs fell out into his lap. He picked it up and read the front once more, Mr. E. Fogg, Esq., that was all, nothing to say whence it had came except for the seal on the back. No mistaking that seal.

"Plenty of time for you after I read the latest news and sailings.", said the man once more aloud. Puss hearing his voice looked around the corner of the door, seeing no one but the man, and not hearing the "psssss" sound went back to her milk. The human was communicating with himself again as he often did; very strange behavior indeed.

Fogg, as we now know the man's name to be, was intent upon the main article of the paper; indeed the central conversation of the coffee and business houses these past two weeks in 1803 since Great Britain had declared war on France, more exactly on the Corsican.

"You French are at it again in this century. Didn't you learn anything in the last century?" once more aloud to himself. This time the cat completely ignored him. Obviously, he was off on one of those days of self-communication.

**Chapter 1**

Fogg mulled over the words that he had just spoken to himself and as he did his thoughts drifted back to that time in the last century when the French had challenged England, or maybe it was vice versa, for the control of North America. The year was 1758 and Fogg's circumstances had found him in New York. He had sailed to North America to personally see to that end of a business venture in which he was involved and also at the request of his sometime employer. Having taken care of that, and establishing his North American accounts with another counting house, he was at large to explore this busy metropolis of the New World; perhaps he might even travel to Boston and Philadelphia, the other two large cities, time permitting.

He had secured lodgings in an inn just off Princess Street and across Broad Way Street from Beaver Street where his business partner's establishment was situated. He decided to walk down Beaver so as to observe the other counting houses and businesses that lined it. One never knew when or what opportunity would arise to invest and this city had the promise of becoming a prominent trade center. Fogg's trip from the ocean, up the great harbor provided by the Hudson and East rivers, had convinced him of that. The two, fortified islands in the harbor, plus the fort at the point where the two rivers converged into the bay, meant that it was not only a safe harbor from the weather but also from man-made problems. The English had strengthened the batteries in all three places so as not to be caught napping as they had caught the Dutch.

He decided that the battery on the point would be a good place to start, so he continued on Beaver until he came to the corner of Broad Way Street. Here was located the old Dutch Bowling Green, where the remaining Dutch gentlemen could be seen during good weather, "kegilin" on the bowling lane as they referred to it. From the Green it was possible to look up Broad Way Street for quite a distance, almost up to the area called King's Farm.

As he approached the landside of the fort, he expected the two sentries posted there to challenge him. From their facings, they were from one of the 35th Foot hat companies. Instead, they simply came to attention and let him pass as it was obvious, in their opinion, that he was an English gentleman and maybe even an officer in civilian clothes, so best not to irk him. Inside, the fort was bustling with activity. There were fatigue parties from several other regiments busy unloading wagons of what appeared to be all sorts of military stores with the exception of powder. All of the powder, except that for immediate defense of the fort, was magazined at the Powder House situated above the Wall and on a narrow spit of land between two parts of the Fresh Water Lake.

Fogg stood watching all of this, amazed that no one even questioned why this civilian was standing in the middle of an English fort, counting boxes and barrels of things being stored. Had it been a foreign fort he would not have been as obvious as to what he was doing. In his sometime other profession one did not act so careless if one wanted to continue in that profession or continue at all. He even thought about speaking out-loud to himself in French, just to see if he would attract any attention but thought better of it.

Fogg's senses made him aware of the person approaching him from behind long before the person announced himself. Fogg had partially turned and was looking over his shoulder as the man spoke.

"I say there, my good fellow, might I be of some assistance to you."

To which Fogg replied, "Actually yes. I am recently arrived from home and having finished my business, for the moment, am on a little exploratory stroll of this unique little city."

"Ahaa! Quite the good thing our paths have chanced to cross. What? You see this quiet little New World town has inherited all of the bad traits and habits of the Old World. Like London, pickpockets, purse snatches, foot-pads, press gangs and the like abound here. Day time is safe enough but best to be off the streets at night unless with an armed guard. Even at that, just a fortnight ago, the watch was beset by a band of foot-pads seeking to overpower them and make off with their arms and accoutrements, maybe even sell them to some press gang.", lamented the gentleman.

Fogg inquired, "Perhaps you could direct me on a short route which would afford me a view of most of this charming place?"

"Better than that, my good fellow, I will conduct you my self, if you like. I was just going up into the town to procure some personal items, but it can wait until later or my orderly can fetch them. This is, of course, unless you would prefer to be left alone."

"No, no, not at all, splendid idea," was Fogg's reply, "but only if you will allow me to be your host for supper at what would pass as this town's best dining establishment."

"A fair enough exchange, my good fellow, a fair enough exchange. Please, allow me to introduce myself, Captain Robert Gris of the 80th Lightly Armed Foot, also known as Gage's Light Infantry after our colonel, Colonel Thomas Gage, late of the 44th Foot." All of this was accomplished with a flourish, stage bow and a large smile.

"Fogg, E. Fogg of London at your service and a pleasure to make your acquaintance." Said Fogg, returning the bow.

Gris raised an eyebrow and asked, "No first name? Just E.?"

"I seldom use my first name, except in business, as I believe my parents thought it to be more poetic than practical. No, my friends simply refer to me as Fogg." It was true that he seldom used his first name, Ethyrial, as most people seemed to think that he was playing a joke on them.

"Than Fogg and Gris it shall be. Gris Fogg. What? Devilish good, I should think. Let us be off on our New York Town adventure! We will draw us a couple of horses from the stable here at the Battery and I can have my orderly return them when we are finished. We will be able to cover more of this island mounted."

They walked over to the stable where a sergeant had a small fatigue party mucking out the stalls. The horses were all picketed outside and had just been groomed. The horses in this stable were mostly for the use of officers and an occasional dispatch rider who was only delivering in the city. Gris informed the sergeant that they would require two horses immediately for the rest of the day. The sergeant looked at Fogg suspiciously wondering what this civilian was doing riding an army horse but he wasn't about to question Gris, who he knew to be a Captain of regulars, despite his odd uniform.

"Yes Sir! Captain Gris, they'll be ready in two shakes of a lamb's tail. Har! You there! Drop that fork and get these two chestnuts ready for the officer and the gentleman. Be quick about it or you'll be mucking out the ox stalls next sodden fatigue party, you will." bellowed the sergeant. "Beggin your pardon, Sirs.", in a slightly mellower tone. "These former inhabitants of Old Start don't understand please and thank you, so's you have to talk at them in language they understand. Skulkers all."

Once their mounts were ready, they were off on the first leg of their journey. Gris thought that they might go out the Water Gate and cut along Pearl Street where he pointed out to Fogg some of the original thirty still standing Dutch-plank houses that were built there just over a hundred years ago. They continued along east to Dock Street until it became Queen Street, which they followed up until they reached the palisade or, as it was referred to, the Wall. On the way, Gris pointed out various landmarks such as the different slips and quays as they were moving parallel to the East River. On the other side, they could see the Wallabout and the ferry from Peck's slip, which was crossing. Gris pointed out that the Long Island went almost 200 English miles east and that the Dutch had some large farms on it. One of the largest was the Rapalje farm that could be seen where the ferry was headed for as the landing was there. The site was easy to spot because of its large Dutch-style barns.

While riding Fogg asked, "Gris, allow me to inquire as to your uniform. You say you are with the 80th Lightly Armed Foot but the brown of your uniform would lead one to belief it was provincial. Not doubting you, just curious."

"Ah yes, does throw one off. You see the 80th is a new regiment, raised by Colonel Gage to help fill the gap between the regulars and the ranging companies. The Frenchies have a great many partisans, what with all of their militia, bush runners and their savages. Their largest regiment in North America is La Marine. Most of the members have lived in Canada all their lives and are in some cases more native than their native allies are. Colonel Gage, who was with General Braddock, learned a lesson from the drubbing they took that day. The 80th is dressed and equipped to fight toe to toe with the French partisans. It is a rumor that we will soon start going out on patrol with the independent ranging companies with half of the patrol made up of Light Infantry. Some even think that some day we will replace the rangers but myself I think we will always need some."

Fogg mulled over Gris' reply for a moment and then asked, "What about the provincials? What is their position in all this? After all it is their homes, farms and businesses that are threatened by this. Where do they stand and will they fight? Will their assemblies contribute to the up coming campaign?"

"Yes, I believe that they will fight and contribute men at least. As for funds and supplies, I am not sure if they have the where-with-all to do so. What do you know about the up coming campaign?" asked Gris wearily.

Fogg's reply was as off handed as he could manage. "It is getting to be campaign season; there are lots of supplies being unloaded at the wharfs and stored in the warehouses. There are many troop transports sitting at anchor in the harbor and both rivers with troops still on board."

"You are very observant of military items ..." Gris replied, "for a civilian business man."

*And you are very astute for an ordinary soldier. I will need to be slightly more cautious until I get to know you better,* thought Fogg.

7

Out loud his answer was, "It comes from having interests in the shipping business and all that. What street is this we are on now?" They had turned off of Queen Street one block back.

"This is Water Street. We will stay on it up to the end and cut through one of the alleys up to where the High Boston Road meets it. From there we can skirt around the Delancy property and pick up the Bowery Lane to get back into the town proper. An alternative would be to cross through the meadows until we pick up the Greenwich Street Road and go back into the town on the west side. What think you, Mr. Fogg?"

Fogg gathered from Gris' statement that above the Wall the land was very open and mostly farms or estates, most likely the latter. The upper part of the town was not as crowed as lower but contained more manufacturing than below. Where they were now passing was just northeast of the Tan Yards and west of the shipyards. Where they finally broke out of the narrow confines of the alley was the beginning of the Rope Walks to supply the shipyards that lay just below them on the East River. The remainder of the ride was filled with observations by Fogg and bits and pieces of local information by Gris. Fogg learned that Delancy was one of the richest men in New York; maybe even the colonies and his daughters were the subject of much attention from all the young English officers. This was rightly deserved for their charm, beauty and poise and not just because of their fathers' station in life. Fogg's only comment on that subject was to himself. *When you are far from home, all young ladies appear to be the most beautiful and desirous in the whole world. Of course to young, second-son officers a large inheritance does not hurt the cause either.*

Out loud he asked, "Does this include yourself?"

"I am afraid that a newly commissioned Captain, like myself does not quite fit into those circles. Besides I am not sure that I would like to be involved under those circumstances. The girls' parents always thinking in the back of their minds that you are just there for the money."

"You, my young friend, are wise for your years. It most surely would not be a good arrangement. Let us get us past the Delancy residence before some mishap of the heart befalls us both!" laughed Fogg.

"Right you are, by all means let us fly!" and with that Gris kicked up his horse and they went galloping past the Delancy estate on the south side across Bullock Road. As they traversed the road, their horses' hooves raised a cloud of dust that was observed from the house by several of the occupants, including the young lady who was the subject of the previous discussion.

The remainder of the excursion was without incident. They went across the island to the west side and rode down a ways toward the Negro's Burial Ground and Kings Garden Ward below that on the south side of the Wall. They went down as far as the Oswego Market area and then cut back northeast by the Commons. Gris said that there was a tavern up there, The Green Bay Tree, that had decent food and they could trust the tavern keeper to treat them well, just as if they were his brothers. When they arrived at the tavern, which was just off of Broad Way Street on Fair Street, a boy took their horses and put them around back, greeting Captain Gris with a great deal of politeness. Hopkins, the tavern keeper, was a man only in his mid thirties, but everyone called him "Daddy". When Gris and Fogg walked into the tavern, he came out from behind the bar, greeted them, and shook hands with Gris, remarking that it had been a while since he had visited The Green Bay.

Gris introduced Daddy to Fogg, saying, "This is my new acquaintance Mr. E. Fogg, recently arrived in New York."

"Oh, then welcome Mr. Fogg. Have you been traveling long?" This surprised Fogg for a moment but feeling Daddy Hopkins grip upon his hand, he replied that under the circumstance he had.

"Then I insist you two gentlemen go up to the private dinning area so that no one may disturb you. There is a fire lit up there as the upper chamber is going to be in use this evening. If you leave your cloaks and hats I will have the boy brush them and then bring them upstairs." They went up to the second floor where there was a room about three quarters the size of the common room downstairs, but much better appointed. There were heavy drapes on the windows and a couple of large settles on both sides of the fireplaces, which were at either ends of the room, with cushions. There was also a side table with bottles, decanters and various glasses upon it.

"What will it be Mr. Fogg? Wine, brandy, rum?"

"I believe a glass of brandy would go well, Brother Gris."

"Then brandy it is, Brother Fogg, brandy it is!"

"How did you know I was a Freemason? I never said or gave any indication," inquired Fogg.

"Actually I did not. I assumed because you are obviously a gentleman and an inhabitant of London that you might be a Mason. So, I let Brother Hopkins test you as he does every gentleman who enters his establishment. He is fussy who frequents the place and he does not encourage the riff-raff to stay. His prices are a little higher than most so that alone helps keep the clientele at a certain level.

Tonight is a Lodge night so supper should be served in about an hour. Of course, as a traveling Brother you are my guest but also since you are 'from home' we shall expect you to stand a round of the refreshment. What?"

"It will be my pleasure, Brother Gris. If I may be so bold as to inquire the name of the Lodge?"

"It is St. Johns Number two hundred seventy-two. It is not as elaborately appointed as some of the Lodges in the bigger cities at home but is equal to some of the less urban Lodges in the smaller cities."

"I had heard that there were possibly some traveling military lodges here in North America. Do you know of any?" Gris replied that he was not sure, but that he would make inquiries when he got up river. To which Fogg indicated that he might just be going upriver himself. He ventured that perhaps he might be able to do a little business in Albany and that he had a desire to see as much of this part of North America as possible. *There are people at home who want to know why this part of the war is dragging its feet. They want to know if James Abercromby is the right man to handle this campaign or should more authority be given to George Howe or is this exactly the right balance. Abercromby may be a General but Howe is a Viscount, related to the King and therefore not easily intimidated.* Fogg had to see all this for himself in order to be able to report to his employer accurately.

Gris' reply to the statement that he, Fogg, maybe going up river was one of enthusiasm. It was a long way from Manhattan Island to Albany and Fogg was turning out to be a good traveling companion. After passing an evening of good fellowship and an excellent meal, Gris and Fogg rode back down to where Fogg had his rooms and Gris went on to his billet with the two horses. They spent some time during the next couple of days doing more exploring and getting ready for their trip up river. Their last day on Manhattan they rode as far north up the High Road to Boston as they could without leaving the island of Manhattan. They had a pleasant meal at the Bronck farm before turning back to make their way down what was once the Lumber Road that turned into a maze of other streets after you crossed through the Palisade but eventually became Lumber Street once more.

## Chapter 2

Fogg and Gris boarded one of the small sloops, at the Albany pier, designed for plying the river and rode the tide up as far as Tappan's Sea, about thirty English miles above New York. The majority of their baggage had been loaded on one of the regular military transports to be brought up to Albany. The winds being favorable and the tide still running, they managed to get up as far as Windsor on the west bank, the sloop's master not being willing to take them to the military pier on the east side due to the tide changing but more likely due to wanting to avoid being looked over too closely. The main trade of most of these river Captains was the illegal transportation of tax-free goods.

Fogg and his companion were able to procure a meal and arrange for a small boat to carry them across the river. From there they took a ride on one of the supply wagons to Viskill where there was a temporary military depot that served as a mount and dray animal relay. Military stores were being sent up to Albany both by ship and by supply trains. One of the largest commodities being shipped up river by wagon was hay and other fodder for the dray animals. The army sat at the northern end of the Hudson River so long that the foraging for hay and such had all but depleted the local area. The farmers had refused to bring in any more lest they should starve their own animals. A great deal of the hay now in use by the army was coming from Long Island, across the sound and up through the Province of Connecticut and over to the Lower Hudson road going north. Armies do not move without supplies, supplies do not move without wagons, wagons do not move without horses or oxen and horses and oxen do not move with out forage, fresh or otherwise.

After staying the night in a laboratory tent that also served as a traveling officers' quarters and a half-way decent breakfast cooked by one of the NCOs' wives, they proceeded up the military road, actually the only road even partially worthy of the designation. The orderly had brought round two decent mounts with rations to last a couple of days if necessary. Fogg and Gris had carried along their own personal equipment and arms. In addition to a customized artillery carbine, that Gris carried, in the saddle boots were two double-barreled, smoothbore pistols of the type popular with officers for hunting small game, which he had loaded with swan shot that morning. He also carried in the frog of his accoutrement belt a small tomahawk and bayonet fitted for his carbine, which he had re-lugged to accommodate it. Fogg had placed his two dragoon pistols in the saddle boots and carried his usual pocket pistol in the special pocket that he always had his tailor fit in the left breast of his coats back just under his arm. His fusil was slung loosely on his back and in addition he carried his dirk high up on his left hip, not in the usual highland fashion and had a skein dubgh stuck into the top of his right boot cover. It was obvious to any on-lookers that the pair were not a couple of recently come to North America fops, despite the quality of their clothing.

As both were accomplished horsemen, their goal was to reach Statsburgh about twenty-five English Miles up river, stay overnight and push on to Kinderhook, another twenty-five EM the following day. This would put them only ten or fifteen EM or so from the large camps at Greenbush and Fort Crailo at Rensselaerwyck. The first day was without incident and they made Statsburgh by mid-day. Gris met an officer of the 44th Foot of his acquaintance there who was on his way down river to arrange for more wagons with drovers to move supplies north, up to Greenbush. He graciously offered them the use of his marquis and orderly in his absence. They slept that night well fed and sheltered, which was fortunate indeed as it commenced to rain in early evening and continued until daylight. After a hearty breakfast, our travelers got off to a late start but with enough time to make Kinderhook by mid to late afternoon.

Fogg and Gris had passed through Rinbeck, a little settlement about five miles from Statsburgh, when they caught up to a supply train that had departed a few hours before them. Their own progress up the road had not been hindered greatly by the rain as they had ridden along the sides of the track where there was a little grass. They had noticed that the center part of the road, if you would call it that, was greatly chewed up by wagons drawn by both horse and oxen.

The train, which consisted of twenty or so wagons and should have been stretched out for at least an eighth of a mile, was bunched up in less than a hundred or so yards. Apparently, when the train had started out the horse drawn wagons had been in front so that they would not be slowed down by the oxen. This had worked until they came to the present stretch of road what was a gradual incline and the roadway had acted like a drain for the great amount of rain that had fallen over night. The horse-drawn wagons had become bogged down and some of the oxen drovers had attempted to pass by on both

12

sides and had become bogged down. A company of the 46th Foot accompanied all of this. Their Captain had gone on ahead with the senior lieutenant and had left the junior lieutenant and the ensign in charge of the detail. The officers, determined to prove their ability to handle the situation, had incurred the wrath of the provincial drovers who now refused to cooperate and had all gathered off to one side and were smoking and discussing the possibility of sitting here until it dried out. After all, the wagons were full of provisions and they were entitled to a day's ration for each day on the road.

When Fogg and Gris approached the train, they inquired from the rear guard of the whereabouts of the officers.

The corporal in charge of the guard, supposing that Gris was a provincial officer from his brown uniform, answered in a surly tone, "I don't know where the sodden officers are. They's mostly up front where it be dry and if you wants them, you best be going up there to look. We're regulars and we don't do any fetch'n for no sodden provincials."

"And what would be your name, soldier?" replied Mr. Gris, politely.

"It's Corporal Weed of the 46th Foot. What be your name, Mr. Doodle?" amid snickers from the soldiers in his guard.

Gris answered, again politely, "Why no, my good-fellow, it is not Mr. Doodle. Actually it is Captain Gris, of the 80th Lightly Armed Foot, and you will stand in the position of most attention when I am speaking to you." The reaction that this simple statement brought showed that these were indeed veteran regulars as the entire guard came to position of most attention, facing the mounted officer. "Now would you care to rethink your answer to my question, Corporal?"

"Beggin your pardon, Captain, Sir! I, we thought from your uniform that you was a doodle, I means a provincial," stammered the corporal. It was a flogging offense to address a regular officer the way that he had.

"That is understandable, Corporal and we shall put the whole incident behind us. Simply direct me to where I may find your officers and we will fetch them ourselves," replied Gris, still calmly.

"Sir! You should find Lieutenant Grice and Ensign O'Neil over where them drovers are, trying to get'em to go back to their wagons, Sir!"

Gris wheeled his horse toward the cluster of drovers and then turned back and trotted to Corporal Weed. He was still standing at the position of most attention when addressing an officer under arms and leaned over and quietly said to him, "Corporal Weed, if ever I hear you address a provincial officer in such a manner as you first addressed me, I will have you brought to the halberds and see that you get the full amount. Do you understand my drift?"

"Sir! That I indeed do, Sir!" replied Weed, now speaking in a slightly calmer voice, realizing that this was a good officer but not one with which to be trifled.

"Good, now when the 46th gets to Lake George, you come look up the 80th and we will see what we can do to get you out of that bright crimson uniform and into a decent brown one, where the action will suit your temperament." And, after a slight pause, "Perhaps we can even see about getting you a red worsted sash to go with it."

"Sir! Indeed I will. Sir!" barked back Corporal Weed, realizing what the good Captain had just said to him.

"Oh, yes, one more thing, remember it is Captain Gris." He wheeled his horse once more and trotted over to where Fogg sat.

"Sir! After this morning, I swear that I'll not forget your name. Sir!" Corporal Weed called after the withdrawing Captain Gris.

Turning back to his squad, "Look alive there, me boys. That gentleman is a soldier's officer."

Fogg, who had only been observing this little vignette, made a mental note that Mr. Gris had the makings of becoming a soldier's soldier, one whom his men would follow without hesitation. He had allowed Corporal Weed to correct his mistake, an act that most officers in the army at the time would not have done. They would have had Weed put under guard and dragged to the halberds at the first opportune time. Captain Robert Gris was one of the new breed of officers that were slowly developing in the English Army. They were using their heads to control their men and not the cat. Instilling a sense of worth and trust between private men and their officers would deliver great dividends in the end.

Fogg followed Gris up through the hodge-podge of wagons, horses, and oxen, to a little grassy clearing along side the road where all of the drovers were congregated. Gris, still sitting his horse, used it to nudge his way into the edge of the group, which was having its own discussion and not listening to the two regular officers who were trying to get them back to their wagons. Gris calmly reached into his pistol boot and drew out one of the double barrels he was carrying there and discharged it into the air. The effect was immediate as all heads turned toward him and fell silent as they realized it was a double barrel.

"Now gentlemen and good fellows, what seems to be the difficulty here?" whereupon they all started to talk at once. Gris pointed his pistol at the drover who seemed to be in charge and was making the most noise. "You, what is your name and station in life?" inquired Gris.

"I am Johanas Eisenbarth, Meister Vaggoner, from the Mohawk Valley and in the New York Provincial Regiment and who might you be?" Gris' reply made Fogg chuckle to himself. He had slipped his hand inside of the pistol boot on the off side of his horse ready for more difficulty, if necessary.

"Well, Vagon Meister Johanas Eisenbarth, I am the fellow who is pointing a pistol, loaded with swan shot at you and asking the questions." Everyone standing around the drover suddenly decided it was better perhaps to stand somewhere else. Swan-shot squares, cut from sheet lead might not kill you outright but would certainly cut you up to the point where you would most likely die from blood poisoning or the surgeon's administration, medicine being what it was. The two regular officers were too dumbfounded by the recent turn of events to react so they were still standing in the blast cone. It took them a few seconds to slowly step back a little.

"Rights you are Sir and what would you to know?" replied the Palatine drover, his accent getting thicker the longer the pistol was pointed at him.

"I would like to know why you are all clustered about here and not doing something about clearing up this situation. There were more wagons getting ready to depart Statsburgh when we left and they should be close upon our heels shortly."

"Well Sir, these English officers told us to pass the bogged down horses and we warned them that the side of the track couldn't hold the wagon loads but they weren't listening. We are all New York Provincial Regiment so they threatened us with the punishment if we didn't do as ordered. We ain't got no officer of our own with us to stand-up for us. You look like you might be a provincial officer what with the brown uniform and the other gentleman in his gray clothes." With this the lieutenant spoke up, realizing that the two men might indeed be provincial officers in some sort of undress uniforms, not highwayman as he first thought, and could be an answer to his problem. His Captain was not going to be too pleased with him as it were and he could only blame so much of it on Ensign O'Neil.

"Yes, my good fellow, can you give us some assistance here?"

Gris turned to Fogg and smiled. "What do you think, Mr. Fogg? Should we pitch in and help sort out this muck up?"

"By all means, Mr. Gris, else we will never, in good consciousness, get up this track today." Gris turned back to the group, replacing his pistol to the boot.

"Yes, and you are Lieutenant Grice and Ensign O'Neil, I presume?"

"Yes, yes, now let us get on with it. What do you propose? Mr. Gris, is it?" sniped the Lieutenant having gained some of his lost composure and assumed the attitude of most regular English officers toward Provincials.

"Yes, my companion is Mr. E. Fogg, a gentleman volunteer on his way up to Albany and Lake George and I am Mr. R. Gris ..." a pause, "Captain in the 80th Foot under the command of Colonel Gage." Both officers straightened up under the gaze of what proved to be a superior officer and a gentleman who obviously had connections with the powers that be.

"Sir! Begging your pardon but we had no way of knowing, what with your wearing civilian cloths and all." Gris just shrugged it off, if he had to explain his brown uniform to every nose in the air regular that they met, it would take all month to reach Lake George. He turned to Fogg and asked what he thought might be the best place to start. Fogg sat for a moment and looked up and down the track, thinking. There was an entire company of regulars sitting about doing nothing and certainly enough dray animals.

"Well, Captain Gris, I think that your earlier suggestion about unhooking the horse teams and replacing them with oxen double paired might start to solve the problem." He had a grin upon his face. It would not do to let Gris' image sink in the eyes of all the regulars and the provincial, for that matter.

"Why thank you Mr. Fogg." Gris was quick on the uptake, "that had slipped my mind altogether. All right, Master Waggoner, get your men to unhitching the horses. Lieutenant Grice, you will send your regulars up to the top of the incline, where they will form a place to secure the horse teams as the drovers bring them up. Master Waggoner, as soon as the first team of horses is unhitched get a double pair of oxen on to that wagon. Tie up the wagon tongue. Next hitch up the oxen in a fan, with a strong line from each yoke back to the wagon. Understood?" Both parties answered in the affirmative and soon everyone was hard at work.

Gris turned to Fogg and said, "Thank you Mr. Fogg, you are indeed a gentleman."

"It was indeed my pleasure, Captain Gris, my pleasure. I thought that the Master Waggoner was going to soil his britches when you pointed your pistol at him. Well, where would you like me to assist?" inquired Fogg.

"I should think that if you might place yourself at the top of the incline, you would have a grand view in both directions. Let me know if you see either the other wagons or the senior officer of this group approaching."

By the time that Fogg arrived at the top of the hill most of the regulars were up and preparing to make some sort of temporary way of containing the horses. Fogg singled out one of the senior sergeants and suggested that they might use the hobbles that hung on each horse's harness to hobble them and they would be fine. The drovers were already bringing the first three teams of horses up. Each team had a drover mounted on the off lead horse and the horses, glad to be rid of the wagon, were trotting up the incline. Fogg could see that the Master Waggoner had already moved two pairs of oxen in front of the first wagon and that his men were in the process of fastening the leads to the wagon. Within fifteen minutes after Gris had started his work parties the first bogged down wagon was sitting on the top of the incline and the second was on the way up to the top. When half of the wagons were up on top of the incline, Captain Gris came up and drew up next to Fogg.

"What do you think, Fogg, shall we be on our way?" Fogg looked over the situation. The wagons with horse teams had been re-hitched and were waiting for orders to move out.

"I should think that Lieutenant Grice ought to start the lead wagons out if he wants to make Lithgow by mid-afternoon and Claverack by evening. I would also guess that you and I will, or at least should, meet his Captain somewhere along the track."

"He is coming up now, so I shall put a little suggestion in his ear, and thence we shall be off," replied Gris as he trotted off to meet the Lieutenant.

Fogg sat watching the Provincial drovers. *These people are better disciplined than they appear, when given the proper guidance. They know the terrain and can read it. If those two snot-nosed officers had listened to them, they would be halfway to Lithgow by now instead of bogged down on this incline. I believe that Gris' assessment that they will fight is a good one. It seems to me that the only victory so far in this war in North America was won by provincials under Sir William Johnson, the only American Baronet and now Commissioner of Indian Affairs. I hope that I will have occasion to meet this Irishman. I believe I can learn much of North America from him.* Soon Gris was back and they set off up the track toward Lithgow.

They met only a small train of wagons returning down the track manned only by the drovers and a squad of Yorkers. Gris inquired if they had seen a regular Captain along their route but the answer was negative. When they reached Lithgow, they inquired of the sergeant in charge of the depot if he had seen the Captain pass by.

"Indeed I did Sir. He exchanged horses as he intended to reach Kinderhook by late afternoon. They had been riding their mounts hard they had Sir."

"They?" inquired Gris. "Who was accompanying him?"

"There was a Lieutenant and two civilians with him, Sir. The civilians looked like gentlemen to me, Sir, but they never said a word. I heard the Captain speak to one of them but it wasn't in the King's English. No, Sir, it was not." The sergeant gave a knowing nod of his head when he said the last part. Gris became concerned with that statement.

"Can you give us two fresh mounts with rations for the horses and where can we grab a quick bite for ourselves? Also, Sergeant, how long ago did they depart?"

The sergeant indicated that the other party was about an hour ahead of them and he directed them to where there was a mess kitchen set up and sent along a private to tell the mess NCO to take care of the Captain and his party. He assured them he would have good, fresh mounts ready when they came back. When they had gotten out of reach of the men Gris confided in Fogg.

"I do not like the thought of a regular officer who might know of the coming campaign in company of two men who do not speak English. They could very well be Dutch and the Captain might have been speaking German to them. I propose that we push on until it becomes too dark in hopes that we can come up to them. We should be able to reach Kinderhook, given we have two fresh mounts. Are you up to a night on the track?" Fogg's reply did not surprise Gris.

"I have spent many a night in the saddle, out on both the road and field. I think we shall do fine." *If you also knew that I was a highwayman for a short period you would not ask such a question. Of course, as a dragoon in the Lowlands I spent a good many night patrols mounted.* "Now let us hope that the food is decent."

The mess sergeant had a kettle of venison stew that was ready to sample. He had made it for himself and the other senior NCOs but the Captain and the other gentleman had approached him inquiring if he could feed them, not like some other regular officers would have done. He gave them each a large plate of stew and a half loaf of fresh bread to share. When they had started to eat standing up, like private soldiers, he offered them the use of his camp preparation table and a couple of kegs to upon which to sit. The gentleman in gray reached inside of his coat and took out a silver flask and told the sergeant to pass over his cup, whereupon he poured a generous helping of fine brandy into the cup. When they had finished, the Captain put a shilling on the table.

"In case you might be needing something extra to keep you warm this evening. We thank you for sharing your fine venison stew with two hungry travelers, Sergeant."

"It has been my pleasure, Sir, and I wish you God's speed."

They did not need to walk back to pick up their new mounts as the Sergeant in charge of the stables had sent them over to the mess area. The Mess Sergeant and the other NCOs looked on approvingly as the two gentlemen checked their arms and equipment before getting aboard their mounts. It was clear to the old soldiers that these were not two run-of-the-mill types who normally came through the depot, fresh off the boat and wet behind the ears. These were two gentlemen who knew that this was not Hyde Park and that there was a war going on here in North America. In less than ten minutes, they were off at a trot up the track toward Kinderhook about eight to twelve miles away depending upon whom you asked.

## Chapter 3

It was already starting to get a little dusk out when they reached Claverack. They asked a sergeant, who was in charge of a squad stationed there, if he had seen the Captain and the other two men pass through toward Kinderhook. He replied that he had seen two civilians pass through but no officers. Their next question was if there was an inn or a place where an officer would stay for the night. The sergeant indicated an establishment just down the street from where they were standing.

"That would be the only place fit for a gentleman. There is a stable in the back and the food is good."

They thanked the sergeant and told him to keep an eye on the road just in case they should miss the officers for whom they were looking. Fogg led the way as they went to the inn and around back to the stable. There was no indication of an army horses being in the stable but they went around to the front to check. The innkeeper was a medium height, burly Dutchman who, while enjoying the trade of gentlemen and officers, was not too disposed to good manners. When Gris asked if he had any officers staying the night, he alluded that it was none of Gris' business who stayed overnight in his tavern.

Fogg tapped Gris on the shoulder, "Captain Gris, let me ask the fellow in his own tongue, perhaps he doesn't understand you," wherein Gris stepped aside. Fogg stepped up close to the Dutchman, took him by the apron strap and pulled him even closer. The man started to struggle until he felt the blade of Fogg's skein dubgh pressing against his crotch.

Fogg said to him in Dutch, "Listen you poor excuse for a human, unless you want to spend the rest of your life singing soprano in the local church you best keep a civil tongue and tell us what we want to know! Now do you have any officers staying here or did you have any pass through here, with two civilians?"

The man, almost unable to speak, whispered, "Yes, yes they were here but they all left together." Fogg pushed the knife a little, "I swear, please do not push that knife any more." Tears were coming to his eyes. Fogg let him go and he fairly flew back away from these two madmen.

Gris untied his greatcoat and replied, "Lead on, Mr. Fogg, lead on. It is only about three miles to Kinderhook and if we do not fall in one of the many famous potholes in this road we should be there in an hour at best."

## Chapter 4

The ride to Kinderhook proved to be a little more than the three miles everyone had told them as they found it necessary to cut a little east to ford the Stockbridge creek. The bridge was partially out, missing enough planks so as to be unusable.

They dismounted and walked far enough out on the timbers to see that the planking had been pulled. This bridge had been built by the military to replace the original timber-framed one. The planking was spiked down as opposed to being pegged with trunnels. It was quicker to build but obviously quicker to render useless. As there were no planks lying about it was a good guess that they had been thrown in the creek and were well on their way to the Hudson.

"It would appear that someone thinks we have too regular a supply route and system working for us. They can not do too much to disrupt the regular supply route on the river but the road is another thing." Gris commented.

"It would appear that they also know the importance of the main commodity transported on this road. Can we ford this creek as some point?"

"I think that if we go about a mile east, Mr. Fogg, we should be able to. If not we can completely ride around it in a couple of hours, if we can see well enough. We will send a messenger back telling Grice to bring along enough planking, spikes, and tools to repair fifteen to twenty feet of bridge."

"Lead on Captain Gris, as you know more of this country than I!"

# Chapter 5

It was a little after midnight when they arrived in Kinderhook. The sergeant at the southern road post verified that indeed two civilians had come through about three hours before and that they had ridden on into the settlement. Gris inquired if the north road had a post. The sergeant indicated that there was also a dray stock and supply depot located at that post. They thanked him and pushed on to the north post.

At the north post, Gris got them an empty subaltern's tent to get in out of the weather and dry some of their clothing and equipment. He also instructed the sergeant in charge of the post that he was to be awoke if any non-local civilians attempted to pass through the post. The corporal or sergeant of the guard was to delay them on any pretense so that Gris and Fogg might espy who they were.

Their accommodations were somewhat luxurious for the place. The tent was somewhat larger than a cavalry tent with a short wall of about a foot. It was designed in the Prussian fashion and had been left behind by a subaltern of the 55th Foot who, in keeping with the other officers of his regiment, had taken to living in a soldier's tent. This one had been pitched and then a plank floor laid in and two camp beds. It had two lanterns and a brazier in it, so once all were going it was quite dry and warm.

Both of our travelers slept with their boots on to avoid them drying out too fast and shrinking. Normally they would have stuffed them with forage to help the drying process and avoid shrinking. They both wiped down their weapons with an oily rag before turning in.

An orderly woke them just at dawn and informed them that the sergeant was detaining two civilians under pretense of a civilian warrant having been issued for two notorious highwayman fitting their description and that the local magistrate had been summoned. He also had two mugs of soldier's tea for them. It was laced with issue rum and local cream. Fogg got out his glass and they sat on the trunk at the end of the camp beds with one flap of the tent open. The two men were mounted on a couple of local farm stock riding horses and carried no visible arms but Fogg was sure that they must have had at least a pistol or two apiece on their person.

"What do you think, Gris? Do they look a little agitated at being delayed? I wonder if they have an accent." Gris stood up and threw his great coat on.

"I think I will find out. I would have to pass them to get to the necessary just the other side of the post." With that, he strolled out of the tent toward the post. Neither man paid much attention to him, as his brown uniform appeared to be either a civilian suit or a provincial uniform. As he came up to them, Gris could hear them discussing something between themselves in what appeared to be Dutch or Palatine. Now he wished that he had let Fogg make the trip to the necessary as Fogg seemed to have a good command of languages. Just as he passed them, he heard a third voice address them in the same language that they were speaking. He glanced over his shoulder and saw that it was Fogg. He heard the word tobac and saw one of the men pulling out a pouch and offering it to Fogg who took it and filled his pipe, all the while conversing with them, smiling and laughing. Gris continued on to the necessary and when he came out the two were just departing. The local magistrate, distressed that he had been pulled out of bed so early in the morning on a fool's errand was stomping back to his house. Fogg was nowhere to be seen so Gris went back to the tent. Fogg was inside with the brazier and lanterns lit finishing his tea and a slice of bread and cheese from his ration pack.

"Help yourself to some food Gris. If we hit the track in about an hour we should be able to come up on our two friends just as they reach Greenbush if they go that far." Gris sat down on his bed, pulled his pack out from underneath, and withdrew a sausage wrapped in a linen cloth to add to breakfast. He called to the orderly for some more tea if they had any and within minutes, their mugs were filled and steaming.

"What do you make of it Fogg?"

"I would bet a sovereign that the gentlemen in question are indeed Belgians working for the French. They both speak perfect Palatine German and claim to be so. However, their inflections would belie the fact. Underneath is the distinct Belgian sound."

"So the inn-keeper was correct in his assumption of their bad French. I would surmise that they are the ones who sabotaged the bridge, most likely pulling up the planks behind them as they went across, and tossing them in the creek," commented Gris.

"It would be my guess, Captain Gris that a closer investigation would indicate that these types of petty harassments are going on up and down the whole supply line. It would seem that General Abercromby would have need of a large force protecting his supply line, even this far south."

"Perhaps when we arrive at the headquarters you might make that suggestion to Lord Howe, General Abercromby still being in New York. For the moment, let us away to Quackenboss Tavern, rouse the keeper and get us a substantial breakfast ere we depart up yon track," all delivered with a large stage bow and sweeping of the hat.

"I think, Mr. Gris, sometimes that you should have taken to trodding the boards at the Strand or some other London playhouse."

"Ah, but it does liven up an otherwise boring military, between campaigns, career. What?" replied Gris with another foppish gesture.

# Chapter 6

It was ten miles to Greenbush, across the Hudson from Albany to the outer perimeter of the east bank camp of the expedition against Lake George and Lake Champlain. Having the advantage of exchanging mounts at every depot, Fogg and Gris came upon the two civilians about three miles out from the first Greenbush outpost. Instead of overtaking them, they hung back within observing distance to see to where they would lead. They followed them until the two passed through the outpost and turned to the track leading to the ferry to Albany. Gris decided that they should go directly to headquarters and report. The weather had been bad, even for April this far north. The area around Fort Crailo, as the van Renssealer house was called, had been laid out with gravel walks to keep the amount of mud and dirt tracked into headquarters down to a minimum. There were boot scrapers and brushes at the doors. Madam van Renssealer, while a gracious hostess, was not above admonishing senior British officers like little boys for not wiping their boots before entering. There were rag carpets laid out in the main hall and into the room used as headquarters and these were picked up, changed and cleaned everyday. The servants scrubbed and washed the stoop everyday in the Dutch fashion. This may be North America in the middle of a war but the van Renssealers had been here since the middle of the last century and Madam was not about to change housekeeping habits.

Lord Howe was not about as yet but was expected momentarily, according to the aide who was in the office, copying dispatches for the elements further north and across the river. The main British camp lay across the river just above Albany in the Cow Pasture. Only a half company of the 60th was stationed on this side of the river and it was rotated every three days. The meadows designated as camp area here were for the expected provincial troops who were still prominent by their absence. Most of the provinces were tardy to report their progress in raising their anticipated numbers.

The aide directed them around the house to the kitchen area where they might have some refreshment while awaiting Lord Howe. He assured Captain Gris that His Lordship would be anxious to see him. In the kitchen, the servants were busy preparing food for the

28

day. The main housekeeper directed them to sit at a large table on one side of the kitchen and offered them tea, coffee or hot chocolate. After the beverages were poured, she inquired if they would like fried eggs with potatoes and onions along with ham, bacon, or fresh trout. Since they had not had a home-cooked meal in a very long time, they opted for everything. When it was served, there was very little conversation as they made the piles of food disappear. They were just finishing mopping up their plates with large chunks of fresh bread, a British officer came into the kitchen. He was medium height, short cut reddish hair in his middle thirties and wearing a soldier's coat of the 55th cut short along with tent cloth breeches and brown canvas marching gaiters. Fogg did not need to be told that this was Lord George Augustus Viscount Howe. Gris immediately rose to his feet and Fogg followed suit.

"Captain Gris, how good to see you. You made excellent time, as I did not expect to see you until tomorrow at the earliest. And this gentleman is?"

"Sir, may I present Mr. E. Fogg, recently of London. He has come north to see some of North America and perhaps even act a gentleman volunteer in the upcoming campaign," replied Gris, formally introducing Fogg. Howe reached out his hand to Fogg in a friendly gesture, who took it in the manner it was offered. A smile crossed Howe's face.

"Welcome among friends and brothers, Mr. Fogg. I did not catch your Christian name."

"Well, Sir, I do not believe Captain Gris offered it. I normally only go by my last name. My parents had a twisted sense of humor when they named me and I seldom use it, but to you sir, it is Ethyrial, if you so wish."

"I believe that all parents have that sense of humor, Mr. Fogg. Augustus is a somewhat pretentious middle name and my brothers are as bad or so they seem to think." The servants had poured Lord Howe a cup of hot chocolate that he was attempting to drink in between sentences. He waved off any food, except for a piece of dry toast that was on a plate on the table.

"Best enjoy Madam van Renssealer's hospitality and Magdalena's fine cooking. Once we move north, we will greatly miss these luxuries. If you are finished let us move around to the headquarters where we can talk and not disturb these ladies in their preparations of what would appear to become a fine lunch." He rose and led the way out of the back door. Not even Lord Howe would dare walk through Madams house in outside shoes.

## Chapter 7

When they entered the drawing room that was converted into the headquarters' office the aide continued working at his desk only glancing up. It was apparent that Brigadier General Lord Howe was not one who insisted upon his immediate military family jumping to attention every time he entered the room or they addressed him.

"Mr. Fogg, may I present Captain Alexander Moneypenny, my Aide and right-hand man. Alexander is meticulous in his paperwork and note keeping. I believe that someday after this war is over he will write a book about our exploits from his journal, right Alexander?"

"If you say so General but for now it is these daily dispatches and orders," smiling woefully. Howe had closed the door when they entered the room and indicated that they should sit in one of the many wingback chairs that were in the room. Howe sat down next to the fireplace and took up a pipe that lay on the stand there.

"Smoke if you so desire gentlemen. Now Mr. Fogg, let me say it is a pleasure to finally meet you." Gris looked surprised at the statement. "Yes Captain Gris, it was quite by accident that you met Fogg but I believe it was propitious that you came up the river together. I have known about Mr. Fogg's arrival for a several weeks now. You see, Mr. Fogg does some work on occasions for a relative of mine. His mission on the way up the river was the same as yours."

Fogg turned to Gris, "I am terrible sorry Captain Gris that I could not tell you but I was to speak to no one about it until I talked to Lord Howe."

"No apology is necessary Fogg. As a matter of fact it pleases me to see a gentleman who honors his obligations above all else."

"Now down to business," inserted Howe. "What have you to report Captain?"

"The supply system is working fairly well in spite of some disruption, which we can discuss in detail further on. The regular supplies come into the harbor and are stored in the local warehouses. There is a delay between their being turned over to the army and I am certain that one of every three or four barrels develops legs and walks away. The powder does go directly from the ships, is stored in the magazine at the lake, and is under guard of the Fourth Battalion of the

30

60th Foot who encamp a part of a company there. This company will accompany the stand of arms and tents up to Greenbush when it arrives." Gris took a brief pause and continued. "A part of the available transport has been siphoned off to support the Louisbourg expedition but we still have sufficient shipping on the river. I do not believe it will slow us up."

Howe interrupted, "And the river road?"

"That is another matter Sir. Perhaps you would like to hear Fogg's impression, he being fresh to North America?"

Howe looked to Fogg and nodded. "Captain Gris is correct in my impression being different. The relay and supply depots seem adequate enough but lack the man power to patrol in between is a serious consideration. I realize that there is no regular cavalry here in North America but I understand that there are a few provincial light horse, especially among the wealthy landowners on the Hudson. Their presence on the road would cut down on the mischief that seems to happen between posts. We were caused to detour at, I believe Stockbridge Creek, due to planking being removed from a bridge. We managed to identify the two people most likely responsible. I would say two French agents who perhaps have been here in the Valley for a long time." Fogg continued, "I would also say that there are newly arrived regular officers who need to realize this is North America and that duty is different here. We assisted a supply train whose senior officers had ridden on ahead and left two very inexperienced junior officers in charge, who had no idea on how to gain the cooperation of the provincial troops who were acting as draymen. Fortunately, Captain Gris handled the situation extremely well." Howe sat and thought for a moment.

"Captain Gris, I will get you assigned to my military family for the time being. Colonel Gage should be over here sometime later this morning and Moneypenny can take care of it. I would like for you and Mr. Fogg to go over to Albany and look around for the two missing officers and the two civilians. I would suggest that you change to civilian clothes. Moneypenny," shouting through the closed door, "write up unconditional passes for Mr. R. Gris and Mr. E. Fogg. Do you have the necessary military papers Mr. Fogg, just in case you might have need of them?"

Fogg tapped his left boot top and replied, "In English ..." and indicating his hat, "...et en Francais."

"Good. Be on your way. Unfortunately, you will miss the grand lunch Madam is preparing. We will save you supper and good luck." With that, he got up and went to his table to commence working on the many logistical details that it would take to get this army and all of its baggage up to Lake George. Moneypenny had their passes ready and they departed the drawing room/headquarters.

When they were out of the door, Gris inquired, "I do not suppose you speak Chinese and carry a commission from Frederick also?" with a broad grin.

"Only the commission part," replied Fogg laughingly.

Gris stripped off his uniform coat and waistcoat and rolled them neatly. He opened his portmanteau and withdrew a tan civilian coat and a brocade waistcoat with which he replaced with his uniform coat. He placed his tri-corn in a oilskin bag and tied it behind the saddle and took out a round hat that was cut down to a three-inch brim with a flat crown. He quickly replaced his white neck cloth with a black silk one tied in an overhand knot. The transformation was amazing. Both had shed their greatcoats as the weather had improved slightly from earlier.

"We will cross the ferry and nose about in Albany. There are regulars, the 35th, encamped above the town at the Cow Pastures or Schuyler Flatts. I think we should start there looking for our two officers. Pity that we did not ask their names back on the track."

The scow ferry trip across the river was uneventful except for a slight chop caused by the wind picking up a little. The weather so far this April had not been exactly conducive for moving an army and all of its supplies from New York to Lake George. Fogg had determined from a fairly modern and accurate map that it was about three-hundred miles. On their trip across, Fogg learned more about the lay of the land from Albany to the lake. The trip by bateaux consisted of at least six portages where each barrel, basket and sack had to be handled twice. Barrels of flour, peas, pork and rice weighed in at two-hundred-forty pounds, butter and lard were stored in firkins at sixty pounds each. The pre-baked bread was stored in barrels that weighed fifty pounds. Add to this tents and tarps to shelter the supplies when they reached the lake plus all else that had to be at the lake head in order for the army to survive in the field.

Bradstreet had given an estimation of requiring at minimum three weeks for one-thousand bateaux, eight-hundred wagons, and oxcarts to transport five thousand seven hundred sixty barrels of provisions from Albany to Lake George. From Fort Edward, it was necessary to transport the bateaux on wagons and the longboats on trucks fifteen miles to the lake head. All of this required several posts to be maintained along the way. The French and their allies were capable of striking deep into the British supply line and almost at any place, despite the constant patrols of ranger units. The patrols that were needed were still sitting in the Mohawk Valley contemplating if they would really get involved in this campaign or not. These were Sir William Johnson and his Iroquois brothers.

# Chapter 8

When Fogg and Gris landed, they rode a short distance north above the Town of Albany to the area called Schuyler Flatts. This holding, like the van Renssealer holding, had been here for a great many years. The Flatts ran about two miles along the west bank of the Hudson from about a mile above Albany Town with a mile long island opposite it. The land was well tended, considering the farming habits of North America where land was a cheap commodity. One of the outstanding features of the farmstead was the large Dutch barn that stood there. Unlike the ones that Fogg had observed down on the Hudson, this one was built in the style that had living quarters for a farmer and his family in one end like the ones Fogg had seen in the Netherlands. He estimated that the building was at least one hundred feet long.

The house was a large brick two and a half stories high with a sunken story below. It had a large porch in the front and a smaller one in back. There were summer kitchens near the back and many blacks to do the never-ending work. When not living in camp, this is where Lord Howe was a guest of Madam Schuyler, widow of Phillipus Schuyler.

In the area called the Cow Pasture the Quartermaster had designated the regulars camp ground. A small element of the 35th, who were involved in providing the guard for the supply wagons that move between Albany and New York and about half of the 55th and 60th were encamped there. More regulars were expected to arrive any day now from down below. Gris and Fogg had made better time than the ships in coming up the river. They rode directly over to the Cow Pasture where they were promptly challenged by a sentry from the 55th at a proper distance from the camp. Gris advised the private to call the Corporal of the Guard who promptly called the Sergeant of the Guard, as two civilians were demanding to be let into camp.

The Sergeant strolled over to where the two civilians were still mounted and boomed, "What seems to be the commotion here? Do you two civilian gentlemen have business with His Majesty's Forces?"

Gris spoke up, "We're curious to know if two officers of the 35th came through this guard post within the last twelve to fourteen

34

hours." The sergeant drew himself up to his full height and sharply pointed out that if they had it was not the business of civilians to ask about such things. The comings and goings of His Majesty's officers was none of their business. Fogg sided his horse up to the sergeant and spoke low enough so that no one else could hear him. The sergeant grinned and inclined his head toward the marquis line inside of the 35th camp markers.

He turned to the corporal of the Guard and said, "Let the two gentleman pass, as it would seem they do have business with His Majesty's Forces." When Fogg and Gris had gotten a way down the track toward the 35th camp, he picked up his foot and exclaimed, "Why bless my buttons! It looks like one of those gentleman dropped a few coins. Well I guess they are too far toward the camp to catch up with them." He flipped one to the corporal. "Carry on, Corporal Wiggins ."

"Right you are Sergeant. See there you sentries start walking them posts, smartly now!" Replied Corporal Wiggins with the air of a man who had just come into some quick and easy money. "Smartly!"

After they had gotten some distance by the Guard Detail Gris turned to Fogg and asked, "What did you say to that Sergeant?"

"I only pointed out to him that he had dropped some coins on the ground right next to his foot and he supplied the rest. That makes him slightly richer than he was when he got up this morning, supposing that he gives one to the Corporal to keep him from asking too many questions as to why he let two civilians into the Pasture so easily."

When they got to the marquis line, they saw two horses tied up to the picket line that were still saddled and not wiped or brushed down. Their lower legs were covered with clay, the same color as those of the horses that Fogg and Gris were riding. The mud and clay on this side of the river was slightly darker. This meant that they had come across on the ferry and rode up the same gravel road leading to the camp. Gris rode over to the picket line, dismounted and ran his hand under the saddle blanket; the horses were still hot and wet. A private was pitching some hay on the other end of the line and Gris called him over, inquiring whose mounts these were. The private looked at Gris a little sullen but did not quite dare to be smart mouthed as Gris looked like he might be an officer in civilian clothes.

"They would belong to the two new officers who just rode in from headquarters, across the river." He jerked his thumb in that direction and added "sir" as an after-thought.

"Thank you, Private. Do you happen to know their names?" The private shook his head no and asked permission to go back to taking care of the horses.

Gris walked over to Fogg, "Well, Mr. Fogg, what do you think?"

Fogg sat for a moment and then said, "Here is what we could do. We go around to each marquis and inquire who or which gentlemen just came in from the south and has a detachment following them. We might simply inform them that we came upon their detail and that they had some difficulty bogged down on the road but were doing well when we last saw them and we thought they might like to know why they were a day late, so far. Act like good Samaritans and see if that draws out anything."

"Excellent idea, Mr. Fogg. Let us do it." and to the private, "Tie our mounts up to the picket line but do not let them eat too much."

The first two marquis got no response what-so-ever. The third was occupied but by a single person who was just getting dressed and wanted to know what the devil they were bothering him for as he had just come in from up river with a patrol. Along behind the marquis line was a much larger one with part of the sides raised and from which many voices could be heard.

Gris cocked his head in that direction, "Sounds like we found the officers mess pavilion and most likely our two pigeons." When they stepped around to the open end, the voices somewhat trailed off. There were at least seven or eight officers in the tent and a couple of orderlies serving food.

One of the older officers looked at their civilian clothes with disdain and said, with a sneer, "The doodle camp is on the other side of the river," where upon his mess mates all roared with laughter.

Gris, with a meekness that belied his true character replied, "Oh heavens no, we are not provincial soldiers. We are simply looking for two officers who may have come from down below ahead of their detachment." One of the other officers, who was sitting on a camp chair with his muddy feet upon an other spoke up.

"What business is it of yours who has just come up the river, if I may be so bold as to inquire? What business do civilians have to be checking up on His Majesty's 35th Foot?"

Gris, still calm and meek replied, "We are only trying to be of help. You see the detachment was bogged down on a quite bad stretch of the track and we wanted to pass on that they had sorted it all out and were on the move once more, although they may be delayed a day due to the bridge being out just down below here. Is not that correct, Mr. Fogg?"

"Quite so, Mr. Gris, quite so. Now if you will just point us to said officers, we will deliver our message and be on our way."

The officer with the propped up dirty boots replied, "You just have delivered your message," and to the other officers, "Damn Grice will never make a decent officer, no sense of duty."

Fogg took a step forward and inquired, "You sir would be...?"

"Not that it is any of your damn business, you country bumpkin, but you are addressing Captain Lieutenant Brownell of His Majesty's 35th Foot." Fogg's only remark was to thank the Captain Lieutenant and wish them all a good day.

When they had retrieved their mounts and were on their way, Fogg said to Gris, "I do not think that those two officers had anything to do with the sabotage. They just happened to be riding with the two civilians who probably flattered them and bought the drinks. Their only crime would be being stupid, self-centered and having bad manners."

Gris agreed, "I am only afraid that they may have talked too much but fortunately they would not have known much about the preparations on this end of the line, having only come up. Well, Mr. Fogg, shall we perhaps look about the petty sutlers camp for a trace of the two civilians? If we find nothing there we will meander down to Albany Town for a look around. What?"

"Agreed, Mr. Gris, agreed."

# Chapter 9

The camp at the Cow Pasture was laid out with the regiments in precedence; that is by numerical order, which indicated their seniority. This method would not provide anyone sympathetic to the French with any indication as to the plan of battle. The only exception were the elements of the 35th, who would not be participating and were therefore encamped closest to the southern end of the camp, due to their parties coming and going with wagons on a regular basis.

The more senior units were on the north or left end. This started with the 27th Foot, followed by the 42nd, 44th, 46th, 55th, and the 60th. The 80th was encamped about one-hundred-fifty yards north of the 27th as they were still in a constant state of training and therefore their coming and goings were less likely to disturb the remainder of the camp. There were various encampments of ranger companies spread out around the landside of the camp and one across the river. The bulk of rangers were already encamped at Fort Edward.

The camp looked very sparse and spread out as the majority of the regulars were still upon the river in transports, making their way north. All of the elements, except the provincials, were expected to appear within the next few days. When all were in place, they would number fifteen thousand strong, enough to take St. Frederick and its outpost Carillon. This would deny the French access to the Lake Champlain passageway into southern New York Province. The ranger companies, reinforced by the newly formed Light Infantry Regiment and companies, mounted in their longboats armed with swivel guns, would control all of Lake Champlain south of Isle St. Jeans, as they had controlled Lake George for the last year. French parties' intent on attacking the supply route between Fort Edward and Lake George found it necessary to land mid-lake and come overland in order to intercept the road.

The camp was set up facing the river with the backs of the camp to the west. This was to facilitate the movement of troops and supplies up river. Troops from down river were debarked from the transport ships at the piers at Albany Town and were marched up the west side road to the camps. The petty sutlers, those with military permits, were set up in the rear of the camp, just outside of the kitchen lines. The other sutlers were set up almost at the tree line of the Pastures with a large space between them, the petty sutlers, and the camps. Although there was a sentry line dividing the two the traffic flowed fairly easily between the two.

Fogg and Gris went through the camp toward the petty sutler line leading their mounts. A few of the soldiers looked at them but none ventured to ask what the two civilians were doing walking through camp. Fogg mentioned to Gris that perhaps they might speak of this to Lord Howe, as it appeared that any civilian could stroll through the camps and gather whatever information that they liked. They stopped and talked to some soldiers of the 55th who were tending the cooking fires. Fogg inquired if any of them had been up river yet. One offered that he had been up as far as Stillwater and expected that they might be sent up there again as soon as the army started to move but didn't know when that was. Above that point on the river, he did not know what was there. Another said that he had been out on patrols a couple of times with the rangers and that they had gone a few miles to the west, north of the Falls of the Mohawk but hadn't seen any sign of the French and their savage allies. They all seemed to be seasoned campaigners and their uniforms were altered to better suit the forest.

Gris and Fogg wished them good fortune in the coming weeks and moved on to the petty sutlers area. Here you could buy everything from soap, not a large selling commodity with the army, to boot black and gun oil, a more popular commodity. Occasionally you could buy brandy, if you had the money and the sutler knew you well. It was illegal for petty sutlers to carry liquor to sell to the soldiers but the provost looked the other way, especially if a spare bottle happened to end up in their forage pockets.

Fogg and Gris split up and went through the sutlers, looking at their wares and talking to them in an attempt to find the two men for whom they were looking. After a fruitless hunt, they met and rode over to the camp-following sutlers by the tree line. This was the most likely place to find unsavory characters. Fogg checked the priming on his pocket pistol and Gris took a small pistol out of his portmanteau and stuck it in his waistband under his waistcoat.

In this camp, as in town, there were no restrictions on what you could sell the army. There were plenty of alcoholic liquids to suit the taste. There was fresh bread baked in traveling ovens, pots of meat cooking over open fires, and what vegetables as could be had in mid April, consisting mostly of root-cellar stock. There were women who would wash, mend clothes, and cut hair for those that had the extra coin to part with plus other services that a gentlemen might hesitate to mention in polite company. The provost patrolled here as they did in Albany Town proper. Their main job was to keep men from deserting and destroying the property of the civilians. One of the most sought after commodities by pilferers was firewood that the sutlers and others had bought and paid for. Soldiers were not adverse to stealing cut firewood and this included fences and boards from out buildings. The boards were used to put under the straw used to sleep on in the tents. The army had supplied some boards but there were never enough. They also had a tendency to sink down into the moist soil and the straw would then become damp and musty. Even airing the tents did not much help straw lying on the ground. Where large bodies of soldiers were encamped, it was not unusual for whole outbuildings to disappear cladding, frames, and all.

This sutlers camp was not organized like the petty sutlers area, as the army had nothing to do with it. It had just grown up around the first sutlers who set up there. A main lane meandered through the camp with small streets that jutted off from it to some of the establishments in the rear of the main lane. They were about halfway through the camp when they spotted several horses tied up in a street at the rear of one of the large conglomeration of tents that passed as a tavern. In with the horses, they recognized one of the mounts that appeared to be the same as one ridden by one of the two men they were seeking. The saddle had a portmanteau fastened behind it that had a sealskin cover with the hair still on it, an unusual practice.

They dismounted just down the street from the establishment and gave a black boy a half pence to hold their horses with the promise of one more when they came back. They also gave him instructions to shout "Fire!" as loud as he could if anyone tried to take the horses. Hollering help in this place would bring very little sympathy or attention.

They walked back to the tavern tents and stepped inside. Although there were some lanterns burning, it took a few seconds for their vision to become adjusted to the light inside. There were several patrons seated at the rough tables having various types of morning sustenance. A couple of them looked like they might work for the establishment in the line of security, probably with a side business of supplying sailors for the ships that tied up at Albany. Back in one corner sat four men at a trestle table that did not fit the rest of the décor, nor did their clothing. One had the look of a man who spent most of his time in mercantile houses in the company of bookkeepers. Another looked like he was probably the owner of the establishment as he was the only one seated in a chair. The other two looked like they had just traveled all the way from down on the Hudson on horseback without benefit of the use of the army's relay stations.

Fogg and Gris sat at a table near the door where they could see everyone in the place. If you left your back exposed in a place like this, you could wake up in the hold of a ship on your way to a very long cruise. The woman who came over to their table informed them that the place had coffee if the gentlemen preferred it to tea or something stronger. They assured her that coffee would do as they were waiting for an associate from Albany Town to meet them here on some business with the army. She brought their coffee and the owner waved her over to his table. They could see that she was conversing with him and glancing in their direction.

Fogg said, quietly and offhandedly to Gris, "I think they have taken the bait."

Gris smiled and replied, "I think that you are quite correct and now if we can reel them in."

"I don't think we should reel them in far enough to put in the creel. They might be of more use to us, Mr. Gris, still swimming around, especially upstream."

"You are most correct and here comes the first one." The one that they had figured for the owner had gotten up and was moving toward their table.

"Gentlemen, excuse me. I am Johann Klompin the owner of this establishment. My associates," gesturing to the other table, "and myself could not but notice that you are obviously two gentlemen and strangers to this area. We thought that you might like to join us for some friendly conversation, exchange of news and so forth." Fogg turned to Gris.

"What say you, Mr. Gris? After all, we have only had each other to converse with for the last few days. Perhaps some new blood will liven up our day a little."

Gris, picked up his cup and gestured toward the other table, "Lead on Mac Duff!" Klompin turned to Fogg and inquired if he was a Scot. Fogg, lifting an eyebrow to Gris, assured him that he was not a Scot and it was just Mr. Gris' strange sense of humor. Gris just shrugged, shook his head, and muttered in Latin "iudicum vulgus", roughly the uneducated multitude.

As they drew near the table, Fogg caught a quick glance between the two that they had followed up the river and decided to broach the subject before they could.

He quickly said in German, "Are you not the same gentlemen who so graciously shared your tobacco with me either late yesterday or early today at Claverack?" The question completely took them off guard and they stumbled and hesitated in answering. Where upon Fogg quickly pursued the matter. "Yes, I know you are the very same," in German and then in English. "These two gentlemen shared their tobacco with me yesterday at Claverack. You must let me buy a round of whatever everyone is drinking in return." To the two pseudo-Palatines he directed, "Verstehen? (Do you understand?)" The heavier set of the two, spoke up for the two of them.

"Yes, we both speak excellent English."

"I'm terribly sorry, but of course you would. You see I only have ever heard you speaking German and made the foolish assumption. Now I really must buy you a drink." Fogg was the epitome of someone who had just committed a very bad breach of etiquette. *I'll bet you do, along with excellent French and Flemish.* The proprietor indicated to the serving-girl that the table would have a round. Fogg spoke up again and introduced himself and Mr. Gris. Klompin introduced the other gentlemen, first the one who looked like he never went out-of-doors. He was Mr. Neville Bruce, of Albany, manager of one of the local mercantile houses for a New York concern. The other two were introduced as two gentlemen from near Windsor who were in the carting business and were looking to expand up river to Albany. The heavyset one was Mr. Felsstein and the thin one with the long nose was Mr. Storch. Somehow, both of their names fit too well to sound real, but then Fogg mused that Fogg and Gris might not sound too real also.

Klompin asked, "What brings you two gentlemen this far north from the comfort and such of New York Town?"

"Business," replied Gris, "just business."

"And what kind of business would that be?" queried Klompin, "If I am not being too bold in asking."

"Not at all," interjected Fogg. "It just so happens that we are, at the moment, in the military-supply business. We have a contract to supply some of the salt pork and other items to the expedition against the French, both here and at Louisburg. The Louisburg one being taken care of, we decided to look into the northern end of this one ourselves."

Klompin cocked one eyebrow, "I thought that there were some Albany merchants who had that contract?"

"Quite true, Mr. Klompin. We understand that their contract is only for the stay of the troops in this camp and Fort Edward, but when the army moves up to Lake George and beyond we will be supplying the remainder. We have worked out a process to make the shipping less expensive to the army. We also understand that the contract for the Provincials will not be as large as originally planned."

"Why would that be!" shrilled Bruce, looking totally shocked at this piece of news.

"Why? Because the Provincial governments have not been able to raise the number of troops that they originally said they would." replied Gris between sips of his coffee. "Instead of ten thousand they are not even able to raise half that and the gossip in New York is that half of those are wanting arms and tentage. It is doubtful that they will be able to reach Albany, let alone march north to Lake George." Mr. Felsstein leaned forward on his bench toward Gris.

"This is true?" he inquired in German.

Fogg inclined his head toward Gris and answered in German, "Mr. Gris does not speak German, but yes that is the gossip, from both the street and the drawing room." He translated it for Gris who nodded his head in agreement. Bruce wanted to know how they were planning on getting their barrels up north cheaper than the Albany merchants. Fogg's only reply was that it was a business secret. From the sullen look on his face, it was apparent that Bruce had some interest in the Albany salt pork business and could see some of his profits slipping away. At this point, Fogg thought that they had reeled out enough line.

Standing up he said, "Gentlemen you will have to excuse Mr. Gris and myself. We have some army contacts to see about moving our supplies up to Fort Edward and thence to Lake George. Perhaps we shall run into each other as we will be here for at least a couple of days, depending upon the arrival of our goods." Klompin quickly offered an invitation to stop by whenever they were in the sutlers camp. He was quick to promote that his was the best food, drink and other forms of entertainment available here at the Cow Pasture. He also added that there were many British Officers and gentlemen who frequented his establishment in the evening.

After they had retrieved their mounts, paid off the black boy and were on their way back to the main camp Fogg turned to Gris saying, "What do you think Mr. Gris? Did our newly found weasel friend Mr. Bruce seem upset that we might be taking away some of his business? I think that Herr Klompin might also have been upset with Bruce's reaction. What say you?"

"I believe that you are quite correct in your appraisal. I also think that there is much more going on here besides bilking the army with bad rations for good money. I think that Herr Felsstein was just a little too interested in there being fewer Provincial troops. His reaction coupled with the small pieces of sabotage on the road would make him and his companions eligible for closer examination. We should pass on this information to Lord Howe and recommend that he put a couple of his people who are in the Follower's camp to watching Herr Klompin's establishment and our two new found friends."

"Before we return to the other side of the river, I think we should ride down to the boat landing," said Fogg glancing over his shoulder, "just in case we are followed to see if we really are what we say we are."

On their way through the camp, they stopped again at the 55th camp and talked to a couple of Lord Howe's officers, inquiring the location of the landing. As they were clearing the 55th camp marker, Fogg leaned down to adjust a stirrup and looked back toward where they had left the officers. A civilian in a green great coat was talking to one of the officers who was pointing toward the landing.

As he straightened up, he said to Gris, "We have a tag-along, green great coat and flop hat. We really need to speak to Lord Howe regarding the ease with which civilians come and go in the camp."

They arrived at the landing, which was a bustle, as usual with soldiers and bateaux men busy moving and loading supplies to be transported up river to Fort Edward and thence to Lake George. Here they spoke with several people, inquiring when the boats would be moving up river, would there be room for some barrels of salt pork that they were shipping to Lake George and so forth. The bateaux men were not quite as free with their information as had been the soldiers. They had a great deal of mistrust for anyone not considered part of their trade. They would simply jerk their head in the direction of an officer and reply. "Ask 'em," and continue with their work.

The bateaux men were a rough bunch, raised by Col. John Bradstreet for this expedition. They were a mixed group of fishermen, smugglers, river pirates and the like. Every one of them was an expert with any type of boat as well as what ever weapon was handy be it a musket or a pike pole. They had an excellent record of being able to deliver whatever the colonel said they would deliver. They would pole, row or sail their boats to wherever he ordered and if required engaged the enemy after they got there. They would prove their worth more than once in the coming campaign months.

Fogg and his companion walked over to the man that they had indicated as an officer. The only thing that set him apart was that he was slightly better clothed and apparently could read and write as he held a journal in which he was recording what went into the bateaux. He had looked up briefly at the two civilians approaching him but paid them no attention until they got close to him.

He looked up and coldly said to them, "If you're not on the King's business you have no reason to be on my landing." Fogg was about to make a retort when he noticed the man's ring on the hand he was holding the journal with. Instead, he stepped close to the man and reached out and took hold of the hand that he was writing with and putting mouth to ear whispered something. The man smiled and whispered something back.

"Well, Brothers, what can I do for you?" Fogg explained their situation as to being followed by a civilian in a green great coat and flop hat and that he was trying to spy upon them as they were conducting their business, which by the way was also, in part, the King's business.

The landing master rubbed his chin, thought for a while, and then replied, "You see these three bateaux here? Well they be going for a trip up the Mohawk as far as Fort Johnson. Now that would probably be a two day trip up and two day back if nothing untold were to happen on either leg of the journey. Would something be happening?" Gris replied that perhaps only a trip as far as the falls of the Mohawk would be sufficient and that they should let him escape at that point. This would just delay him reporting to his employer.

The landing master held out his hand to Fogg and said "Done, Brother and if you need any assistance getting yourselves or your property up river you know where to find me. The Colonel can also be counted on to throw you a cable to give you a tow up river. I'll be right here at this landing."

Our two travelers walked their mounts until they were clear of the landing. Once mounted, they headed south to the ferry. There was no sign of their tag-along friend in the green great coat. He seemed to have miraculously disappeared. Once they reached the east bank of the river, they reported to Lord Howe all that they had seen and heard and their suggestion for tightening the security of the main camp. Although it did not appear in the written orders for the next day, the traffic of civilians through the camp became restricted to only those who had a pass issued by headquarters or a senior staff officer. There was also a rumor in the camp about a civilian who claimed to have been "pressed" by the bateaux men for a voyage up the Mohawk. It seemed he had made his escape at the falls when the bateaux men were getting ready to portage the bateaux. When questioned, the bateaux men simply smiled and shook their heads in disbelief at such a preposterous story. Lord Howe's men in the Follower's camp reported a great deal of activity among the main conspirators and lots of coming and goings of people who looked more at ease in the woods than around a British army camp and they seldom stayed more than a couple of hours and were off again. They always headed northwest out of the camp, through the treeline. One of the watchers even claimed that he had heard a couple of them speaking what sounded French with the two "Palatines" from down river.

## Chapter 10

Instead of re-crossing the river and going on up to Schuyler's to stay, our two stalwarts opted to stay at the Headquarters over night. The next day they planned to manufacture some paperwork to support their stories and then to find lodgings in one of the taverns in Albany so as not to appear too attached to the army. Lord Howe had approved the plan before leaving for Schuyler's and had given Moneypenny instructions to assist them, as he did not plan on coming over to this side until afternoon as he felt the necessity to visit the 55th in camp. Lord Howe may have been second in command of the army but he was never too busy to look to the welfare of his own.

The next morning as Fogg sat having a mug of coffee and writing out some bogus commercial records to help cover their story, he looked back upon their adventure so far. Today was May 9th and they had left New York five days ago. Fogg's original mission was to observe and report directly to his employer on the state and operations of the army in New York Province, especially the expedition that was headed for Lake George and Lake Champlain. In addition, he had been drawn by accident into a counter espionage operation. He also was surprised to learn that Lord Howe knew of his mission, which would make it much easier for him. His newly acquired "partner" seemed well suited for the operation being not only well versed in the military but also fluent in French and familiar with the country. He also had the complete trust of Lord Howe, a definite plus.

By late morning, they had completed all of their counterfeiting and were ready to move across the river to Albany Town and find lodging. Moneypenny had directed them to the establishment for which Mr. Bruce worked. They had decided to seek his help in finding lodging as it would put them and their morning's work where it would do the most good. They had no difficulty finding the place as it was situated down by the quay area. Bruce was surprised to see them, especially standing in his place of business. He was equally surprised and pleased to find out that they had sought him out as they wanted to include him in a portion of their business deal. The day before in the tavern tent, he had seen some of his profits slipping away but now here they were coming back to him.

Fogg opened the conversation about lodgings with, "Perhaps, Mr. Bruce, you would know of suitable lodging for Gris and myself while we are here in Albany Town. Perhaps something convenient to both the ferry and the road to the Cow Pastures as we have arrangements that can only be made at army headquarters and the landing."

"Finding the lodging is a simple matter as I have an, er, cousin who runs a lodging that caters to gentlemen such as you. As you know, the ferry is just down the street a little to the south and the road to the Pastures is just there to the left However, access to the landing is now somewhat restricted due to the army having closed off the road and requiring passes from either the headquarters or senior staff officers. They have even increased the patrols around the perimeter of the camp. My friend Klompen has felt a loss in his business from the camp as even officers are being restricted in their movements."

Gris spoke up, "Well it shan't be a problem for us as we have carte blanch movement throughout the entire military establishment due to being a prime supplier. It also helps that a couple of our partners stand rather well in the government." All this with a slight grin and a wink of the eye. This also seemed to make Bruce perk up. *These are valuable friends to have, indeed,* thought Bruce, *I will have to pass this information on to Klompen as he may find a use for them.*

"I'll take you over to my cousin's and introduce you and you can settle in. The King's Arms is just around the corner from there on Market St. where they serve food and drink. It is a place that is frequented by some of the better gentlemen of Albany Town. I also have another cousin who works at the army landing as a clerk. He might be of some assistance to you as he eases things for my firm."

"What is your cousins name?" inquired Fogg.

"I'll get word to him. Better he contacts you than you to be asking about him at the landing."

"Quite right. No need to draw undo attention to him by having two complete strangers asking for him. We are off to the landing this afternoon to check on some supplies that should be going up river, providing that they have made it this far from New York."

Bruce's business establishment was on the corner of Quay and Mark Lane and they only had to go one short block west to Dock Street, then north along Dock to Maiden Lane. The second house on the north side of Maiden Lane was the home of his cousin, Mrs. Bruin, who according to Bruce was a widow. At first, she seemed confused as to what Bruce was saying about her renting out rooms but a slight sharp incline in Bruce's voice seemed to jog her memory.

She explained that the last lodgers had just left this very morning and she would need to clean up the room and change the linen, and if they would come back in an hour she and her son would have it all finished. She suggested that perhaps they would care to go around the corner to Market and have something to eat for midday at the Arms.

"An excellent thought, Mrs. Bruin as we had a very early breakfast. Come Mr. Gris let us be off. We will be back in an hour and one half."

Bruce, still flustered by his cousin's hesitation chimed in, "Yes, gentlemen, by all means. An hour and a half should be more than sufficient. If you leave your baggage here I'll have, er my cousin's son take it up the stairs when the room is ready."

"I should think that if it is only around the corner we can leave the mounts here. Perhaps Madam has room for them in the back in her shed for a couple of extra pence per day? The boy does know how to take care of fine horses, does he not? As you can see, they are on loan to us from the army, including the furniture. If the boy just puts the horses in the back and takes off the portmanteaus and saddle bags we will remove the firearms ourselves." With this remark, Gris shot a sharp look at the young man who had been standing there all this time. "Understood?" The boy mumbled something that sounded like an affirmative answer, which satisfied Gris who flipped him a sixpence.

Fogg added, "There is another one in it for you at the end of our stay, if you do as you are bid." The boy again mumbled what might pass for an affirmative answer but this time with a slight smile on his otherwise dour face. Fogg and Gris turned with a slight nod to Mrs. Bruin and departed out the door. Fogg stopped at the corner of the house and took out his pipe, filled the bowl and lit it with his burning glass, as the day was bright and sunny. While doing this he and Gris listened to the voices coming through the windows from inside the house. When he and Gris had heard enough they moved off up the street. Once around the corner he and Gris looked at each other and gave a chuckle.

"Me thinks that the widow Mrs. Bruin is a very distant cousin of our Mr. Bruce. Perhaps kissing cousins at the very least," said Fogg trying to contain himself. Gris, who was attempting not to appear a complete fool from laughing.

He replied, "I surely hope that they do indeed change the linen as I do think that they are much more than kissing cousins. From her last remark it may be a while before Mr. Bruce gets to plough the widow's furrow again." With this remark, neither could retain themselves and they had to stop so as not to stagger down Markets St. and scare the local inhabitants.

They found the King's Tavern a pleasant enough place, for a country tavern. The food was plentiful, the tableware simple but clean, an oddity in itself. The keeper attempted to gouge them as they were obviously gentlemen, but Gris having been in this part of the country put up a vigorous argument. When they said that they would like to make arrangements to have at least two meals a day in the tavern for the remainder of the week, paying in advance, the price came down. There were a couple of officers of the 35th Foot sitting one table over in the corner having a meal. They looked over at Gris and Fogg but did not seem to be too interested in them. Shortly, they were joined by two more officers from the 27th Foot who, from their conversation, had just come up river as part of the advance party. They had sent the other ranks on to the camp under the command of a junior lieutenant and a sergeant. The two from the 27th were eager for information on when the army was moving, etc. and were not overly quiet about it. The two 35th officers did not seem to care how loud they were either. Fortunately, they didn't know anything as the 35th was only involved in guarding the supplies that were being ferried up and down the lower Hudson. Everything that went up river went under the watchful eyes of the bateaux men and boats that required extra guards usually had a contingent of the 55th on board.

When they had finished, our two adventurers paid their bill and left a small advance to assure that they would be fed. The publican took their money and thanked them. He indicated that they would have their meals at the table in the far corner, near the fireplace, but away from the more common frequenters of the tavern. Fogg indicated to him that they would not mind sharing their table with army officers, above the company grade. The publican allowed as he did have several senior officers who did come in to partake of food and drink. He also added that they need not be worried about being bothered by ladies of low virtue as there were very few of them in Albany and none in his establishment as his wife did not allow unescorted ladies in the tavern. They thanked him and left to inspect their new lodgings.

Upon arrival at the home of Mrs. Bruin, they discovered that Mr. Bruce had departed soon after they had. The widow and her son had indeed straightened up the room, which was in the back of the house. It was quite large for a Dutch-style house and contained a double bed with a kass in one corner and pegs on one of the walls. It also had a wash stand with pitcher and bowl and clean linen towels. The windows had been thrown open and the room aired. Indeed, they had changed the linen. Their traveling baggage was sitting in the room. They expected the remainder of their belongings to arrive in a couple of days from New York. It was destined to go to Lord Howe's headquarters on the other side of the river. They went down to the shed in the rear of the building and retrieved their firearms from the horses. When they were back upstairs, they checked their baggage to see if it had been tampered with. As expected, they found pieces of broken horse hair, indicating that the bags had been opened. The papers that they had arranged in a particular fashion were disturbed and the couple of pieces of short horsehair were missing. Gris looked around and found them lying on the wash-stand by the window.

He said to Fogg, in French, "These quarters are all that we could ask for, thanks to our friend Mr. Bruce."

"Truly," Fogg replied, "we were lucky to make Mr. Bruce's acquaintance. It is fortunate that his cousin, and I might add a lovely lady, had this room emptied this very morning." They heard a slight creak in the room that was across the hall in the front of the house that shared a common wall with their room. They smiled and knew that the bait had been taken. "Let us be off to the landing at the camp and check on our goods."

# Chapter 11

On their ride to the camp, they discussed the possibilities of how many people were now involved, or at least suspect, in the circle of enemy agents. It was quite possible that some were only guilty by association. It would certainly be a Gordian Knot to unravel, but unlike the Gordian Knot it would not do to simply cut it as that would leave too many pieces lying about that could possibly reassemble itself. Better yet that when the time came they should catch as many in their net as possible. It was possible that some links could be eliminated altogether and made almost impossible to replace. They were about to do so shortly.

They had been traveling north on Market Street and when they arrived at the parameter of the camp at Patroon Street, they were challenged by the guard post there as to their business traveling north. They were still about a quarter mile from the Cow Pasture and could see patrols marching in the area between them and the camp. Lord Howe had indeed tightened the security around the camp. They showed the sergeant who had challenged them their passes, who in turn took them to the Subaltern in charge of the post. He was sitting in a tent doing paper work. He came out to inquire as to how they had obtained these particular passes and what business they had that would give them such a carte blanc to the army.

Fogg put on his iciest stare and suggested that he, as a Subaltern, might inquire directly from the signer of the passes as to what business it was. Then as the poor young fellow started to stammer and backtrack, Fogg praised him for taking such precautions to ensure the security of the army. As he was now very confused, he returned the passes and ordered the sergeant to remove the chevaux de frise blocking the road. Fogg and Gris kicked up their mounts and continued down the road.

Gris remarked, "I'll wager that poor young fellow will never question your right to pass that post ever again. Probably still quaking in his boots and attempting to chastise the sergeant for bothering him. Doubt if he'll have much luck with that as that sergeant looked like he had been on a few campaigns. By Jupiter, Fogg, you would have unsettled me."

"Doubt it," replied Fogg. "You are made of sterner stuff and would probably have shot me on the spot as a spy.... for the Chinese!" Where upon they had a good laugh. The sound of their laughter made the young Subaltern turn red as he stomped back to his tent. The sergeant turned away from the young officer to hide his smirk and bawled out to the corporal to get that barrier back into position before the King of France were to come riding down this road and demand entry into His Majesty's camp.

When they arrived at the landing, they dismounted and walked over to where the landing master was standing, who greeted them with, "Gentlemen, it is good to see you. I have no word as yet to when it might be possible for you to go up river."

Fogg took him by the arm and drew him close, mouth to ear, and said, "We need to speak with you away from your people. It is on a matter of urgent safety of your post." This immediately got his attention. He dismissed the clerk he had been talking to and they moved away from the boats to an area where there was no one standing and it was clear for several yards.

Fogg continued, "As a Brother we felt that you should be aware of the fact that there is a clerk in your charge that is not quite on the square. We do not have his name as yet but he is a cousin of a Mr. Neville Bruce, whose company on Quay Street is one of the army suppliers."

"That was him, Justin Bruin, that I was just conversing with."

"Bruin? Did you say Justin Bruin?" queried Fogg.

"Aye, that's his name. Why do you look so surprised?"

"Because we have just secured lodging in a house owned by a widow Bruin, another cousin of Mr. Bruce. Do you know her?"

The landing master thought for a minute, "Doesn't ring a bell but then I'm not an Albany man and stay away from that town as much as possible. I never use the ferry below town as we cross the river in our own boats when necessary to go to headquarters. Matter of fact, when you gents want to cross the river you have only to come up to the landing here and we can accommodate you, mounts and all. Clerk Bruin, he is an Albany man. Not one of our bateaux men but he can read, write and figure, which is more than most of my boys can do. His cousin probably made it possible for him to work here at the landing. I didn't hire him, he just showed up one day with the right paper work."

"I should think that it might be advantageous to you and the army to assign him to a job that would take him away from the landing," suggested Gris.

"Well if he is causing mischief on this end where he can get stuff shipped up river with out too much ado, perhaps if I put him on the other end of the river he won't get into so much mischief. I have a fellow on the other end who is on the level, that would be more than glad to keep an eye on him. If he still is a problem there, my bateaux men know how to loose unwanted cargo between here and the Lake."

"Excellent idea," replied Gris, "but wait a day so it is not connected to our visit. It should also not get around that we have any knowledge of this business." The landing master tapped his chest and our adventures understood his meaning.

"Me, Sir I'm a man what takes his obligation seriously."

"Now if we might take you up on that boat ride across river?" queried Mr. Gris.

"Right you are Sir. I have one almost ready to go across with some supplies and my daily tally for the Brigadier. He keeps good tabs on where the army stands. He's the reason this army will probably get to the Lake and off on the campaign on time. Now if them lazy Provincials would just get up here."

A bateaux man came up to the landing master and said, "Coxs'n is ready to shove off, with your permission Sir."

"Tell the Coxs'n these two gentlemen are going across with you. You can leave your mounts here, as it is only a longboat going over. You can requisition two temporary mounts on the other shore and I'll hold yours here until you return. Needn't worry about your tack or arms as I'll put a watch on them over by my berth, there." He pointed to a tarpaulin erected over some saplings.

They followed the sailor down to the longboat that was waiting. It was loaded to the gunwales with supplies. The coxswain indicated that they could sit on the supplies and they shoved off. The wind was light and they made a rapid trip across the river. The only thing they did notice was that the tide was still slightly effective, even this far up river. Fogg inquired of the coxswain how far up the river they could still feel the tide. He informed them that it slacked off just before or about even with the mouth of the Mohawk. Fogg also inquired if the river was deep enough at the army landing to accept ships from down river. He was informed that it was indeed at high tide but at low, it was not quite reliable to do so hence they used the Albany piers. It was better than having had to build a new set of piers at the landing. The small beach at the landing was capable of handling the boats used to transport up river. They could handle several dozen at a time and it only took twenty minutes or so to load a boat using the gin poles and oxen to move the heavy items, like cannon and salt pork barrels, and such.

When they reached the other side, they found that it was only a half mile to the headquarters so they walked. They noticed some activity over in the area that would be the Provincial camp, which indicated that maybe some of them were at last starting to arrive. When they reached headquarters, they inquired of Capt. Moneypenny if this were the case. He indicated that some Massachusetts men had arrived but they were from just over the border so they had not come too far. Moneypenny announced to Lord Howe that they were awaiting his pleasure and he had them ushered right in.

"Well, gentlemen, how goes everything so far? Anything interesting to report in this espionage affair?" was his greeting to them. He had laid his coat aside and was only wearing his waistcoat. He was wearing brown marching gaiters and common shoes. Except for his bearing, he looked like almost any private soldier on fatigue duty, sans cap.

Gris, being the staff member spoke up, "Yes General, we have uncovered a few more individuals that most likely are involved. It would include, as best we can guess, the original four we told you of plus at least three more, including a woman. There are quite possibly more who act as messengers but we have as yet to discover any of them. We have taken one other person, semi into our confidence in keeping with our cover."

"And what do you make of all this, Fogg?"

"General, I think that Captain Gris' assessment is quite correct. I think that we should play this out as long as possible. We may be able to use it to feed false or confusing information to the enemy. We have taken the precaution of eliminating one cog in the wheel so as not to corrupt our supply line north. This will take place tomorrow and the fellow will be on the down side of the northern supply line where he cannot cause too much mischief. If he does, the bateaux men will take care of him. They all seem to appear loyal to Bradstreet and his officers, so I should think there is no worry there. I would put some of the rangers to watching who comes and goes from the establishment of Herr Klompen in the Followers camp. My guess is that they come and go through the northwest corner so as to cross the Mohawk above the falls and then move off to the north skirting the river outposts. They could meet with French messengers from the north any where in the mountains west of Fort Edward. We know that they are not using the passage north of the Sacandawga because that is controlled by Sir William's Mohawks."

"Excellent! What do you think we should do to make the most of the situation? I have received word that General Abercromby will be here, possibly by day after tomorrow. When that happens, I shall be ready to move on up river. I will most likely set up my headquarters between the second and third portage between Saratoga and Fort Edward. I am ordering Major Proby to move four companies of the 55th past the falls above Saratoga. That is where I will be. I would like you to remain on this mission and cause as much confusion as possible to this espionage ring. If necessary, you might even travel up and down the supply route north, as far as Fort Edward to see what you can ferret out. Any thing you need, simply let Moneypenny know. I have told him to give you whatever you request. Now on about your unsavory business and good hunting," he said dismissing them with a good hearted grin.

They both stood and with their hats saluted him. He returned the salute with more of a wave then a salute. Both understood why his troops admired him so much and why he was getting one-hundred-ten percent out of the army moving north to the Lake. They stopped at Moneypenny's table on the way out and gave him a list of items they would need, one of them being a half dozen barrels of salt pork marked with "F & G Military Suppliers - Pass on to Lake". They needed those as soon as possible. Moneypenny assured them that they would have these barrels at the landing by this afternoon or sunrise tomorrow morning at the latest. They also needed some more hard cash to replace what they had spread around already. He went over to a Dutch cupboard called a kass and took out a bag of coins, which he deposited on the table.

"You will need to sign for this as it is His Lordship's own money." Fogg requested a piece of paper and wrote out something upon it.

Handing it to Moneypenny he said, "This is a note of credit, drawn upon the indicated counting house in New York. His Lordship can use it to replace any funds that he advances to us. It will come from a special account established for that purpose by my original employer, who Lord Howe is aware of. As you can see it is open ended so that I will not have to write one each time. It simply orders them to honor any requests from His Lordship." Moneypenny thanked him and put the note in the box in the kass.

"Next one of His Majesty's ships that goes down river, I shall send it upon as I would not trust any of the commercial Captains to carry out such a mission." They bid Moneypenny adieu and departed up toward the East landing. When they arrived there was a boat just coming across to their side of the river. Within the hour, they were back at the army landing and had retrieved their horses.

## Chapter 12

There was a great deal of activity at the landing and in the camp. The camp equipage of the 27th and 55th had been loaded on the boats yesterday and were in the process of departing up river. There were soldiers from each of the aforementioned regiments in the vicinity of the landing. Two messes, ten men were assigned to each boat that had their regiments' gear on board. They were to provide the hands necessary to row the boats up river and provide extra arms on each boat in case of attack. On the return trip, it only took three bateaux men, a coxswain, a bow hook, and an extra hand to bring the boats back down river as the current accomplished most of the work.

The equipment of the 42nd had been loaded on wagons and was departing up the west road. A quarter of the regiment was moving north as a security force with it. Their trip was a little longer as they would leave the river just above Schuyler's and cut across to the ford just above the Cohos' Falls. After crossing the Mohawk, they would cut back to Half Moon and proceed along the Hudson again. These wagons would eventually go all the way north to Fort Edward where they would become part of the train that would move the army from there to Lake George. The Scots who were accompanying the wagons were in high spirits. They looked forward to getting out of camp and moving toward the mountains. They had been cooped up long enough on the ships coming up the Hudson and then sitting in camp with its constant round of guard mounts and fatigue parties.

From the amount of men missing from the 55th camp it was apparent that Major Proby and his four companies had already departed for the second portage at the falls above Saratoga. It was obvious that the remainder would go up the river shortly as they were now encamped with less than one third of their tents and were messed seven soldiers to a tent. There was talk of the 4th Battalion of the 60th Foot moving north tomorrow or the next day, depending upon the number of boats available.

The weather through April had been extremely wet, but had started to moderate a little. The rivers were at a good level for both the use of the boats and the fords not too deep for the use of the wagons. If the wet weather returned, the roads would soon become impassible for the wagons and the army would have to rely upon the river.

The logistics of moving both the army and the supplies from just Albany to Lake George was a tremendous undertaking. The estimated number of troops was twenty thousand if the provincial governments came through with what they had promised. If they adhered to their original time line, the army would be at the Lake in three weeks, about the middle of June. It was estimated that it would take one-thousand batcaux, eight-hundred wagons and ox carts to transport five thousand seven hundred sixty barrels of provisions. The trip required that each barrel be handled five times before it reached the Lake. There were not this many wagons or boats to be had. There were carpenters at the Lake building bateaux to transport the army down the Lake to attack Carillon and St. Frederic and then to be shifted over to controlling Lake Champlain. Lord Howe's latest estimate was now the end of June and at the latest the first week in July.

Fogg suggested to Gris that they take a ride over to Klompen's Tent Tavern, have a drink, and see what the atmosphere was like there now that it was obvious that the army was on the move. The atmosphere in the Followers Camp was one of hustle and bustle. There were some sutlers that were already tearing down their tents and packing it up to move up river. Unless the army put some restriction upon the road, it soon would be clogged with civilians attempting to move up river with the "cash cow".

Klompen was busy directing his people in starting to pack up the tavern for moving. He was greatly pleased to see them as he knew that they would have reliable news on the armies movement.

"My friends, my friends. Come, sit and have a drink. What is your pleasure? Brandy, wine, ale what ever."

"Perhaps two small brandies would be appropriate," replied Fogg. "What or should I say why are you packing?"

"The army is moving. By tomorrow there will be few left in camp. You mean you don't know of this?" asked Klompen incredulously.

"My good fellow, you jump too soon. Do not believe the rumor mill. There are at least another three regiments on their way up the Hudson, even as we speak. It is also said that the New Jersey and Pennsylvania Regiments will be coming into camp in less than two days and will be camping upon this side of the river. All of the New England regiments will be in their camp by the beginning of next week," was Fogg's answer to Klompen's question.

58

Klompen took the bait, "This is true? Why, why that means nearly," counting on his fingers, "four or five thousand more soldiers. Here, in this camp, wanting all sorts of things. Excuse me for a moment. There is a job that needs to be started." He went over to the barmaid who had waited on them and was now busy packing things behind the plank bar. He semi whispered instructions to her in Dutch and then came back, smiling, to sit with his guests. "Last minute business to be taken care of. You have perhaps saved me from loosing a lot of money by acting to hastily."

"Well, Herr Klompen you have been decent with us so there is no reason we should not have returned the favor. Let these others depart hastily and there will be more business for you. One should look after their friends. Right, Mr. Gris?"

"Perfectly right, Mr. Fogg, perfectly. One hand washes the other so to speak, what!"

"Absolutely. Now Herr Klompen, you are an Albany man, are you not?"

"Yes that is true, Herr Fogg."

"Then perhaps you can be of another service to Gris and me. We need to get some papers up river to Fort Edward, quickly. How would you do this?"

Klompen thought for a few moments, "I can get this done for you. It so happens that I have, er some papers that need to go up to Fort Edward. I have a man up there who is a Petty Sutler. My messenger will be leaving late tonight by the land route. He should be in Fort Edward by tomorrow afternoon at the latest. Have your papers here before ten o'clock and they will be there by tomorrow."

Fogg replied, "Good enough. We will have them here before ten o'clock." Reaching in to his pocket, he pulled out four Spanish dollars and laid them on the table. "That should help cover the expense of a couple of trips, if necessary. Ja?" Klompen scooped them up, glancing around to see that no one was watching and thrust them into his waistcoat pocket.

"Ja, Herr Fogg, ja," was all he could manage. Throwing that kind of money around in a camp could get your throat cut, if you were an ordinary citizen. From the attitude of these two, attempting to cut their throats would probably end with getting your own throat cut. Fogg had the bearing of a highwayman and Gris acted like someone who had been a soldier, a very good soldier, at one time. With that, the two stood up and departed with out any further words.

Once mounted and on their way back through the army camp, they spotted Klompen's bar-maid at one of the Petty Sutlers who appeared to be putting his establishment back together. It appeared that Klompen had more than one "legitimate" partner.

Fogg remarked, "I thought that is what I heard Klompen tell the girl. The prospect of another few thousand soldiers here should keep Herr Klompen and company in place for a while. It will be at least a week before he realizes that there is not going to be that many and another week to move his operation up to Fort Edward. We need to have some rangers dog his messenger all the way to Fort Edward so we will know who the contact is."

"I have a better idea, instead of rangers, as we are not sure who to speak to, let us use a couple of the better 'hunters' from the 80th. Come," and he headed for the 55th camp. They went to the quarter guard of the 55th and Gris went inside and spoke to the officer. He produced paper and pen and Gris quickly wrote out a note and sealed it with his signet. The officer called in the Sergeant of the Guard who took the paper and gave it to a Corporal with instructions to deliver it to no other than Captain Gladwin of the 80th upon pain of being reduced back to private soldier.

Gris remounted and said, "Done." The whole transaction had taken less than ten minutes.

"Alright Mr. Gris. We now have to go back to the lodging and manufacture some paperwork. Do we know anyone at Fort Edward that we can send it to?"

Gris pondered for a moment and then said, "Yes, let's send the whole packet to Colonel Bradstreet.!"

"Is he at Fort Edward?"

"I do not have the slightest idea if he is good, if not, well then it will take a while to reach him," smiled Gris. "The better for our purposes."

They arrived back at their lodgings to find Mr. Bruce there talking with Mrs. Bruin. He was all flustered because of the news of the army starting to move up river. Fogg put his mind to rest with the same tale that they had told Klompen. He embellished it by saying that they had heard that news at the army headquarters across the river this very afternoon. Fogg also inquired if the boy was around as they had to send some papers back to Klompen that he was going to have delivered to Fort Edward for them. Mrs. Bruin said that he would be back within the hour and then he could deliver their papers for them. Bruce said he would let the boy take his horse that was just down the street in a public stable. Our two adventurers excused themselves and went up to their rooms, lit the candles and closed the door. Gris took some paper out of his portmanteau and they wrote out instructions for shipping their barrels up to the lake and authorizing Bradstreet to hire a private drover if necessary or he might use his own men and they, Fogg and Gris, would reimburse him when they came up. They also wrote out a bill of laden for the barrels that Moneypenny was going to have marked and sent up river. They added one more barrel than there actually was to the bill in case they might need to make a public case of it. It was not unusual for private contractors to try to bilk the army out of a little extra money by using false shipping documents. They had just finished the papers when a knock came at their door. It was Mrs. Bruin, looking somewhat disheveled and flustered, saying that the boy was back if their papers were ready.

Fogg replied, "Yes, I am just putting them into the letter carrier now." He had also sealed them with a special sealing wax that had a touch of horse glue in it. If tampered with it would tear fibers from the paper leaving a mark. He handed her the letter carrier with a bow, saying, "There you are madam and may you have a pleasant evening." After she had started back down the stairs he closed the door and said to Gris, "Me thinks that with the boy gone she and Mr. Bruce will continue the pleasant evening that it looks like they have started already."

Gris' only reply was, "God, I hope they are quiet about it as I am exhausted." Fogg put the one chair in the room in front of the door so that anyone opening it would make a scraping noise. "Tell me Fogg, slept in many publick houses have you?"

"One or two, my friend, one or two." *More like one or two hundred. Highwaymen do not live in one place too long nor sleep too deeply. Spies either.*

As has been the habit of soldiers through out the ages both only undressed as far as their shirts and breeches with their boots and weapons close to the bed. Gris put his pocket pistol under his pillow. Fogg had rolled up his great coat to act as an extra pillow and had his dirk between it and the pillow. He lay on top of the bed covering with his maud spread over him. Gris had done likewise with his own blanket. It did not take long for them to fall asleep.

The slight creak of the stairs caused both of them to be wide-awake, hands on weapons. A muffled whisper in the hall way and the sound of Mrs. Bruins' door softly closing told them that attacking them was not what was on the minds of the two occupants of the other room. They both rolled over and started to go back to sleep. Within a couple of minutes, the rhythmic creaking of a rope bed again disturbed them. This was followed in a few more minutes by some muffled grunting and moaning, which was all punctuated by a very muffled scream, like into a pillow. Then silence.

61

"Thank God," whispered Gris. They heard the boy return about midnight and Mr. Bruce departed. All was quiet until morning except for the rounds of the wardens.

## Chapter 13

May 10th started without much incidence. Gris and Fogg walked over to the King's Arms just after sunrise for breakfast. The publican, true to his word, had their table ready for them. Both had coffee and within a few minutes he brought them each a plate with a slice of ham, fried eggs and a white mass that Fogg had not yet encountered in his brief stay in North America. He looked at them and pointed his knife at them and asked, "What are these?"

Gris laughed at the comment and replied, "That my dear fellow is hominy, a local culinary delight."

"Hominy? What in the name of the good Lord is hominy? Is it animal, vegetable or mineral?"

"Hominy, my friend, is lye bleached corn, boiled into this pudding-type dish you see here."

"How do you eat it? More to the point, why would you eat it? Maize or corn as you colonists put it is animal fodder."

"I am afraid not, on this continent it is consumed as regular human food. See, you put a lump of butter on it and then you grind some pepper on it, add a dash of salt and there you have it. As some old housewives say, it will stick to your ribs, get you through a hard day in the fields or saddle." Gris stuck a large spoonful of the hominy in his mouth and said, "Mummm, delicious."

Fogg followed Gris' instructions, plopped on a large slab of butter, ground on some pepper and added a dash of salt. Putting about half of the amount Gris had on his spoon he gingerly tasted it. It was a little different from some things he had eaten but tolerable.

"Needs more pepper," was his only comment.

They finished off breakfast and decided that they would take a short ride up river by way of the river road at least as far as the Mohawk and maybe even up to Halfmoon. Gris said that the 42nd wagon train should be camped just above there where the Coho's Falls road came back to the river.

As they stepped back into the alley that lead toward their lodgings, three men appeared at the other end. Fogg felt, more than saw, the two who had been lurking just down the corner from Market St.

His only comment was, "I think these boys want to play. I wonder if they are up early or up late. Do we shoot them or cut them up?"

"Let's see, if it is a Royal Navy press gang we best not completely do them in. Now on the other hand if they are either a private press gang or some of our friends from the Followers Camp, no one will miss them. What do you think Fogg."

As the group got closer Fogg replied, "I have never seen a Royal Navy press gang without at least a Petty Officer in charge and I do not see any here." He could see that one of the group was armed with a short hunting type sword and the rest had pulled out knives. Gris had glanced back at the ones behind them and commented that they were armed only with knives.

All this time, our two gentlemen had continued walking toward the group in front. This group had hesitated when they saw that they were not going to frighten them into turning and running into the pair behind them. Fogg told Gris to take the two coming up behind on his command. They continued walking toward the three in front who now had stopped completely. Fogg said to them in a clear, loud voice, "Get out of our way you wharf scum."

The one with the sword, brandished it and hollered back, with a quiver of fear in his voice, "Strong talk for unarmed men. We only means to take some of that money you been throwing around."

Fogg's only reply was, "I guess they are not a Royal press gang. Now!" He had already taken the pistol out of the pocket on the inside of the coat by reaching through the slits in the tails with his right hand and his left had pushed that tail back far enough so that he had his hand on his dirk. He raised the muzzle of the pistol and shot the loudmouth with the hunting sword between the eyes. In a blur of motion he drew the dirk, dropped the pistol back into the pocket and shifted the dirk to his right hand.

Gris had turned and reaching into his coat pockets drew out his pistols cocking them as they came out and neatly shot first one of them in the heart and then the other in the face. He quickly returned the pistols and a fighting knife miraculously appeared in his hand from out of his sleeve. The fellow he had shot in the face was still alive and screaming, clutching his face. Gris put him out of his misery with a quick cut across the throat.

Fogg's two remaining attackers froze in their tracks when all three pistols seemed to bark simultaneously. They had lost some of their stomach for quick riches and fear paralyzed them. They had thought that this was an easy mark, two dandies. Fogg was upon them before they could move, he slashed the one on the left across the

64

neck and chest and knocked him down. The other had gathered his wits enough to attack, as he had no place to run. He thrust at Fogg who deftly stuck him under the elbow, forcing the knife up and as he did so he ducked under the arm and slashed his assailant across the back of his knee, severing his hamstrings. The wretch let out a scream of pain and collapsed on the alleyway, dropping his knife, and grabbing his leg. It was all over in less time than it takes to tell of the incident.

Fogg crouched down to the man who was still shrieking and cuffed him across the face.

"Who sent you? Speak up or I'll cut your other leg." The poor wretch was still wreathing about grabbing his leg in pain but had controlled his sobs.

"No one sent us. One of me mates, him," jerking his head toward the one with the sword, "saw you yesterday in the Arms with a purse full of money."

"Was it worth it?" asked Fogg. "You are the only one left alive." He stood up and kicked the knife out of reach of the man. The shots had caused a few of the inhabitants to peer out of their windows or doors and a few even ventured out into the street. One patrol of the military watch must have been not to far off as within five or so minutes they appeared. They had heard the shots and had thought that it was one of their patrols who was in trouble. Since the army had been in Albany, patrols had been jumped by gangs before, trying to relieve them of their weapons and any thing else that they could steal.

The Sergeant in charge stepped up to the fore and demanded, in a loud authoritative voice, "What seems to be the trouble here? Who are all these here fellows lying about? Who are you two gentlemen? I'd bet from your clothes youse was to be the victims, ehh?"

Gris stepped forward. "That would seem to have been the intent, Sergeant. My companion, Mr. Fogg and I are military contractors. We were coming from breakfast at the King's Arms and these fellows seemed to think we were easy prey. If you would care to see our passes." He started to reach inside his coat, "they are signed by Lord Howe." With this comment the Sergeant pulled himself a little straighter.

"No, that won't be necessary, sir. This is not the first time we have had trouble with this gang. I recognize that one there with the hunting sword, no doubt stolen from some gentleman. I guess they won't be bothering any other citizens. That one is going to need a crutch to walk, ifin' he don't die from blood poison. We'll cart him off to the local magistrate and he can deal with him. Good day to ya sirs. All right you local citizenry, the show is over for now, go on about your business. We'll get these vermin off the street as soon as possible." Fogg and Gris started to walk away and the Sergeant called after them.

"Begging your pardon sirs." He had the hunting sword and its case in his hand. "One of you gentlemen should take this as it will only get sold for grog or some other entertainment by either one of my boys or some crooked warder. It is truly a fine weapon that should be carried by a gentleman." Fogg took the sword and handed it to Gris.

"Next time you won't have to get so close as with that fighting knife. Thank you Sergeant."

Gris took it and said, "At least it didn't get bloody."

When they got back to the house Mrs. Bruin was up and asked what was all the shooting and commotion .

"Just some ruffians trying to make a dishonest living. According to the patrol, they seem to have accosted the wrong gentlemen this morning. Dreadful business, four of them dead and the fifth fellow probably crippled for life." This was the only comment that Fogg made about the incident. "We will be gone for the rest of the day and most likely will not be back this evening." They went upstairs and retrieved their firearms, bedrolls and greatcoats. When they came back downstairs their hostess gave them a tow sack.

"Here, gentlemen, is a small snack for you should you get caught short. It is just some bread, cheese and sausage, not much but enough to take the edge off until you find a suitable place to eat."

## Chapter 14

Gris had been up to the falls of the Mohawk but never up river so they had decided to take the track that ran along side the river. There was a road that led to the Mohawk just after Water Fleet but it came to the river way above the Coho's Falls. It led off to the left and another branch led off to the right. The right branch was the road that also lead to the Cow Pasture camp. They stopped briefly at the army landing to see if their problem at the landing had been taken care of. The landing master tipped his hat to them and gave them a sign that they recognized as his having been faithful to his charge. They continued on up past the Patroon's house and van Arrem's where the other road to the ford above the Coho's Falls branched off to the left  It was necessary above here to take one of the scows over to the first island in the delta of the Mohawk. During dry weather it could be forded on foot if you didn't mind getting your feet wet. A man on horse back could keep his feet dry. It was necessary to take another scow from the second island to the third. From the third to the north bank it was fordable. This ford passed just west of a set of rapids of which there were two in this part of the river. The various transporting by scow took a considerable amount of time as in both cases they had to wait as the system here was run by the civilians. The army either went over the Coho's Ford or transported up river by boat.

There were several houses along the road and from the scow and the islands they could see that there were more along the river on the west side. The only house that they saw on the east side was part of the van der Hayden farm. In all cases the large Dutch barns dwarfed the houses. It was ten o'clock in the morning before they sighted the first road coming in from the Coho's Falls ford. It was only a short trip from there to Halfmoon, which consisted of barely a half dozen houses, scattered out opposite the small island in the center of the river.

The 42nd train had encamped just above the settlement and just above the large rapids. There was another road coming in from the Mohawk at this point. They were there to control that road and to assist in getting the boats up past the rapids. When the river was too low they would help portage the bateaux which were loaded on trucks. When the river was high enough for the boats to float they helped pull the boats up river by rope. There were three sets of large rapids between Halfmoon and Stillwater and the boats needed assistance at all three. With the river as it was now during a rainy stretch it was only necessary to pull them up river. This was a much easier job than having to portage them.

At the larger rapids it was necessary to unload the boats, put the contents in wagons and then draw the boats up and reload after they were above the rapids. Once above the falls at Saratoga it was a continuous ride to Fort Edward.

Our travelers rode up to the guard post and were challenged by the Corporal of the Guard. They produced their passes and he had them wait while he sent a private off for an officer or a sergeant to read them. A short stocky sergeant appeared in a few minutes and took the passes from the corporal. He looked them over very carefully and inquired if their final destination was to be Fort Edward. Fogg replied that they intended to go no further than Stillwater on this trip and would be back down tomorrow but before continuing they required to speak to the Officer in Charge. The sergeant again eyed them suspiciously and asked why.

Fogg, who had been surveying the camp spread off to the west, turned in his saddle and replied in Scots Gaelic, "The King's business."

The sergeant pulled himself a little straighter and answered back respectfully, "Then pass on through, Sir, and you have a good day," in English and to the privates on the barricade in Scots Gaelic, he said "Open that barrier and don't keep the gentlemen waiting about all day." To Fogg in the same tongue, "You put them in King's uniform and their still poachers and cattle thieves, Sir." Fogg and Gris trotted off through the now open chaveaux and went toward the camp. There they found a Captain and Lieutenant of the 42nd looking over a rough map of the area from the ford at Coho's to Halfmoon. As they dismounted the two turned the map over and rose to meet them.

Fogg addressed them as he stepped down, "Good day to you gentlemen. Allow me to introduce my friend Mr. Gris and I am Mr. Fogg. We are suppliers for the army. Here are our credentials," handing them the passes. The Captain looked at the signature and handed them back with out reading the rest.

"I should guess that gentlemen like yourselves, bearing passes signed by his Lordship, ought to at least be offered a seat."

"No thank you, Captain," replied Gris, "we've been sitting enough for a while."

The Captain chuckled and queried, "What may we do for you on this fine June day?"

"We understand you came here by way of the Coho's Road. We are wondering if the ford on the Mohawk was easy enough for your wagons. Also is the ford guarded?"

"Taking your questions in order, yes, yes and yes."

"Well put and to the point, Captain. Now if you could be a little more specific. Is the road in good shape for this weather? Was the water at the ford below the wagon beds? Were there troops stationed at the ford itself?"

"The road is in very good shape for this weather. I would say that whatever is underneath allows most of the road to drain well. Our wagons did not dig it up too much and the lads did not complain because the mud was too deep. As for the ford itself, the water has not risen to a sufficient height to reach the bottom of the wagons, despite the rain earlier. In regard to your last question, why do you want to know if there are troops at the ford?"

"We may be sending some of our own wagons up that way and would like to know if the ford is secure. I would not like to have my draymen in the middle of the Mohawk and then attacked by brigands or much worse the French and their allies."

"I assure you Mr. Fogg that there are no French and their red hellions in this area. The 46th Foot has a detachment at the ford and I have patrols going back and forth on this road at irregular times. I also have patrols moving up and down this side of the river between here and Stillwater. At least half of my detachment is out at any time. We have heard rumors of French partisans off to the west in the hills but have yet to see or be bothered by them." Gris, who had remained quiet to this point spoke up.

"What is the road like between here and Stillwater?"

The Captain replied, "It is in good condition. You can take wagons up and down on it with out too much effort. If you are using horses, you might want an extra pair in harness. Oxen, well two will do if you are using Dutch wagons. May I ask why you are not shipping your goods upriver by boat?"

"Actually we have not yet decided on how we are shipping it," Gris replied. "Our trip is to calculate our options. Our contract calls for us to get it to Fort Edward and from that point on it is the concern of the army."

"I would suggest that you might consider the wagons. As you are aware, there is a shortage of boats on the river. I would think that as the army requires more boats it would be commandeering as many civilian boats as there are. A great many of them may even be taken above Fort Edward to the Lake.  If your wagons are out on the track, carrying army provisions, they will be exempt from being pressed into army service."

"Very sound advice, Captain, we will give it a great deal of consideration." was Gris' only reply.  "What say you Fogg, shall we be on up the track?" Fogg nodded his head in reply and as they turned to remount the highlander Captain spoke up.

"Excuse me, Mr. Gris.  Do you have a brother who is an officer in Gage's Lights?  You look awfully familiar."

As Gris settled himself in the saddle, he answered nonchalantly, "That would be my cousin, on my father's side. Deuced family resemblance and we are both named for our grandfather Gris.  Some people even say we could pass for twins." The Captain nodded his head and seemed satisfied with the answer.

"Sorry to have bothered you but it is indeed a remarkable resemblance.  Well, good trip and perhaps we will see you in a few days, on your return."  They wheeled their horses and headed back toward the river.  The horses wanted to run so they let them out until they reached the junction where the track ran north.

As they turned onto it, Fogg looked at Gris and made only one comment, "Cousin?  Remind me to never play cards with you for money."

Gris smiled and said, "Actually it is somewhat the truth.  I do have a cousin named Robert Gris, who by the way, is a handsome fellow also with a remarkable resemblance to me.  However, he is most likely in Philadelphia or Baltimore making lots of money supplying the army with horses. Mostly other people's horses."  With that, they settled in for the ride up to Stillwater.  Their job on this mission was to observe how well the army was moving both men and supplies and where there were any hitches in the system.  They had been satisfied that the Highlanders would keep their section of the road and river secure.  The 17th stationed at the ford above the Coho's Falls were seasoned campaigners and with their constantly being in contact with the 42nd that section would be secure.  In their report to Lord Howe they would suggest that the ranger patrols might extend farther west or that perhaps Sir William's Mohawks might be convinced to set up ambushes along the trails on the foot hills that the French partisans were using.  Gris had heard tales of English long-hunters who made it a practice of stalking the French and their allies for the purpose of the bounty on their scalps.  They would make the ideal ones to range these trails but he had never actually met one nor anyone else who had actually met one.  Perhaps they were just Mohawk Valley tavern tales.

## Chapter 15

The river was full of traffic as was the track up to Stillwater. There were boats of both men and supplies moving this fine bright day. There was a small set of falls at Halfmoon that required the boats to be unloaded. If the boats were designated to go on up river they would be hauled out of the river and placed on trucks and taken above the falls and the rapids just above the falls. The supplies that they had in them were transported up to Stillwater by wagon. The boats were then hauled up each set of rapids by rope. A crew was left on each boat to row it up to the next set. At Stillwater they would be reloaded and continue up to the falls just above Saratoga. At this point is was again necessary to portage around these falls. Only the boats designated for use on the Lake were transported around the falls. There were a group of boats that shuttled back and forth between portages. This cut down on the unnecessary man-handling of boats at every portage. Supplies were handled on an average of five times between Albany and Lake George, ten if you counted loading and unloading. All this required a great many men stationed at various places along the route. It also required a great many animals at strategic places in order to haul both wagons and boats. The country was such that with each place there were animals plus all sorts of support people for the animals and the wagons. Trucks and wagons were lucky if they made a round trip between stations with out some sort of repair being necessary.

All this was the Herculean job that Lord Howe had taken on. General Abercromby made sure that everything made it to Albany from New York and General Howe made sure that it made it to the Lake. This was the largest force of His Majesty's troops ever to be assembled in North America. Even in Europe it would have been a logistical nightmare. Here was a country where roads were almost non-existent. The road that followed the river on the west side north to Saratoga was an exception. It had been widened by Lyman in 1755 and allowed two wagons to pass each other in most places. The rivers and streams were the real thoroughfares of the North American Continent. This war was really over who would control these as they were the way into the heart of the continent and therefore the trade routes with the native population.

71

Each one of the major waterways that penetrated the mountains and passed on into the interior was guarded by somebody's fort which was wanted by somebody else. This struggle had been going on, in one form or another since the beginning of the 17th century. In 1609, Samuel de Champlain paddled up the lake that would later bear his name. The same year Henry Hudson sailed up the river that would bear his name with both claiming land that belonged to neither one in the name of whichever king they served. It was only recently that it had reached its present proportions of European size armies in conflict. For almost one-hundred-fifty years they had let the native population do the killing for them and now they had started a war that would spill over into Europe. Each government would do its damnedest "For King and Country" and to hell with the native population and the settlers who were just trying to make a life.

## Chapter 16

The track, as it would not qualify for a road in England, was full of wagons and troops stretched out all the way from Halfmoon to Stillwater. Fortunately, there was room to ride alongside it. The wagons were mostly carrying supplies and provisions that were being portaged around the rapids and falls. It was possible to carry four to six of the size barrels that were used for such things as flour, rice and salt pork. They, the barrels, weighed in at between 200 to 250 pounds each, depending upon what exactly they were carrying. Wagons carrying butter and bread could carry more containers in number but the overall weight remained the same. Butter was shipped in sixty pound firkins and bread in fifty pound barrels. Dried peas were shipped in covered baskets. Someone estimated that every boat that comes up from Albany with supplies requires between six and eight wagons to transfer the goods around a set of falls. It required at least two sets of trucks to transport an English bateaux around the falls.

Not only was it necessary to haul all of the provisions for the troops in this manner, but it was also necessary to haul all or most of the provisions for the animals that did the hauling in this manner. The average draft horse required twenty lbs. of hay and nine pounds of oats as well as green grazing. A team of four horses required almost the equivalent weight of what they could haul in one trip to sustain themselves for a week, not counting the green grazing. Oxen required slightly less as they were not quite so discriminating about what they munched on as were the horses.

The average bateaux was approximately thirty to thirty-two feet long, a little over six feet at the beam with almost three foot height. They had between seven to nine sets of oar pins but usually only had half of these occupied during a normal trip. It could carry 33 men and their provisions for a maximum of a month. Carrying provisions only and a five man crew it could carry two tons. This would equate to, according to some estimates, about fifteen barrels of flour. Based on these figures it would take well over a one thousand bateaux to transport the army and its supplies up to the Lake in time to launch the force on schedule. Due to the shortage of both boats and wagons it was necessary for Lord Howe to set up a chain of supply points between Albany and Fort Edward. As the bulk of the army moved up to the debarkation point on the Lake it would pull the majority of its supply train tail up with it. They would leave only enough boats on the river to maintain a communication line with Albany. It was hoped that the new boats being built in New York would be ready to take over the supply transportation, which if all went well, would extend to Fort St. Frederic on Lake Champlain. Once having moved above Lake Champlain they could rely on the St. Lawrence River and the Royal Navy to supply them.

The threat to the French had always been that the English would put together an expedition large enough to sustain itself and invade Canada from the south by way of the Hudson, Lake George and Lake Champlain. It was to this end that Fort St. Fredric and Fort Carillon had been built, and the English Fort Wm. Henry had been destroyed. Now one of Montcalm's greatest fears was being realized as the English had assembled two invasion forces large enough to sustain themselves and attack from two different points. One point, Louisburg, was designed to deny the French Fleet a safe harbor on the North Atlantic coast and also the use of the St. Lawrence River to supply their armies in the interior. Montcalm did not have enough French Regulars, Troupe de Terre, to defend against both attack points. His forces would have to consist of a majority of Troupe de la Marine and la Milice to face the English Regulars who made up the bulk of these two invasion forces. Montcalm, like his English opposites, did not have a great deal of faith in provincial troops. Both the French and the English generals had a great deal to learn about their provincial allies. This was the basis for the conversation between Fogg and Gris as they made their way up the track toward Stillwater.

At the rapids just below Stillwater, they stopped to let their horses rest. They dismounted and stood on a piece of elevated ground where they could watch a party of men who were hauling a bateaux up the rapids. There were two men on the bateaux, one at the bow and one at the stern using an oar as a tiller. At first the bateaux appeared to be empty but on one of its dips toward shore they could see that it had what appeared to be a medium size field gun in it, tube, carriage and all. There was a rope attached to the bow post and run to the shore where about thirty soldiers had a grip on it and were hauling it slowly upstream. There was a drummer tapping out the pace and the bateaux was slowly making headway against the current. They watched for about fifteen to twenty minutes while the horses rested and grazed on the spring grass. Several parties of troops marched on by them on their way up river. One group of highlanders were marching barefoot to keep from getting their shoes wet and muddy as

74

the track was not quite dried out yet. They seemed to be the only ones not grumbling about having to walk when there were plenty of wagons and boats to carry the officers' baggage. The highlanders were happy that their stint in the transports was over and that they were getting out of the lowlands. They were looking forward to getting in to the mountains that reminded them of home.

As they stood there watching another bateaux being rigged to be hauled up river their attention was drawn to a point up at the head of the rapids by a group of soldiers pointing in that direction. There was a longboat just entering the rapids. Gris took out his glass and trained it on the boat.

"It is a party of rangers running the rapids," he remarked, "and from the green coats they would appear to be from one of the Rogers brothers' companies." They could now see that there were several men in the boat, all facing forward. The coxswain had the tiller and there were two standing near the bow with long poles to help keep it off any rocks. The coxswain picked his way down the rapids as if he had made the trip several times before.

The passengers were all whooping and a hollering and having a fine old time. Bradstreet's men did this all the time and thought it was a good break from the monotony of poling and rowing. Apparently, it was considered a great pastime by the rangers who also spent a great deal of time in their longboats.

"It must be a dispatch boat as it is continuing down river. Shall we Mr. Gris?" asked Fogg as he turned to mount.

"Yes, it is only a short distance to the camp at Stillwater from here. Just above the rapids. We should arrive just in time for lunch. Perhaps we can bully our way into the Officers Mess."

"I'd rather the Sergeant's Mess. They have better food and usually more of it. They also know everything that is going on with an army," replied Fogg.

"Well we will never bully our way into a Sergeant's Mess. I guess we will need something to sweeten the pot." Gris answered Fogg's statement. He turned around in his saddle and reached into one of the saddle bags, withdrawing a bottle of whiskey.

"This was brewed and aged in the highlands. Yes in the highlands of the Hudson River and aged at least for a couple of months. It ought to get us a seat at any Sergeant's Mess, even in the Guards." With that he kicked his horse up and they went flying past the columns on the track because this was fairly open country.

## Chapter 17

When they came within sight of the camp, just above the small falls, they slowed to a walk. Along the way they had passed some of the four companies of 42nd and 55th Foot who had left Albany the day before. The troops had gone as far north as Halfmoon and continued on to Stillwater the next day. They were commanded by a Major Campbell and a Major Proby. Fogg knew that Campbell was the Laird of someplace in Scotland but couldn't remember which place. The sixteen wagons that accompanied them had slowed down their progress due to not having enough horses. The teams had been made up of only four and the continuous uphill progress of the track had slowed them down.

The camp at Stillwater consisted mostly of companies of the 42nd and 55th. Some of the troops coming up the track now were destined to go on to Saratoga and garrison the supply depot there. There were some pioneers and carpenters here at Stillwater working on the beginnings of a blockhouse and storehouse laid out by the engineer Montressor. By the time it would be finished the majority of the army would be up at the Lake and it would become a vital link in the supply chain.

When Fogg and Gris reached the outer perimeter of the camp they were challenged by the guard post. The soldiers of the 55th eyed them with caution. Here were two men, obviously gentlemen from their kit, mounted upon two army horses. It was possible that they were officers and it didn't pay to challenge officers too forcefully.

The Corporal of the Guard stepped forward, coming to the position of most attention under arms.

"Might I see your passes, sirs." The members of his guard detail were standing at the same behind him. Fogg handed his pass to Gris who was closest, who then handed both to the Corporal. Here was a Corporal who was going to make sergeant someday as he took both passes and read them, his lips forming each word slowly. When he got to the bottom and saw more than read the signature, he straightened up even more. Here were two gentlemen carrying passes signed by the very colonel of his own regiment, Lord Howe, himself.

He handed the passes back to Gris, "Pass on through, Sirs. May I direct you to any particular point in the camp?"

"Yes as a matter of fact you may. Could you direct us toward what would pass for the Sergeants Mess," asked Gris.

"Aye Sir. Would that be the 55th's Sergeants Mess or the 42nds Sir."

"The 55th's would be the one."

"That would be the camp furthest up, Sir. Just beyond that small stand of trees. Sir."

Gris stood in his saddle and looked toward where the Corporal was pointing. "Thank you, Corporal. One more question. Is that the tent of Colonel Donaldson?" pointing to a subaltern tent.

"Aye Sir. That would be his tent. Sir." They thanked the Corporal once more and rode off toward the direction he had indicated as the Sergeants Mess. There was a small tarp erected at one of the field kitchens with a small plank table set upon a couple of barrels. There were three sergeants in the process of getting some food and a fourth soldier who appeared to be doing the cooking.

When our travelers dismounted, the person cooking inquired, "May I be helping you two gentlemen? If you're looking for the officers mess it would be that way. Sirs," pointing toward the tents closest to the river, where there was a marquis canopy pitched.

"Actually we are looking for the Sergeants Mess and I assume that this is it or at least one," stated Fogg.

"Yes Sir. It would be one but why would two obvious gentlemen like yourselves be looking for a Sergeants' Mess?"

"Well in my experience with armies, I have found that if you want something done or the best rations, you seek out the sergeants. And you would be Sergeant?"

"Sergeant Thomas Sanford, Colonel's Company, 55th Foot at your service. Sir!" Gris stepped forward and held out the small sack he had in his hand.

"Here is a little something to add to the Sergeants Mess, for medicinal purposes, of course." Sergeant Sanford took the proffered sack, opened it and looked inside.

"Of course, Sir, for medicinal purposes. We have great recourse for such, camped so close to the river. Damp night vapors and such." He opened a chest and stowed the sack safely inside. "And now if you two gentlemen would care to pull up a couple of them empty kegs, it just so happens that we have some tasty Sheppard's Pie, compliments of a local mutton that decided to volunteer for His Majesty's service. Wandered right into camp it did. When I asked it if it was volunteering to become Sheppard's Pie or Mutton Stew it said, 'Sheppard's Pie'. So I accommodated it," whereupon the other three Sergeants all laughed and nodded their heads in agreement.

One of them spoke up, saying, "That would be Sergeant 'Cookie' Sanford, able to charm all sorts of local livestock into a pot!"

Pointing to the one who had just commented, 'Cookie' Sanford replied, "And it don't look like you are none the worst for it either." This sent them all into fits of laughter. Fogg and Gris sat down, took out their camp utensils and commenced to eat the offered bowls. The pie was indeed excellent. The Sergeant-Cook pulled a loaf of fresh baked bread out of a basket that sat on one of the chests and placed it on the makeshift table. They both broke off a large chunk to help sop up the thick broth. One of the Sergeants reached under the table and pulled out a wicker covered bottle while another got them two stoneware mugs. The one with the bottle filled up the mugs, commenting "Local cider" with a twinkle in his eye. Fogg picked up his mug and held it up to sniff it before drinking. It was cider made sometime during the winter and having sat in a root cellar until recently. It had been strained and was a clear golden color. He took a sip, letting it sit in his mouth for a second or two. It was not as strong as he had thought as somehow the maker had halted the process so that it had just a slight buzz to it.

He held up the cup and said, "Excellent, simply excellent. I might even say damn excellent."

As they ate they conversed with the Sergeants who were joined by a couple of more, who took bowls and stood eating. This was a combined Sergeants mess from several companies as Stanford's prowess as a cook was well known in the regiment. Fogg inquired as to their opinion of the alterations that Lord Howe had caused to be made to their uniforms. The general consensus was that all the changes were good except that perhaps their coats had been cut too short. They all hoped that they would receive new issue coats for the coming winter. They all had great faith in Lord Howe. He had supplied all-new, special-made, cut down hats for them. Their cocked hats were all stored, along with their halberds and hangers. The frogs for their hangers were now carrying a smaller version of the regulation camp axe fitted with a leather covering. Each man had been issued a belly box in addition to his shoulder box. They carried in their haversack additional cartridges bundled into packages to refill their box if emptied. All wore brown marching gaiters and soldiers coats. It was impossible to determine the officers from the other ranks. The officers wore their sashes under their coats and their gorgets dropped into their waistcoats. Most of the officers were carrying slightly shortened regulation muskets, yet some were carrying musketoons and fusils. The entire regiment was going to store its tents at Fort Edward, to be brought up when they had taken Carillon and Fort St. Frederic. Each man was issued a waterproofed tarp in which to carry his blanket. This tarp would serve as their only shelter. A soldier would sit upright with the tarp held up by his ramrod, wrapped in his blanket, cradling his musket to help keep the lock dry. All the muskets had been fitted with a cow's knee, a piece of leather taken from the knee area of the cow skin, oiled to be more water proof and with a single leather thong that wrapped around and tuck under itself instead of tied to hold it in place.

All of this information was imparted in bits and pieces while our two travelers ate their Shepard's Pie. It was apparent that the Sergeants of the 55th Foot were proud of their regiment's adjustment to North America. It was even rumored that Lord Howe had been out on patrols with the rangers, especially Major Rogers' own company. They thanked the Sergeants for their generosity and donated a shilling each to the Sergeants Mess fund. This was enough to keep the mess in luxuries for a goodly period of time. Sergeant Sanford extended to them an open invitation to dine in his mess at any time they were in the vicinity of the 55th, warning them that out in the field it might only be boiled peas and salt pork.

They gathered up their mounts and walked on to where the Corporal had indicated Col. Donaldson's tent to be. He was not there but his aide indicated that he could be found over at the marquis top by the river. They mounted and rode over to where the marquis top had been pitched for an officer's mess. There were several officers seated under the fly, some eating and others just passing time. One of them rose to greet them.

"May we help you gentlemen? You seem to be somewhat astray, this is a military camp." His tone somewhat denoting an air of disdain for civilians. The more elderly looking officer sitting in the far end of the fly spoke up.

"There, there Mr. Ashe. Can't you see that the gentlemen are riding army mounts. This is not something easily come by outside of headquarters, now is it." He stood up and walked over and extended his hand. "Indeed, what may we do for you. I am Colonel Donaldson and in command of this little encampment here on the river."

Gris took the lead. "Yes, Colonel Donaldson. Allow me to introduce Mr. E. Fogg and I am Mr. R. Gris. We are suppliers to the army and travel under a pass from Brigadier General Lord Howe. Our purpose in stopping here at your mess is an obligation to deliver a packet of letters from His Lordship into your hands personally." Gris was still holding onto the Colonels hand and he felt the Colonels grip change to which he also responded. The colonel leaned over and whispered something in his ear and Gris indicated to Fogg to deliver up the packet that Fogg had been carrying in his coat tail.

"Won't you gentlemen sit down and have something to eat or drink while I look these over?" indicating the packet.

Gris responded, "No thank you Sir. We have eaten already and are eager to get on a little further up the river. We will be returning back this way later today or perhaps tomorrow and may take you up on your hospitality then. Gentlemen," he said, touching his hat. They both walked out and mounted and started on up the river road. They planned to be at the camp at Saratoga by sunset. This is where they would spend the night and also connect with a patrol of Rangers from Robert Rogers Own Company. They had orders for them from Lord Howe also.

## Chapter 18

By the time they arrived at Saratoga the sun was just starting to touch the horizon. They were challenged by the lower picket post and had to wait for a Sergeant from the 42nd who could read English to pass them through. The majority of the Scots could not read English, with the exception of the officers and some of the senior NCOs. It was occasionally a problem also that some of the Highlanders could not speak English at all or very well. They had learned the commands but other than that could not understand anything but simple terms.

The Sergeant pointed out the direction of the Ranger Camp to them and they rode until they came to within a couple of hundred yards of the area. They dismounted and led their mounts until they were challenged again, this time in New Englander English. The challenge was slightly more than a raised whisper. In the failing light it was difficult to tell where it came from until a man stood up out of a clump of brush, his musket pointed in their direction. Gris answered him back with a slightly more nasal twang in his voice than usual.

"Friends, we've come from down river with a dispatch from Lord Howe to the officer in charge here."

"Stand fast where you be." The words were almost running in together so that it sounded to Fogg like "Stanfstwereyabe". As yet, he had not met too many of the Yankees. God, I hope I can learn to understand them and vice-versa. I would hate to get shot by some damn Yankee who didn't understand me. The sentry gave a low whistle like some sort of bird. Another figure appeared out of the underbrush further back and came up to him. The first sentry whispered to the other who disappeared back from whence he had come. Within a few minutes he came back with another man and they motioned to follow them. The second sentry took and tied up their mounts in a small stand of hardwoods just off from where he was stationed. Their guide indicated that they should be quiet and he led them off down a path for about fifty or sixty yards whence they came to another small stand of trees. Situated in among the trees was a party of about twenty-five rangers. There was no camp as such. They were all sitting or lying down leaning on their packs eating cold rations. They were not uniformed in a military sense but were in that they all wore similar type clothing. There were boxed frocks of the type worn by farmers and dray men for the most part dyed with butternut or iron grey. Some were wearing waistcoats over a couple of linen shirts, the one on top being raw or tow. A couple had on dark colored sailor jackets and other types. Their head gear ranged from everything from workman's caps to cut down flop hats. There was even one or two Scots type knit bonnets.

They were led over to a man who was sitting almost in the middle of the camp. He was leaning against his pack and had his musketoon laid across his lap. He motioned for them to sit down and offered them a piece of jerky.

They refused and he leaned forward and in a whisper, " I'm Sergeant Ross, Major Rogers Company. The sentry said you had a dispatch for me?"

Gris leaned forward, "Are you in command of this detachment?"

"Yes. There are two more detachments, one about four hundred yards north and another about the same south. Ensign Wynne is in command of the south one and Sergeant Fenton is in command of the north one."

"Perhaps we should deliver these to Ensign Wynne as we were told to deliver them to the senior Ranger officer present at Saratoga," replied Gris.

Sergeant Ross leaned forward and replied, "You are speaking to the senior Ranger officer present at Saratoga. Ensign Wynne is from the 60th, a member of the Cadre Company and only ranks as a Sergeant when in the field with us. Now, the dispatches or get out of my camp as we are about to go out on an ambush." Fogg handed him over the dispatches and looking him straight in the eye inquired as to the nature of the ambush.

Sergeant Ross, still whispering said, "Seems like word has come up from down below that there may be some Frenchie spies moving back and forth between Albany and the Lake. We're moving off to the point on the foot hills where the path goes north. My orders are to watch the trail and follow the messengers to see who they contact, if anybody at Fort Edward. If they bypass Fort Edward we shadow them to the Lake."

"Sounds a little dicey," replied Fogg.

"They ain't never give us the slip, except once. They had the bad luck to run into a patrol from the Stockbridge Company just west and north of Edward. Stockbridge weren't aware of what was happening so they shot um up and took a few scalps. By the time we come up on them it was too late and the only one to live through the ambush was shot in the face and couldn't talk."

"Did he recover enough to talk later?" asked Gris?

"There weren't no later. He was wearing a Stockbridge knife and case hang'n around his neck. Seems that them Stockbridge was a little touchy about that. They took him off into the woods to talk to him about his manners." The Sergeant started to stand, "Well, gents we got to go. Maybe we'll see ya up at the Lake sometime or up at the Island. Look us up, the Ranger camp is easy to find." Fogg and Gris wished them good hunting and were led back to where they had left their horses. When they got back nearer the regulars camps they realized that they were not challenged. The regulars were thinking that the Rangers had the land side covered. When they arrived at the 55th camp they looked up the officer in charge and mentioned to him that the Rangers were out hunting French and that his back door was unguarded. He immediately put out a picket line and sent a runner to the 42nd area of the camp to tell them to do the same, at least until first light.

He offered them a tent to sleep in for the night but they declined, instead asking where the Sergeants Mess was located. Having been pointed in the general direction, they led their mounts over to a fire that appeared to be slightly larger than the rest. There were a couple of Sergeants sitting on the ground by the fire. They started to stand up when our duo approached. Gris motioned them to remain where they were. They hobbled their mounts and took off the saddles and other tack. Fogg, who was finished first, walked over to the fire and asked if they could spare some hot tea and perhaps a hunk of bread for two weary travelers. One of the two rose up on his haunches and said that all they had to offer was hot coffee and perhaps some cold biscuits. With that, a man stuck his head out of the tent and inquired what all the fuss and commotion was about.

"A couple of gentlemen travelers looking for a cup of something hot to drink and a place to throw down their blankets," was the reply that the Sergeant who had rose to meet them.

The head from the tent nodded and said, "There's some pea soup in that pot near the fire. It would still be warm as I only pulled it from the fire 'bout an hour ago," with that the head disappeared. The Sergeant, who had done most of the talking, motioned to the pot and asked if they would like some. They accepted the offer, as they had not eaten since leaving the Stillwater camp. The Sergeant took a couple of tin cups out of the utensil chest and half filled them with the thick gray soup. He then took a ladle and dipped some hot water out of the other pot that sat near the fire. He handed the cups to Gris and

Fogg who using their own camp utensils stirred the mixture until it was thin enough to drink. This was portable soup made with local gray peas. It didn't taste any different than yellow or green peas but was more easily eaten in the dark as the color didn't matter then.

While eating, they inquired if the troops going up river stopped here for long or did they just pass on through. From what they had seen, it did not look like the grass was flattened and dead as it would have been if there were a lot of men staying over night. They asked if they ever saw much of the Rangers. The answer to that question was hardly ever. They mostly just took it for granted that they were out there. Occasionally, a couple would come into camp and do some cooking and then disappear back out into the woods. Mostly, the duty was just patrolling the road and occasionally having to unload boats of supplies for the depot. There was also a lot of dray stock here at Saratoga and they had to constantly keep a watch posted on it. The locals were not above driving off an ox or two as once slaughtered you could not tell if it was army property or not. Horses were relatively safe from pilfering, as they were too easy to trace. There were at least a dozen families living in this area and they were on the one hand glad to see the army posted there as it made it somewhat safer from attacks by the French savages. On the other hand, they were constantly complaining about missing items such as fences, vegetables from root cellars, and the occasional chicken. Those with daughters kept them locked up and out of sight as well. Any place that the army encamped, it was always a mixed blessing.

When they had finished their soup, Fogg took out a small bottle of brandy from his saddlebags and poured some in the two Sergeants' cups and then his and Gris'. He took out his pipe and filled it and passed the tobacco around. When he and Gris finished their brandy and pipes they rolled up in their greatcoats and turned in. They had taken great care to secure their arms from the damp. Along about false dawn they heard a couple of shots off toward the south and then all was quiet again. They surmised from the direction that it was below the lower Ranger post, most likely from a nervous sentry.

When it got light enough, they were up and mounted before the camp was awake. Only the sleepy eyed sentries saw them head south, back down river toward Albany. They had delivered their dispatches and seen enough of the operations at the depots up along the river as far as Saratoga. Lord Howe had placed the right regiments to watch this series of lower depots. The 55th and the 42nd were doing their duty well. As the army moved up river, it would pull its supply train up with it. The garrison at Fort Edward and those left behind at the Cow Pasture would then be in charge of making sure that the supply route stayed open.  As the main army advanced up to the Lake and pushed the French north, the supply route would increasingly become longer but safer.  Denied the use of the lakes the French would eventually only be able to launch attacks from Oswegatchie by way of the Black River and the Mohawk.  Once Webb finished building the fort at the Great Carry of the Mohawk ,that route would also be closed to raiding parties.  A lot was riding on the throw of the dice at Louisburg and Lake Champlain.

## Chapter 19

A great deal of Thursday, May 11th was consumed by the return trip down river to Albany. They did not stop except to eat some of their traveling rations, just below Stillwater. They remarked that there was a great deal more troop movement on the river then the day before. When they reached the Cow Pastures they also noticed that there were more troops in camp than when they had left

It was just mid-afternoon when they stopped at the landing to obtain a ride across the river to Lord Howe's headquarters. There was a scow going across so they took their mounts with them. When they approached the van Renssealer home, they were stopped by the sentry post on the road. They could see that there were at least a dozen horses tied up at the back of the house with half as many orderlies taking care of them. They produced their passes and were ushered through the post. They tied their mounts up at the picket line and walked around to the front of the house. There were two sentries at the front door who challenged them.

Gris stepped up to them, "I am Captain Gris of the 80th Foot. Inform Captain Moneypenny that Mr. Fogg and I have returned from up river.". While one still barred the door, the other one disappeared inside and returned within a few minutes informing them that Capt. Moneypenny would see them. The one barring the door stepped aside.

Moneypenny now had three clerks in his office, all busy copying documents for distribution among the army. Moneypenny rose and walked around from behind his desk and extended his hand.

"Good to see you back. His Lordship was wondering how you were faring. As you can see our little family has increased. General Abercromby has arrived from down below. He is in with Lord Howe at the moment. We are finishing the arrangements for him and his staff. We were aware of his coming up river but did not have the exact day of his arrival until early this morning when a dispatch rider came in with news of his transport on the river. As you probably notice there were additional companies across the river."

Fogg replied, "I take it that the Inniskillings outside are part of the General's entourage? I take it also that he brought mounts up river with him. There did not appear to be that many fine mounts in the area before. What else is worthy of note?"

Moneypenny gave his brief smile and replied, "Most observant Mr. Fogg, but then that is what Lord Howe's relative relies upon from you. See those clerks all scribbling away? Well, they are writing out the orders for the army for tomorrow and several of the items are going to have most of them wringing their hands and shaking their heads. I quote, 'It is Major General Abercromby's orders that the regiments do not carry their colours, nor camp colours to the field this campaign. That the officers do not carry their sashes, but wear their gorgets on duty. That no officer carries more camp equipage than a soldiers tent, a small portmantle, blankets and bearskin.' I'll see if Lord Howe wants to see you right away or have you wait." With that he went to the door and rapped softly. They heard a muffled voice from within reply. Moneypenny slipped through the half open door.

Within a couple of minutes Moneypenny reappeared and motioned for them to go in. They went through the open door and were greeted by Lord Howe who had risen from his chair. He and General Abercromby were sitting at a table that was under one of the two windows in the room. He extended his hand,

"Gentlemen, gentlemen, come in. May I present Major General Abercromby, Commander in Chief in North America. Captain Robert Gris, 80th Foot on detached duty to me and Mr. Ethyrial Fogg, a Gentleman Volunteer who comes very well recommended. They are both working on an extended project for me." The General was gracious enough but did not rise to shake their hands. Fogg was well acquainted with the General, not personally but information wise. James Abercromby was fifty-two years old, born in 1706 and had entered the army at a young age. He also held a seat in Parliament, had been the Lt. Colonel of the Royal Scots in 1746, and had served in the expedition against Port L'Orient. In '55 he had become the Colonel of the 50th Foot and in '56 was promoted to Major General and seconded to Lord Loudon in North America. Abercromby was known as an admirable "second" due to his logistical ability. It was rumored that he was not in the best of health, but that made him not so much different than most men his age in this day and place. Fogg thought that he looked a little pale and puffy and that he certainly was overdressed, wearing a laced coat even though it looked like a field coat. He was definitely of the "European school" of general grade officers. Both gave him a slight bow and said in unison, "General". *The General is wondering why am I being introduced to this junior officer and a civilian* was the comment that went through Fogg's mind.  Lord Howe broke the silence that seemed to hang in the air.

"General, these two gentlemen have been engaged in some intelligence gathering for me.  They have uncovered a possible, no, more likely probable nest of rodents in Albany and following our army up to Fort Edward, and possibly beyond.  They have recently returned from a sojourn up to Saratoga, I believe, and most likely have good intelligence on our supply efforts and the actions of the French to thwart us."  The General seemed to become slightly more interested in them at this point.

"Let us hear a brief verbal report, if you would, Captain Gris."  Gris recounted all of the events that had transpired on their sortie up river, omitting a great deal of detail.  There were parts that he thought should only be heard by Lord Howe as the General would most likely not be interested in all the trivia that made up contre-espionnage, the in vogue word for in what they were engaged.  When Gris had finished, General Abercromby sat there for a moment, hands folded in his lap, not making any comment.  He then slowly looked at Gris and then at Fogg and finally to General Howe.

"Well General, I think that this all falls under your responsibilities.  Therefore you should deal with all of it as you see fit.  Do you think we should involve anyone else in it, any of the senior officers, say Gage perhaps?"

"I do not think that it would be wise to include any more people in the matter than we have at the moment.  These gentlemen are at great enough risk without including any unnecessary persons. So far they have limited their contacts to only men that they are positive they can trust, men with a certain obligation.  It is for those reasons that we have put nothing in writing and do not plan to.  I am afraid that if even senior officers were informed that it will somehow leak out, perhaps through bat men, orderlies or clerks.  If I was a Frenchman and I wanted to get information I would attempt to get it through those channels.  A little female attention to a soldier who as a rule can not obtain it has the effect of opening a spigot, in more ways than one."  Howe's last comment was made with a smile based on his knowledge of the common soldier.

"Well then, that's it isn't it!  However you see fit General, however you see fit.  I am off to inspect the camp.  I should suppose that by the time I return my quarters will be ready.  I am having my headquarters marquis set out on the east lawn so the house can protect it.  My clerks will move in as soon as it is up and of course they will be quartered in it."  With that he arose and departed.  Howe indicated to Gris and Fogg to sit.

88

"Well, gentlemen, would you now care to give me all the details? I am sure that you omitted some items of significance." Between the two of them they covered all of the details from their encounter in the alleyway to their return. They remarked on how there was a mixed bag of officers. The newly arrived ones having very continental attitudes about campaigning in this country and the old hands being too busy to have the time to instruct them. The NCOs are the ones who take up the slack and consequently the blame when things go wrong. The Rangers that they had met seemed to be capable of doing their job as did the bateaux men. As yet they had not met any of the provincial troops so they did not have an opinion. The General informed them that General Abercromby did not have a very high opinion of the ability of the provincials. His greatest reliance on them would be to relieve the regulars of the normal fatigue duties that kept an army going.

Fogg questioned, "Is that wise, Sir. They will make up almost or more than half of the force. Some of these people have been fighting the French and their Red Indians for years, have they not? Good Lord! Sir William Pepperell and his New Englanders took Louisburg in '45 and without the help of any regulars. The only successful campaign in '55 was Sir William Johnson and his provincials at Lake George."

Gris commented, "Sir, I have seen the New Jersey Provincials while in New York. They are as well equipped and trained as any regular regiment fresh out of England and are used to campaigning against the French and their forest allies."

"We are not at the point of landing as yet and a great deal may and will change ere we see the Citadel at St. Frederick or its outpost at Carillon." replied the Viscount. "There are some tactical aspects of this campaign that have as yet to be disclosed and discussed among the Military Family. I need not caution you that what you have just heard is in the utmost confidence and should be locked away in that place where all deep secrets are faithfully kept. Now back to the primary discussion ... do you think that the Rangers were able to intercept and follow any French parties to the north? We most likely will not receive any word for at least another day unless they take the express to deliver it."

"Express?" Gris looked at the Viscount questioningly.

Fogg spoke up, "I think that the General means by the longboat we observed the other day on our way up the river. I would dare say that it can be a very short trip in the hands of skilled boatmen. Shooting all of the rapids most likely cuts the trip down to a few hours."

"It is no wonder that my relative relies upon you, Mr. Fogg. There is very little that you miss. I believe that you have fallen in with a most valuable mentor Mr. Gris." Then to Fogg's surprise, "He can even be helpful to you if you would like to learn Sanskrit, Hindi, Arabic and Urdu. Picked up any of the Red Indian dialects as yet, Mr. Fogg?" the Viscount commented with a large grin.

Not showing any surprise, Fogg replied, "None as yet, Viscount. I have not had the opportunity to even see one, let alone listen to them speak." *I see that Cousin Georgie has well briefed you on my accomplishments. I wonder if you know the rest and why I am of such service to your relatives. I would bet that you would be very surprised if I called you by your nickname unknown outside your family, Red Augie.* "You flatter me General; I am not quite as accomplished as rumor has it. I stumble when attempting to speak Hindi."

Howe laughingly countered, "You are too humble, Mr. Fogg and truly a gentleman. Now I shall turn you two loose among the miscreants and let you do your work. Keep the Frenchies from knowing too much about us. Neutralize them where you can and eliminate them where you can not. Mr. Gris, follow the lead of Mr. Fogg as he has a great deal of experience in these matters." They stood and departed to the other room. Moneypenny asked if they needed anything and informed Fogg that he had been able to send his letters down river. They allowed that they had enough funds to cover them for a goodly time span. They asked to be kept abreast of what ever seemed of importance. They informed Moneypenny that he could send packets across to the Landing Master on the other side at the Army landing and that they would receive them un-tampered. He informed them that he had a dispatch rider who was completely in the trust of his Lordship that could deliver any messages to the Landing. They departed the Headquarters and headed back toward the east landing.

## Chapter 20

On the short ride back to the East Landing they noticed some activity in the area that was designated as the Provincial Camp. There appeared to be a dozen or so tents and shelters set in somewhat of a military order. They guessed that it might be some advance party of one of the larger provincial units or perhaps even some close-by elements from New York or Connecticut. It was assumed that if the provincials were to participate they would need to start arriving in camp soon. There had been controversy regarding payment, arms and equipment, the controversy varying with each colony. One of the biggest stumbling blocks appeared to be arms. As far as General Abercromby was concerned, they could show up without arms as they, the provincials, were there to support the regulars by doing all of the fatigue details such as loading and unloading supplies, hauling wagons, rowing the boats, etc. In the General's mind the fighting would be up to the real soldiers, His Majesty's Regiments of Foot.

The scow was just returning from the west shore where it had deposited General Abercromby and his entourage. Within the half hour they were at the west landing. They made a point of contacting the Landing Master who informed them that some of the paperwork, and consequently the supplies themselves, were departing a bit smoother than previously. He also informed them that young Mr. Bruin had proved to have a problem with being posted to Fort Edward and therefore had been transferred to the depot at the Lake. It seems that the poor lad, being unfamiliar with the woods, had wandered off and was captured by some of the French and their Red Allies. A new clerk showed up, who was also an Albany man, but he had refused him. His new clerk was a New Englander who had all the desirable qualities that he liked in a clerk. He listened to instructions and kept them to himself.

Having concluded their business at the landing, they headed for town and supper at the King's Arms. They put their mounts in the care of the black stable boy and gave him a h'penny to rub them down and give them a ration of oats. They were not to be unsaddled and he was to keep a close eye on their gear with the promise of another h'penny when they came out. They brushed the dust of the road off and went on into the tavern. It was crowded with both locals

91

and people who were following the army along with a goodly number of officers, despite the new restrictions. In the course of the evening they were to find out that they were, for the most part, newly arrived from down below. Fogg and Gris were ushered to their table, which true to his word the publican had kept clear for them. They dined on roast turkey stuffed with chestnuts, boiled potatoes and candied squash. All topped off with a local ale that somewhat bit you back. After they finished, the publican brought them a glass of brandy from his own stock, or so he said. It was tolerable and warmed the soul.

As they had been eating their supper they had listened to the various conversations going on around them. The talk among the close by civilians was speculation about when the army would move, now that Abercromby was here. Some were eager to see them leave and others reluctant to have them depart. The business men had made a great deal of money from dealing with the army. The remainder of the population had found them to be an extra burden on an already taxing existence. This was still the gateway to the frontier despite the settlements that were west along the Mohawk. That was Indian country ruled by Sir William Johnson. Certainly there were a few Palatine settlements stretched out as far as the German Flatts but still all in all it was Indian country and for the most part they were welcome to it.

The officers, on the other hand were full of piss and vinegar, boasting on how they would be in Montreal by this coming fall. It seemed that Abercromby's army had expanded to fifteen-thousand regulars with another ten-thousand provincials looming just over the borders on their way to join the regulars at Albany and Fort Edward. Sitting at a table opposite from Fogg and Gris were two men who seemed detached from the rest of the crowd. They wore clothing that looked as if it would be more at home in the bush than here in town. They were wearing jackets that were more in the fashion of highlanders or sailors. One of them was a deep grey color and the other was a cross between a brown and a grey. They were both wearing Indian-style gaiters or leggings and both carried hunting bags and horns. Hanging on the back of their chairs were regular accoutrement belts with a small camp axe or tomahawk stuck in the hanger frog. Along with the belts were hung another with a belly box attached. Their firelocks were resting in the corner directly behind them where one of them could see them.

Gris called the publican over and whispered something in his ear. He disappeared behind the bar and shortly came out with two glasses of brandy and delivered them to the table with the two strangers. He put them down and our travelers could see that they questioned from where they came. The burlier of the two looked sharply across the room, said something to his companion and pushed back his chair and got up. Fogg let his hand slip off the table and rest on his dirk.

Quietly he said to Gris, "I hope this is a long lost cousin or something equal as he looks a little formidable."

"Hardly," was all that Gris said. The man walked up to the table without saying a word. The officers who were closest to them glanced at him but went back to their conversations.

The man, addressing Gris said in a stern but quiet voice, "We don't take kindly to strangers buying drinks where I come from."

"I should think that you would be used to strangers where you come from, as none of you know who your fathers are," replied Gris, rather flippantly. *Oh, God! Here we go!* went rapidly through Fogg's mind. The man threw back his head and let out a peal of laughter. He grabbed Gris by the shoulders and pulled him up out of the chair but instead of throwing him across the room he clasp his arms around him. Gris burst into laughter and returned the bear hug.

"Israel Putnam, you old bastard. I didn't recognize you at first."

"Nor I you Robby Gris and it takes one to know one and who might your silent and astonished friend be?"

Gris extricated himself from Putnam's grasp, "Mr. Israel Putnam allow me to introduce Mr. Ethyrial Fogg, late out of England by way of New York town. Mr. Fogg will be going north with us. Call your companion over and we'll discuss it further."

Putnam looked around and said, "Perhaps you should join us as our table seems more isolated. I guess these town folks and officers don't like to get too close to bush runners." They picked up their glasses, cloaks and hats and moved over to the other table. Putnam sat back down and introduced the other man as Caleb Greene. In the act of he and Gris trying to crush each other his waistcoat had pulled open at the neck, revealing a silver gorget.

"Israel, what is that I see around your neck?" Putnam glanced down and quickly tucked it back and buttoned up the waistcoat to cover it.

"It doesn't pay to advertise too much. I'm a Major in the Connecticut Rangers and Caleb here is a Lieutenant. We are on our way across the river as soon as we leave here to report to Lord Howe."

"Well it's a good thing we ran into you. We will save you a boat ride. Lord Howe stays on this side of the river at Schuyler's. Do you have horses?" asked Gris.

"No, we came down by boat."

"We'll get a couple of mounts for you as it is about four miles up to Schuyler's. It is above the Upper Cow Pastures. We'll go up with you," leaning closer to Putnam, "as Fogg and I are at the moment working for the Viscount. Once out on the track I'll give you more details." Fogg called the publican over and instructed him to add the bill from this table to theirs. Putnam objected but Fogg assured him that he insisted. When the publican walked away he informed Putnam that the army was actually paying for it. That Putnam thought was a good idea.

All four left the King's Arms and went around to the stable area, retrieving Fogg's and Gris' mounts. They doubled up and went down a few blocks to the wharf area where the King's Stable was located for use by authorized officers and couriers. Gris had no problems procuring two more mounts using his pass accompanied by six pence for the sergeant in charge, enough to get a bottle of brandy or some other luxury not ordinarily available to a sergeant. Once out away from everyone and on the road to Schuyler's they commenced to tell Putnam about their mission after inquiring if Lieutenant Greene could be trusted.

Putnam turned in his saddle to Greene and asked. "Brother Greene, can you be trusted with a secret or two?" Greene, very solemnly, made two gestures which assured his traveling companions that he could be very trusted. They told Putnam of their progress so far, their trip up river to observe the security of the camps and the road. Putnam interrupted them at the point of telling about the encounter with the rangers. This was the very object of his trip down river to report to Lord Howe directly. It seems that the party led by Sergeant Ross had dogged a couple of messengers from their ambush point at Saratoga up to opposite Fort Edward. Here the messengers had met with a party of French irregulars and Indians. They had all started on their way up toward the Lake but at a point opposite with Halfway Brook the whole had run into a party of rangers returning from the Lake sweeping the area west of the road for just such an opportunity.

The French, their allies, and the messengers scattered. The messengers made the mistake of heading back due south and ran into Sergeant Ross and his party. They were immediately subdued and Ross and his party made contact with the other ranger group. Together they returned to the ranging company post at Halfway Brook where Putnam happened to be on his way back to Fort Edward. Putnam and his party took the two messengers back to the island at Fort Edward that was the headquarters of the ranging company battalion under the command of Major Robert Rogers. After being questioned by the Major and a couple of other Ranger officers and making no progress they tried another ploy. While standing outside of the tent, but within earshot of the two prisoners, they decided that they could not gain any information from them here on the island. They then declared that they would let the Stockbridge Company take them out from the island and let them entertain the two guests. The very mention of the possibility of a party with the Stockbridge was enough to loosen the tongues of the two messengers. It appeared that the northern end of the messenger route was just a few miles down the Lake from the site of the former Fort William Henry. It was situated on one of the mountains overlooking the Lake in view of the British encampment. The observation post was on the south side of the mountain top. It consisted of a half dozen men in a cold camp. On the North West side where they were hidden from observation was the main camp that usually consisted of a quarter company of La Marine and two dozen Irregulars. They were a portion of the force of Canadian partisans commanded by Joseph Marin de la Malgue Putnam was on his way to obtain permission from Lord Howe for Major Rogers to neutralize this post.

During the remainder of the ride they learned a great deal about the operations of the ranging companies from both Fort Edward and the camp at the Lake. The rangers at the Lake had been, of recent, kept close in to form a screen for the work parties who were employed a distance from the main camp or too near the woods. It was the practice to put out a ranger screen 75 to 100 yards out into the woods. This practice was limiting the use of a valuable intelligence resource. Rogers had no idea what was going on down Lake and over into South Bay or Wood Creek section of the lake the French called Lac du Champlain. Over the winter months of '57 and '58 the ranging companies had been busy reconnoitering and harassing the French. Rogers' companies and Putnam's Connecticut Rangers had both been out on scouts that had resulted in men lost, either killed or captured but now they were ready to commence their activities again. Rogers and an eighteen man patrol had been to Crown Point and taken three prisoners. A British party under a flag of truce had been sent to Carillon and all scouting and raiding activities had been held up. Putnam was requesting orders to have the all the ranging companies released to reconnaissance duty. There were enough to do both if the work-detail guards were supplemented with regulars who could be trained to do this type of duty. The 55th, 60th and the 80th were examples of what could be done with regulars. It was obvious that too many of the regular officers did not understand the type of force they were fighting here in North America. They were still operating in a European mind set. Hopefully the Viscount would be able to change all that when he got to the Lake.

## Chapter 21

When they arrived at the Schuyler home they were informed by a lieutenant that Lord Howe had just sat down to his supper and that he did not intend to disturb him. Fogg intervened by requesting that the lieutenant would do well to give the Viscount this message and let him decide what to do about it. The lieutenant taken aback by Fogg's forwardness and insistence inquired as to the message.

"Tell His Lordship simply this, 'Gris, Fogg, urgent news, lake' and I warrant he will respond favorably." The lieutenant repeated the message, somewhat incredibly but never the less left to deliver it. Within a couple of minutes the lieutenant returned and said that Lord Howe would be right with them and they were to wait in the drawing room to their left and Mrs. Schuyler requested that they please wipe their boots and stay on the rag rugs. They went into the indicated room which had a fire burning in the fireplace to help keep down the dampness of the evening. Putnam and Greene, in true woodsman fashion, had brought their firelocks into the house with them. Gris suggested that perhaps they might stand them in the corner by the door for now. A slight knock came at the door and it opened and a black servant entered carrying a tray with four steaming mugs on it. He offered it to them explaining that it was hot mulled cider made from apples from the Patroon's orchard. There was also a dish of sweet butter for those who liked it that way. They each took a mug with a large spoonful of butter in it. Putnam tasted his and remarked that it needed more mull and proceeded to take out his mull horn and put a couple of pinches into the cider. He offered it around but the other three declined. They stood about the fireplace drinking their cider and the Viscount appeared within fifteen minutes.

"Gentlemen, my apologies to have kept you waiting, but Madam Schuyler insisted that I finish my apple upside-down cake. She serves it with a very thick whipped cream. I am sure that there is plenty left if you would care for some." Fogg assured him that they had just finished eating about an hour or so ago and that Madam Schuyler had served them hot mulled cider while they waited. Gris inquired if Lord Howe was acquainted with Major Putnam of the Connecticut Rangers.

Lord Howe stepped over to Putnam, extending his hand and remarked, "No, it has not been my pleasure but I have read of Major Putnam's exploits in dispatches. I am sorry that you lost so many men in the beginning of the year Major Putnam. I trust you are back to strength now?"

"Yes, General, we are almost back up to strength. Our men are chafing to get back to the job we do best, reconnoiter and harass. I have been sent down to apprise you of the situation on the Lake. In keeping with the suggestions of the Misters Fogg and Gris, we had put patrols out to shadow the messengers from the camp at the Pastures to wherever they were going on the Lake. One of our patrols was doing just that when the messengers met up with a larger French party. They was all moving north when they ran into a ranger patrol moving back in a sweep to the south to Halfway Brook parallel and on the west side of the road. The French scattered and the messengers cut and run in the direction they knew best, south and smack into the patrol led by Sergeant Ross who were following them. Ross quickly joined up with the larger party and they high-tailed it over to the post at Halfway Brook and then on down to the Island. We, Major Rogers and myself, questioned the two prisoners but was getting nowhere. The Major decided to see if they might change their minds if they thought that he was going to turn them over to Captain Jacobs and his Stockbridge Company. Well, they didn't take too kindly to that suggestion and started to talk like a bunch of women at a church social." He paused to let Lord Howe make a comment.

"Go on Captain, go on," urged His Lordship. He had sat down in one of the wingbacks and indicated to the others to sit. Putnam now had the floor and continued his tale. He laid out for the General the same information regarding the French observation camp that he had told Fogg and Gris on their way up to Schuyler's. He also pointed out that if the Rangers had been free to patrol the lake and area as they had been, the French would not be sitting so snug and close by. The Viscount asked him what he thought they should be doing. Putnam indicated that in his opinion, and most likely Rogers', that they should be running patrols with two goals. One would be to gather information on the French strength at Fort St. Frederic and Carillon and the second goal would be to harass the French as much as possible in their own neighborhood. The Rangers had been doing this for at least a year and now that they had stopped it, by itself, was a good indication to the French that something was in the wind. The lessening of pressure on the French in the vicinity of their own posts simply allowed them to strengthen their position to resist the forth coming campaign. As Putnam finished Lord Howe sat quietly staring at the fire. The rest of the little group sat waiting for his reply or comment. Putnam was still standing where he had finished. Lord Howe seemed to suddenly become aware of the group and stood up.

He took Putnam's hand and said, "Thank you Major Putnam. I shall have Moneypenny write out a set of instructions for Major Rogers that will allow you to re-commence activities on the Lake, actually on both Lakes. We want the French to be too busy worrying about their own base of operations to be causing us consternation at ours. I plan to move my headquarters on up the river and to the Lake shortly. By the time the remainder of the army and General Abercromby are there I want the French activity in the area of Lake George camp curtailed. You may also tell Major Rogers that I also would like a detailed reconnaissance of the ground between the foot of Lake George and Carillon. Thank you, gentlemen. I shall see you all tomorrow across the river. Good night." With that he left the drawing room.

"I guess that means that we can turn in," said Putnam, "we just need to find an empty tent. I saw a nice big barn on our way in. I guess the Schuyler's would not mind if their horses shared some straw with us. What about you gentlemen?"

"We will be on our way back to town. We have a small room that we have paid for but have hardly used. You could bivouac out on the floor if you like," replied Fogg.

"No thank you Mr. Fogg, the straw sounds better. We can be up before dawn and work our way back down to the landing through the Ranger camps and check on the boys." With that Putnam and his companion took up their guns and departed toward the barn with their mounts in tow. Fogg and Gris mounted and rode off toward Albany town. When they arrived at Widow Bruin's, the house was totally dark. They put their mounts in the lean-to out in the back and rubbed them down with straw and fed them. They went in through the back door and quietly crept upstairs. They avoided the stair that creaked and were able to get past the other bedroom without disturbing the occupants, who from the sound coming from the room, were otherwise occupied. When they got in their room and had closed the door and struck a light, Gris commented that it was no wonder that Neville Bruce was so thin. Fogg inquired as to why he made that observation and Gris answered, "Lack of sleep!" With this comment they both barely refrained from laughing out loud. They turned in as it was going to be a short night. As he lay there starting to fall asleep, Fogg's thought drifted to how quickly the pace of things were picking up. He envisioned that he and Gris would soon be knee deep in muck before this month was out.

# Chapter 22

Fogg and Gris were up early. Today was Friday, May 12th and they needed to be up at the civilian camp by mid-day to see what , if any, news or rumors were floating about. They made their way over to the King's Arms for breakfast. As it was still very early, six-thirty in the morning by Fogg's watch, there were few people on the streets and in the tavern. The publican, true to his word had their table set up for them. He assured them that it was set for any meal which they chanced to stop by. He said that he had fresh bread, just baked, eggs right out of the hen house, ham, bacon whatever they wished. He said he also had corn pan bread. The latter made Fogg raise an eyebrow questioningly. Gris assured him that he would find it as delightful, if not more so as the grits from the previous day. They decided upon the ham with eggs and the pan bread along with coffee. Gris remarked that Fogg was starting to eat like a home grown colonial and by the time he returned to England he would have to plant his own corn field just to maintain his present diet.

By a quarter to eight they were on the road up to the Pastures. There was a great deal of activity in the military camp as the remaining elements of the  4th Battalion of the 60th  were getting ready to depart up river. Their baggage was going up by boat and the men were going to march over the Cohos ford and on up to Fort Edward. The 60th, like the 80th, was composed mostly of men recruited in North America. A great many of them were recruited in towns and villages from the frontier areas and were no strangers to the hardships of North America. They didn't seem to pay a great deal of attention to everyday annoyances as did their English brothers. The black flies and mosquitoes didn't seem to care to feast on them as much as they did the regular English soldier. However no one asked them why so they didn't bother to tell them.

They were well equipped and their uniforms were distinct in the absence of regimental lace. Their red coats had no white tape on their blue turn-backs. Their company of Light Infantry wore cut down caps with a usable flap on the front and the turban was a folded up arrangement to protect the neck in inclement weather. Instead of a white linen shirt the Lights were wearing a blue and white checked shirt under their sleeved waistcoats. The uniform coat had been cut down and its sleeves removed and wings like grenadiers sewn on to it. They also carried a belly box along with an altered shoulder box.

Fogg watched as the Lights went trotting on by up the road, passing the hat companies to get out in front of the column. Gris remarked that this was something that had been learned from the Indians. They would trot for an amount of time and then walk for an amount of time. Using this method they could travel great distances in one day. Here in the North American forests the Light Infantry would perform duties that light cavalry would in Europe. Fogg suggested that perhaps they should make a quick stop at the landing to see if Lord Howe had crossed over to the headquarters yet. They learned that he had crossed over very early and had left a message for them. The message was a quick note that said simply, "Move up river tomorrow. Headquarters at Saratoga." They left instructions for the Landing Master to send a man for their baggage and send it up to Lord Howe's camp. They themselves would be leaving first light tomorrow and would not need anything that they were not carrying with them. They decided that they would spend the night in the Ranger camp and, if Putnam were still there, move on up with him.

They departed for the civilian camp to find out what news was from up river. When they arrived at Klompin's tavern tent they found the establishment in a state of disruption. Klompin was nowhere to be found as neither were Misters Felsstein and Storch. All the bar tender, who appeared to be somewhat in charge, knew was that they had received a message and had departed, he knew not where. His instructions were to move the tavern up river to Fort Edward where they would be in touch with him. Fogg inquired as to any news if their messages had been delivered at Fort Edward. The answer was that he did not know but it appeared that the line of communication between Fort Edward and here had broken down and he suggested that perhaps they should consider departing camp also. They thanked him for his advice and answered that they would do just that.

When they had got out of the civilian camp they stopped again at the landing and wrote a note to be delivered to Lord Howe. It said: "Outcome of Putt story, communication broken, parties departed unknown. Advised we move upriver. In process. F." They then rode on over to the Ranger camps in search of Putnam, who wasn't difficult to find. He and a party of Rangers were getting ready to move on up to Fort Edward. They were going to ride up as far as Saratoga, pick up a longboat and proceed to the fort. Gris and Fogg were a welcome addition to the party. They drew trail rations and were set to depart with the hour. They would not be stopping until Saratoga.

# Chapter 23

Just above Schuyler's, they cut across the road that crossed the ford in the vicinity of the Cohoes Falls and thence on over to Half Moon. On the way they passed the 60th Light Infantry, who by that time, were just approaching the ford. Fogg remarked to Gris that he was amazed at the time that the Lights had made since they saw them earlier, about a mile every fifteen minutes. After crossing the ford it was only a few miles more to Half Moon. Fogg, Gris and the Rangers only slowed down going through the encampments at Half Moon and continued on the twelve miles to Stillwater. There was a great deal of activity on the river with boats backed up at all of the portages. They were waiting to be unloaded and then either hauled or trucked around the rough water themselves. It was clear that there were not enough men stationed at these portages to get the glut of boats up river fast enough. They were sure that when Lord Howe passed through tomorrow that he would see the problem and get more men working on correcting it. It was a great waste of regular troop manpower. If the Provincials had come into camp this would be a good job for them as they were used to this type of transportation problems. Everything that moved by water in North America moved this way.

As they made their way up toward Stillwater the road became more congested with troops, ox carts and wagons. There were regulars who would just march around a wagon that was mired down or stuck on an incline. Officers barking at the drovers to get out of the road, to make way for the foot companies. In some cases they even were halted waiting for the wagons to move as opposed to moving off the road around them. Both sides of the road had a space cleared back in the areas where there was brush and trees and in the other areas it was open fields. Fortunately this was still a relatively safe area where the French raiding parties did not penetrate but as one drew progressively north the possibility became greater. At one point, Putnam remarked that the regulars probably would all get killed, scalped or captured if they didn't learn anything before passing from Fort Edward to the Lake. Little did he know at the time how prophetic he would prove to be.

By the time they reached Stillwater it was a little past noon so they stopped to rest the mounts and get something to eat. There was a Ranger camp where they were greeted heartily, as Putnam was a soldier's officer. They had some cold meat and bread, washed down with strong tea laced with a little rum. They also swapped out a couple of mounts who had proved to have loose shoes and not up to the pace. They departed a little after one o'clock, after both they and the horses had rested. There was some congestion on the road but not as much as down below. At an area known as the Meadow there were some drovers who had pulled their carts off the road and their oxen turned out to graze. There were also some drovers who were coming back down river with trucks from delivering longboats up to Saratoga. They had tied the trucks in tandem so one team of oxen could pull down the road empty what required several teams to pull up loaded. Gris inquired as to the traffic on the road above the Meadow. They informed him that it was light until you got above Saratoga. Just above the Batten Kill it was necessary to transfer over to the east side of the river. There was a ford but it wasn't passable this time of the year. You had to cross by water borne vehicle, either bateau or one of the several scows that were stationed there for that purpose. There was a system of ropes set up to speed up the process. Everyone except officers helped pull the boats across the river. The river at this point was less than a quarter mile across. The party pushed on to the crossing which was just above the camp at Saratoga. Fogg and Gris wanted to see first hand the crossing and Putnam needed to cross as his longboats were on the other side. They parted company with the plan to look up Putnam when they finally arrived at the Lake. He promised to take them out on a scout so that they could see Lake George for themselves.

The situation at the crossing was a smaller version of the situation below at the rapids. Troops and provisions were starting to pile up. This did not even take into account the Provincials who as yet had not arrived at Albany. The rumor was that twenty thousand would soon fill up the meadows on the east side of the river at Fort Crailo although they had only seen a few New York Provincials when last there. Gris was of the opinion that only a quarter of that number would eventually report for the campaign as it was also rumored that the provincial legislators were all dragging their feet in fulfilling their quotas. It seemed they were waiting for the Crown to foot the whole bill. *I'll need to inquire of Lord Howe*, thought Fogg, *exactly what his take of the provincial situation is. I'm sure HM will want to know what the colonial opinion is of Mr. Pitt's grand plan.*

After viewing the situation at the crossing their immediate need was to establish a temporary camp until Lord Howe came up. Gris suggested that they set up near the farm located just by the falls near the Fish Kill. It was back far enough from the road as to be slightly quieter and they could probably sleep in the barn as opposed to outdoors, as the weather looked like it might drizzle a little later. When they arrived at the house they found that it had been commandeered by some regular English officers and the barn was occupied by a quarter company of regulars. The family that lived there was taking shelter in a shed attached to the back of the house. In a conversation with the man, Gris learned that the house belonged to the Schuyler's and that he was just a tenant who took care of the Patroon's property in this area. The family had three children and another on the way and the shed was damp and drafty. Fogg decided that Lord Howe would like them to correct a situation with one of his host's tenants. Gris just shook his head and mumbled something about, "... these fellows are about to get a lesson in Fogg diplomacy..." recalling the confrontation in the alley.

They went around to the back door of the house and entered into the pantry/buttery area. There was a Private there preparing vegetables who started to speak. Gris just put his finger up to his lips making a soft shhh noise and motioning toward the door with his head. The fellow dropped the carrots he was cleaning and quickly departed out the door, most likely for the barn to retrieve help. Fogg went through the door into the family part of the house, where there were three officers sitting at the table with a couple of bottles of brandy sitting on it. One had his feet up on the table and was tilted back in his chair the others were facing the fire place.

The one with his feet upon the table looked up in surprise, "I say, this house is taken by His Majesty's regulars. Provincials may bivouac in the barn, with the rest of the unwashed multitude." slightly slurred and laughing at his own cleverness.

Fogg kicked the chair out from under him, grabbing him by the collar of his waistcoat, "On your feet, youngster! You're moving out." Gris opened the front door of the house and Fogg propelled the unbalanced young man out the door, sprawling into the dirt at the door yard. He turned to the other two who had managed to get to their feet one attempting to draw his sword which hung on the back of his chair. Fogg pushed back the tail of his coat exposing his dirk, placing his hand upon the grip.

Gris spoke up, "I would not do that, young sir. I saw him do in three ruffians in Albany Town the other day with that very dirk."

At the same time he pushed his own coat back to expose the pistol hanging under his arm.

"I believe that you are all seeking quarters elsewhere. This house belongs to the Patroon who is the host of His Lordship, Brigadier Howe. He might not take it kindly that you treated his host's property and employees with such carelessness." At this point in the dramatics a Sergeant and two Privates burst into the rear of the house and through the door into the main room.

As the Sergeant took a step toward Fogg, Gris warned him, "I would be most careful Sergeant, that is an officer you look like you are about to offer to strike!" The sergeant stopped in his tracks and held out his arms to halt the pair behind him.

"We was just coming to see if we could be of any assistance, Sir," replied the Sergeant coming to the position of most attention. It was plain to see why he was a Sergeant as he knew when and to whom to answer. Fogg saw from the facings on the two Privates that they were from the 55th, Howe's regiment while the officers were from the 44th, Gage's old regiment now under command of Major Eyre.

"Well Sergeant, if your men could help the officers remove their baggage down to the crossing, as they will be going over to the other side where their regiment is encamped, I would greatly appreciate it. I will see that Lord Howe gets a full favorable report of your actions here today," replied Fogg. The one who had been ejected into the door yard was now managing to get up.

"Stand where you are, Sergeant. What regiment do you belong to, Sir? Do you think you can come into here and just bluff your way into dry, comfortable quarters? I have not seen you in any of the camps or officers messes. Produce your proof and beware the penalty for impersonating an officer of His Majesty's Forces," drawing himself up to as much dignity as he could muster, covered with dirt.

"I am not in the habit of answering to inferior officers, from inferior regiments but I shall be glad to oblige." He reached into his inner right pocket and with drew a leather wallet from which he produced a folded paper. Would you do the honors, Sergeant?" handing it to the sergeant. The sergeant unfolded the paper.

"What does it say Sergeant as to last name, rank and regiment?" inquired Fogg.

" It says, E. Fogg, Major, 1st Guards, Sir!"

The fellow standing in the yard seemed to melt where he was standing. Not only had he questioned a superior officer but one from a Household Regiment and probably a staff member to boot. His career in the army was over for sure.

"Does that satisfy your curiosity? If so, I would suggest at this point you all gather yourselves together, dress properly as officers should and move on toward the crossing, keeping in mind that as yet I have not inquired as to your names and therefore cannot identify or report you to Major Eyre." This put a little more fear into them because he had identified their regiment. The Sergeant had already gathered up their belongings from the house and had called up a couple of Privates from the barn to help get them down to the river.

"Sergeant, get a couple of your men to help the farmer, his wife and their children back into the house. There are at least two bottles of brandy on the table that might come in handy if any of your men are having effects from the night air this close to the river," ordered Fogg.

With a forced cough, "I could use a little myself, Sir, and thank you very much, Sir. The lads will appreciate your looking out for their health. Sir."

Fogg turned to Gris and said, "Well, Captain Gris, shall we move into the shed?"

"By all means, Major Fogg, by all means. Can't wait to hear His Lordship's reaction to this, your leading an insurrection of the 55th against officers of the 44th. God's fish, that was fun!"

## Chapter 24

After getting settled in the shed, with the help of the Sergeant and a couple of Privates from the 55th, who carried some straw down from the barn out of which to make beds, he and Gris went back down to the river to observe more of the troop movement. They wanted to have a good report for His Lordship when he came up tomorrow.

The situation at the river was getting worse by the hour as troops arrived and needed to wait for transport across the river. Bradstreet's men were doing the best that they could with the boats that they had available. Fogg suggested that they attempt to send a message down river to Lord Howe apprising him of the situation. Perhaps he could at least be prepared to deal with it when he came up. As luck would have it, they spotted Putnam who was still on the west side of the river. Fogg called to him just as he was getting into a longboat ready to shove off for the other side.

"Putnam, glad we caught up with you. We have need of a favor."

"Name it, Brother Fogg, and I'll see what I can do." was Putnam's reply.

"We need to send a message down river to His Lordship. Can you dispatch one of the Ranger longboats to carry it? It is the quickest way."

"That I can accomplish, Brother Fogg. We have a couple of boats that are stationed here just for that very purpose. You get the message written out and I'll take care of the rest," answered Putnam.

Fogg took out his traveling stationary kit from his saddle bag and sat down on a nearby barrel to pen off a message to Lord Howe. He explained that as you came further up the river the more congested the supply and troop line became. He also explained that there was a shortage of water transport to carry everything across to the east side. It appeared that once troops and supplies reached the other side, the problem seemed to correct itself, although he and Gris had not as yet been over to that side. They could see from the west bank that as people disembarked they moved on up the river. He folded the message and gave it to Putnam.

"Brother Putnam, it is most important that your messenger puts this in His Lordships hands tonight. By the time he gets down river Lord Howe will most likely be at either Schuyler's or at the 55th camp. If he does not find him there, he is to use the army landing and cross over to Craillo. If he is given a hard time at the landing, he is to look up the landing master who is a Brother. He will tell him the message is from Fogg and he will take care to get him across."

Putnam, replied, "I will see that it gets delivered to His Lordship. I'll instruct the whale boat to standby at the landing, just in case they need it to cross over the river." He started to walk toward the boat and turned about. "By the way Fogg, my friends call me Putt," he said with a large grin.

"Well, Mr. Fogg, it would seem that Brother Putnam has the situation well in hand. Now I think we should wander back to our humble abode and see what we have to scrape together for our dining pleasure," said Gris as he stepped aboard his horse.

Stowing his writing kit back in the saddlebag, Fogg swung up onto his mount and replied, "By Jupiter, Mr. Gris I do believe that you are correct in both assumptions. Perhaps the 55th might have some of that stew they were starting to put together that a couple of pitiful looking gentlemen could beg." With which they trotted off up the track to their bivouac. When they arrived at the farmstead, the tenant farmer who lived there came out and asked if they would like some supper. He said that he was much obliged to them for restoring his family to their home. Gris assured him that he owed them nothing but the man insisted, carefully pointing out that it was from his own larder and not that of the Patroon. They went inside and the woman was setting places at the table for them. She had taken out what appeared to be her very best dishes and flatware. Sitting on the table was a large pot of mutton stew, several loaves of cheat bread, a block of cheese, and a small tub of butter. The man apologized for it not being more, whereupon Fogg assured him that it was more than enough and that they thought that they would be eating a cold supper if they had not been able to procure some from the men of the 55th Foot. The man informed them that they were indeed lucky as the soldiers had departed immediately after they did. The man indicated that they had moved out north, up river.

"They must be on a special assignment," was Fogg's only remark throwing a quick glance at Gris who outwardly seemed to ignore it.

After they had finished their meal and thanked their hosts, they retired to the shed. On the way, Fogg said he thought that they ought to have a look at the barn where the 55th had been staying.

Inside it was easy to spot where they had been camped. There were several piles of straw laid out on the normally empty threshing floor. They kicked around some of the straw looking for anything left behind but came up empty handed. They were getting ready to leave when Fogg saw a shiny object lying almost behind one of the anchorbeam posts. He reached down and picked it up, turning it over in his hand. He held it up for Gris to see, it was a crucifix.

"Do you suppose one of those lads was Irish?" queried Fogg. Gris took it from him looking it over closely. It was silver and on the back was a touch mark.

"Maybe we can find someone who knows what this touch mark is. There are more than a few Irishmen in Lord Howe's regiment. We need to inquire from His Lordship if he had a patrol on a special assignment to travel up the west side. If not, then we have another mystery on our hands," Gris stated, very soberly.

"Yes, Mr. Gris, and one that would pose monumental circumstances. The Sergeant seemed genuine enough but one can never be too sure when engaged in this business."

It was about nine o'clock when they made their way back to the shed and spread their bed rolls. Before turning in they checked their weapons. Fogg drew his dirk and placed it under his greatcoat that he was using for a pillow. Gris did the same with his recently acquired hunting sword. Fogg picked up a barrel stave that was in the shed and leaned it against the door. They blew out the lantern and rolled up in their bedrolls.

About three hours after they had turned in, both were awakened by the barrel stave sliding down the door as it opened outward. The small amount of light from outside showed three figures in the doorway. Both men grabbed their weapons and rolled away to the sides of the shed, clearing their bedrolls just as two shots rang out, hitting the empty space where they had been lying. Fogg had rolled to his left and immediately sprang to his feet putting him next to the doorway. He reached out of the shadows grabbing one figure and jerking him forward into the room, at the same time striking him in the face with the large brass pommel of his dirk. He let the figure go, pushing it away from the doorway into the vicinity of the corner of the shed.

Gris came out of the dark charging the remaining two knocking them out the door following through with a slashing attack of his hunting sword. He felt the sword strike flesh and bone, which caused a shriek from the unlucky target. Fogg was immediately out the door behind Gris but the other attacker had been hit so hard that the momentum caused him to roll backward a couple of times. The cries of his fellow attackers caused him to panic and he sprang to his feet and was away into the dark like a flash. Fogg fired his pistol at the fleeing shadow but to no apparent avail.

Gris went back into the shed, took out his tinder striker and lit the lantern. Fogg had only struck his assailant in the face with the butt of his dirk, knocking the fellow out. Unfortunately, he had fallen face first into the corner of the shed onto a froe that struck him in an artery in his neck. During the struggle he had expired. They went back out to look at the other attacker that Gris had cut. He had not fared any better as Gris had hit him in the neck and in the thigh, both wounds were enough to do him in.

"Damn!" exclaimed Fogg. "We might have found out who sent them and why." They dragged the one from inside out of the shed and laid him next to the other one. Both were wearing military small clothes but had on fatigue smocks. There was nothing to indicate which regiment they belonged to, adding more mystery to the affair.

"Well, these fellows could be from two sources," commented Gris. "They could be from the 44th and hired by those officers we pitched out of here today or they could be from what might be a rogue element of the 55th."

"They could also just have been some soldiers who intended to rob two civilians. However they knew we were in the shed which means that they had been watching us for some time. Maybe someone is on to us. Perhaps we will find out somewhere between here and Fort Edward. If the 44th Foot officers seem surprised to see us we will have a better idea. Also, perhaps Lord Howe will be able to shed some more light on the subject of a detachment of the 55th going up river on the west bank."

They heard a voice calling from the back door of the house. It was the farmer warning them not to shoot as he was coming out. They assured him that he was safe and he came out with another lantern. They asked him if these two were any of the 55th who had been staying in the barn. After looking them over carefully he commented that he could not be sure as he had not seen all of them. He got a tarp from the shed and covered them up. The farmer told them not to worry about them as he would put them in the cart and take them down to the army camp in the morning. Fogg instructed him to wait until Lord Howe came up so that he could see the bodies himself. With that, they went into the shed, gathered up their bedrolls and gear. They put out the lantern and moved to the barn. They spent the rest of the night up on the sheave loft over the threshing floor. The rest of the night passed quietly.

## Chapter 25

They were roused the next morning by the lowing of the two cows in the barn who were greeting the farmer, coming to milk them. Fogg and Gris climbed down out of the loft. The farmer asked them what they had done with the bodies. They went outside and sure enough they were gone. Gris looked around the spot where they had been and checked about the shed and the path leading toward the fields for any sign of footprints.

"It looks like there was more than three of them. Two were wearing shoes, not army issue and the rest, maybe three or four were wearing moccasins. One of the moccasins had a patch so the owner was probably a white man. Indians don't patch moccasins, even on the war path. Usually carry an extra pair or will go bare foot. White men do not have tough enough feet to do that, even the ones who have lived with the Indians for a long time. Not exactly sure but I think that the moccasins are Huron. They are the same as the Iroquois wear. They don't like to admit it but they really are cousins."

"Would that lead you to believe that they might be French and if so what are they doing this far south," queried Fogg, "and why would they be after us?" *Maybe it was a mistake to show my papers to the Sergeant yesterday. Or perhaps those officers said something down at the landing.*

The farmer went back to take care of his livestock, leaving them alone. They decided to go down to the landing and wait for Lord Howe to arrive. Gris went to the house and left some money for the farmer and his family. Hard cash was something of which that these tenant farmers saw little. The woman thanked them for being so helpful and generous.

At the landing, the army was just starting to stir. There was a party of Rangers at the landing just having some breakfast. Gris recognized the Sergeant in charge from yesterday and inquired if there were any of the Stockbridge Company on the other side of the river. He said that he had a couple of them on this side and whistled. Three figures arose from the other side of a stack of boxes and walked over to where they sat. They stood silently staring at the Sergeant and the two white civilians. Gris explained what had happened and asked if they would go back to the farm and look about for more signs or evidence. The one who seemed to be in charge simply nodded his head and they turned and took off at a trot, back up the track toward the farm. The Sergeant of Rangers assured them that if there were anything to be found that they would find it. Gris told him that they would be at the landing until Lord Howe came up and to let them know as soon as he had any news. Fogg asked if there was an officers' mess set up anywhere as they were also looking for three officers from the 44th. The Sergeant pointed off to a laboratory tent set up just north of the landing with a cluster of subaltern tents off to one side of it. "Temporary officer country," was his only remark.

"Shall we, Mr. Gris?" asked Fogg, already leading his mount up in that direction.

The officers mess was an artillery laboratory tent. As there was a shortage of artillery officers there was more artillery equipment than necessary, except for guns. There was enough guns but not enough qualified people to man them. It had been necessary to draft men from foot regiments to fill the lower stations on a gun. The artillery tent made an ideal mess tent with its roll-up windows and copious size. There was a fly mounted behind it to use as a food preparation area and the kitchen area had been dug directly behind the fly, contrary to regulations. As it was breakfast time, there were over a couple of dozen officers in the tent. When the two civilians entered the tent the buzz of conversation seemed to end abruptly and all eyes turned toward them. One of the batmen came up to them and politely informed them that this mess was only for regular officers of His Majesty's forces.

From the far end of the table came a voice, "It is all right, Smith. These gentlemen are officers. Come, sit up here at this end Major Fogg, Captain Gris." It was the officer from the 44th that they had pitched out of the house yesterday. They walked up to that end of the table where two younger officers rose and offered them their seats. They declined, instead taking two camp chairs that were sitting in the corner. The men at the table shifted to make room for them.

"First off let me apologize for my behavior yesterday and secondly let me introduce my self." Fogg held up his hand, interrupting him.

"No apology necessary and it is better if we do not know your names or rank. If anyone asks we can truly say we do not know," all with a grin. Fogg held out his hand to the officer who took it and shook it firmly. Gris offered his and received the same.

"And now, gentlemen, what's for breakfast?" asked Fogg using the contracted slang that seemed to be popular among the colonials.

"Today it would seem to be bacon, mixed into the eggs, along with some onions. There is also the ever present grits that the provincials seem to be so fond of. No offense Captain Gris, you are a provincial are you not?"

"If you mean by having been born here in North America, yes. If you mean by regimental posting, no. I am an officer of the 80th Foot."

"Does that mean that the 80th is on the way up the river, then?" queried the 44th officer.

"Captain Gris and I are part of the advance party of the Quartermasters," replied Fogg, "sent ahead to see to the smooth transportation of men and supplies across the river and on up to Fort Edward."

"That would seem to be an odd assignment for two gentlemen of your caliber, what?" came the reply.

Fogg quickly returned, "Not really. You see I have had a great deal of experience in my younger days in the Lowlands. While not quite the same as North America, it required a great deal of water transport and its associated problems. I am instructing Captain Gris here in what I have learned from my experience and he is instructing me from his experience of having grown up here. A good exchange, wouldn't you say, Captain Gris?"

"Yes Major, I would indeed." With that their breakfast arrived and they pitched in, their dining companions leaving them alone to let them eat.

They had barely finished with breakfast when there was a commotion outside. Several of the younger officers seated at the end of the table nearest the entrance got up and went outside to see what was the cause. One stuck his head back in the opening and announced that Lord Howe had arrive in camp. Fogg and Gris got to their feet and started for the opening when Howe entered.

"Gentlemen! Please be seated. Mr. Fogg and Mr. Gris, come with me if you please and we will discuss this logistical problem." With that Howe turned and departed the tent. Once outside and far enough away from the tent he stopped and turned about. Moneypenny had joined the circle.

"Give me your report, Mr. Fogg."

"It would seem, your Lordship, as you have probably gathered from below, there is a bottleneck at each of the rapids or anywhere it is necessary to deal with the river. Either there are not

114

enough men to haul the boats up the rapids or if the rapids are large to haul them out and transport them to the next smooth part of the river. The officers in charge of each part of the process are not attending to their duty. I do not mean the senior officers but the company grade officers. It seems to be the attitude that this fatigue work is for the men only," reported Fogg, turning to look at Gris.

"Fogg is correct in his assumption, my Lord. I believe that there are more than enough boats on the river to do the job and if there were not and Colonel Bradstreet knew of it there would be. I think that they are being misused. I would suggest that the best way to straighten out this snarl is to get some New York Provincials up here to run the ferry business, along with a few more boats down from Fort Edward. I would also start to replace the regulars who are stationed at the rifts with provincials as they become available. The provincials are more experienced in doing this type of duty, even the townsmen." Howe stood and looked at the ferry landing for a moment and then back at the two of them. He took off his round hat and ran his hand over his closely cropped red hair. He then turned to Moneypenny.

"Alexander, did you get all of that?"

"Yes, General," replied Moneypenny.

"Good, write out orders to see that it gets accomplished. When they are finished, sign my name to them and get copies to all of the appropriate places. There should be provincials coming into camp in another day. I want them moved up river as soon as possible. The Yorkers can move today if we send the dispatch down in a boat. See that it gets to either a ranger officer or one of Bradstreet's bateau officers. Tell them I expect to see Yorkers up here at this station no later than tomorrow afternoon. Now, gentlemen, any other news that I should know about?" They told him of their encounter the previous evening, and that they had three Stockbridge rangers out looking for more information. They also inquired if there was a special 55th detachment that would be going up the west side of the river to Fort Edward. They explained that they had eliminated the 44th officers as they were not the least surprised to see them at breakfast. His Lordship was not aware of any special detail but would inquire from Col. Donaldson to see if by chance he had sent one up the west side.

"Very good, gentlemen. I think that from here on up you should start wearing your uniforms. Major Fogg, you will find a uniform over in the baggage wagon. I have taken the liberty of procuring one from the Royals and had the buttons rearranged, the tails altered and removed all of the lace. I believe they shall fit well as I had a set of your cloths to check them from. Do not look so surprised. You know how larcenous my family can be," with a wide grin. "I will be set up over there with my lads," pointing to a spot well removed from the officers country. They went over to the baggage wagon, from where Moneypenny was retrieving his lap desk.

"Captain Moneypenny, His Lordship says there is a package for me on the wagon," asked Fogg.

"Yes it is right here. Oh, by the way it is now acting Major Moneypenny, as of two days ago. General Abercromby appointed me Major of Brigade. Also my name is Alexander."

Fogg held out his hand, "Congratulations Major Alexander Moneypenny. A well deserved promotion. Keeping up with His Lordship is not an easy task."

"Indeed it is not. As you fellows no doubt are finding out," was Moneypenny's reply accompanied with a brief laugh, handing a rather large package wrapped in tent material to Fogg.

"Wear these in good health." With that he instructed the driver to follow Lord Howe up to the camp area, he himself going over to the officers mess to get some breakfast and start writing out the orders required.

Fogg and Gris led their mounts over to one of the toilet tents that were set up by the officers mess. An orderly came over to inquire if they needed anything. Fogg said some hot water would be nice as they would like to wash and shave. Within a few minutes he had it there and they managed to get two days of dust and beards off. Gris had brought in his portmanteaux and had laid out his regular waistcoat and sleeved waistcoat along with a clean blue and white checked shirt. Fogg untied his package and took out the cut-down uniform coat, holding it up to look at it. It had not required much to make it look like a Guards uniform, being practically the same. The biggest change was in the tails that had been cut off and the coat ended just at crotch level. The cuffs had also been made slightly smaller to fit closer to the sleeve. The waistcoat had been shortened so it did not hang below the skirt of the coat. There were a pair of blue wool breeches along with a pair of field breeches made with tent cloth. Included also were a pair of soldiers' raw linen marching gaiters. Gris told him to wait a moment and went back outside to his saddle bag. When he came back in he had a pair of Indian leggings or mitasses made of elk skin.

"These will hold up much better in the bush and will also make you look like you have been in North America for a while. They do not have any distinctive decorations so will pass for almost any Indian-made ones, in case the need arises. Wouldn't want you to get taken by any Lake Indians wearing Iroquois leggings," said Gris with a smile.

By now they had finished dressing and had rolled up their civilian cloths and stowed them. As they walked through camp they drew a lot of stares. Most of the regulars had not seen any of Gage's men before and Gris in his brown uniform and "leather cap" stood out. Fogg was also a curious figure wearing his altered uniform and a hat cut into what was referred to as a castor hat, due to the flap in front resembling a beaver tail. It was to become the headgear of the light infantry companies then being formed from each regiment.

They led their horses on up to Lord Howe's camp and gave over their extra clothing to the man in charge of the baggage, with instructions to send it back down river to be stored with the 55th officers' baggage. They then went down to the ferry crossing to see if there was any news from the Stockbridge scouts. Just as the Sergeant was telling them that the Stockbridge rangers had not came back in, they appeared coming down across the meadow behind Lord Howe's camp. The three of them trotting along in single file.

"You see that Sir," said the Ranger Sergeant pointing to them, "they can run like that all day long and still slit your throat without waking you from your sleep. The damn French Indians can do the same thing, so learn to sleep with one eye open," with a knowing nod of his head.

When they came up, the one in charge remained standing and the other two sat down. He said in perfect English that they had picked up the trail leaving the farm with no trouble. It appeared that the party had not thought that they would have trackers looking for them. They followed the trail for about two English miles where it joined another party coming from the direction of the river. It appeared that they had stayed there for a while and perhaps even had some food. There was a mix of shoe and moccasin prints. A couple of the moccasin prints belonged to white men but the remainder belonged to Iroquois from Lake of the Two Mountains, Catholic Mohawks most likely. The shoe prints were made by both French and English soldier shoes. They also had a button from a French uniform waistcoat. The two parties had split and the one with the English soldier shoes had headed back to this camp. They had followed it right back to the upper edge of the clearing, pointing in the direction from which they had come. With that, he sat down with his companions. The Sergeant said something to them in Mahikander and they got up and started to leave.

The one who had been the spokesman turned and said, "One soldier have crack in bottom of shoe. Leather is split like this," making a diagonal line on the bottom of his own foot "Easy for Indian to find," and with that they walked away. Fogg and Gris stood there staring at each other for a moment.

Fogg turned to the Sergeant, "Are they going back to Fort Edward?"

"Yes Sir, they are," replied the Sergeant.

"Well, there has been a change in their orders. We will get you either written or verbal from Lord Howe. They are to become part of Lord Howe's military family until further notice," was Fogg's quick reply.

"There is a Ranger officer on the other side of the river. I'll have it delivered to him. In the meantime, I'll send the boys up to His Lordship's camp. Please pass the word along as the regulars don't seem to cotton to having the Stockbridge around their camps," as he went calling after the three Stockbridge rangers.

They went up to the mess tent to find Moneypenny who was still working on getting all of the necessary orders written out. He had collared the clerk who was helping to make copies. Fogg explained their recent discoveries and requested the proper orders to keep the three Stockbridge rangers on this side of the river close to Lord Howe. Moneypenny complied without any hesitation and within minutes they were back off down to the ferry crossing with orders for the ranger officer on the other side. This made for a very happy ranger sergeant who now was not sticking his neck out for a couple of decent officers but regulars never the less.

Next they went up to Lord Howe's camp and informed the officer in charge of the guard detail of the arrangement with the Stockbridge. They were to have the run of the camp and anyone who interfered would be dealt with not only by themselves but by Lord Howe. They briefly stopped at Lord Howe's tent to inform him of their latest findings.

It had been a very busy day.

## Chapter 26

Very little of consequence happened during the next couple of weeks. Everyone was involved in the normal activities required with maintaining an army this size in the field and at the same time moving it up river a piece at a time. Major Moneypenny, as Brigade Major had to return to Headquarters at Fort Craillo. He had only come up river for the one day to assist in Lord Howe's getting settled. One clerk remained behind and Howe sent Moneypenny on the Hudson Express back down river. The Hudson Express was a wild ride in a longboat with a party of rangers or the bateaux men. It did not take very long to make the trip as opposed to coming back up the river. The rangers and bateaux men would draw lots to see who would get to make the trip.

The men were busy with getting themselves and baggage up the river. It seemed to the men that they spent all the time putting supplies into boats, only to have to take them out again after a short trip and then repeat the process over again. Others were busy repairing the road or cutting and hauling wood. The carpenters and blacksmiths spent hours repairing broken or worn equipment due to the conditions of the roads.

Colonel Bradstreet required a great many men to get the bateaux that had been built in Albany up the river. They could be hauled over the rifts but they had to be removed and trucked around the sets of falls. There were also several courts-martial and punishments that went with the discipline of the army. The Indians had presented a problem as the soldiers could not tell one from the other. A party of supposedly French Indians had walked right into camp and right back out again with several bags of supplies. The General issued an order that all of the British Indians would henceforth have a band of red cloth tied to their firelocks.

The various regiments were required to shift the location of their camps once during this period as the ground became fouled and churned from all of the foot traffic. The straw used for the tents would become moldy despite airing the tents on a daily basis when weather allowed. The process for airing the tents consisted of rolling the tent back to one end in the case of the bell tents and rolling it up vertically to the middle with the few two ended tents. The entire

119

camp would take on a strange effect when this was being done. It looked like someone had planted a field of frames on which to grow some white crop.

The presence of possible French and Indian activity caused the General to restrict movement around and between the camps. No one was allowed beyond the out sentries without permission from Major Proby. During the night, special guards were mounted over the bateaux and longboats. The regular ferry was kept on the east bank at night. Work details were accompanied by rangers and covering parties. The rangers formed an outer screen far enough removed to give adequate warning. Detailed orders explained how they were to react if attacked. The work party was to withdraw to the head of the camp and form two deep while the rangers and covering party were to withdraw while skirmishing. The guards mounted in the two redouts were to hold their ground, leaving the picquetts to respond. Amid all of this, the largest army that the English had ever assembled in North America moved, slowly but surely up the river to Fort Edward. On Thursday, June 1st, Lord Howe with three companies of the 55th and three of the 42nd crossed the river and marched up to Fort Edward while their baggage was sent up by bateaux.

To the three Frenchmen, and their dozen Indian companions watching from a nearby hill, this signaled that it was time to withdraw to the rendezvous on Lac du Saint Sacrement and thence to the outpost at Carillon. Howe was on the move.

# Chapter 27

While Lord Howe and the troops moving up to Fort Edward crossed the river and went up the east road, Fogg and Gris had another assignment. They, along with the three Stockbridge rangers, six men from Rogers unit and six from Gage's, were to traverse the west track up to Fort Edward. They were to shadow the army on the other side of the river, the plan being to intercept, any Frenchmen doing the same. They waited until a half hour after Howe and his force started their march up river and departed camp by cutting back to the farmstead where they had originally stayed. This way it would appear that they were heading back toward Albany. By the time they made it back to the river track the tail of the column could just barely be seen. If they could maintain this distance, they would be in a good position. Fogg and his force moved cautiously up the track. Two of the Stockbridge were in advance on the lookout for any signs of activity along the track. Prior to starting out, Fogg had set up his force into two sections, one commanded by Gris and the other by himself. Gris had the men from Gage's Light Infanrty plus one of the Stockbridge rangers. Fogg had the Rangers along with the other two Stockbridge. Fogg told the Ranger Sergeant in charge of the detachment that he was to speak up if he thought that Fogg was about to do something that he, in his bush experience, seemed to be the wrong action to undertake. They moved up along the track separated by about one-hundred yards, taking turns leap-frogging past each other. This way it was difficult to determine exactly how many were in the entire party.

Just above the islands, below the Moses Kill, they made their first discovery. At the site of a small settlement that had been deserted during one of the earlier French Wars they came upon signs of a camp. The Stockbridge quickly discerned the footprints as being the same as those discovered weeks before near the farmstead at the Little Falls. However, these were fresh, no more than a couple of hours old. They also included some shoe prints that both the Rangers and the Stockbridge said were French. All in all, there may have been twelve to eighteen men in the party. Further searching showed that they had all moved on up the track together.

Fogg gave the order to move out but at an even more cautious rate. The Stockbridge advance scouts moved slowly, stopping every few feet to look around and listen. They moved one on one side of the track and one on the other. Whenever they came to a curve, the one on the opposite side would drop down and creep forward until he could see around the curve. Only when they were sure that it was clear would they move on, signaling to the rest to follow. They proceeded this way all the way to the Snook Kill without any sign of the enemy. They could still catch glimpses of the army column across the river. They were now only a few miles from Fort Edward. As they approached one bend in the track, the Stockbridge, who was with the main party, held out his hand in the signal to stop. Everyone froze where they were. He slowly motioned them down to a crouch. Through the use of sign language the advance scout, who had given the first signal, relayed to the other that there was a party of French and Indians ahead down by the river. The other one slowly crawled backwards down the track until he was far from the bend. He rose to a crouch and silently trotted back to the main party. After a brief conversation in whispers to the one who was with Fogg, the one who spoke English turned to Fogg and whispered in his ear.

There was a party of the French and Indians down by the riverbank. They were hiding in the brush, using a glass to observe the column on the other side of the river. They appeared to be counting the troops and wagons. He said there were less than there were in this party and that perhaps the rest were a little further up or were waiting in ambush to cover the watchers if they were surprised. Fogg turned to the Sergeant, told him what the Stockbridge had said and asked his opinion. He said that he would go with the latter opinion as they were prone to separate their forces to catch any enemy nearby unawares. He had been at the second snowshoe fight. Fogg signaled for Gris to come up cautiously. When he reached him, he relayed the same information that he had received from the Stockbridge and the Ranger Sergeant. Gris agreed with them. They should wait until they had a very clear picture of what the French were up to and only if they were all together should they even consider attacking them. If they were just counting troops, the intelligence would not be very useful as there were not any more than six-hundred men in the column with Howe. It would prove more useful to the French to wait until the army arrived at Fort Edward to count troops. Perhaps they were observing the column for another reason. They may have been trying to determine if Lord Howe was with the column. He had left his horse at the ferry crossing and was marching with the men. His uniform was not any different than the rest of the 55th common soldiers.

Fogg instructed his men to get back just off the track, his group taking one side and Gris and his group a little further down the other side. The second Stockbridge had gone back up to his original position and he and his companion did the same thing, carefully brushing out their footprints, including the ones leading up to their positions. The men all sat quietly, in spite of the insects. The Rangers had given everyone some oil that seemed to drive away the bugs. When asked by Fogg what it contained they said "Don't ask!" so he left well enough alone.

It had only been about fifteen to twenty minutes when the Stockbridge laid his hand on Fogg's and slightly inclined his head up the track. At first, Fogg could not see anything but slowly he caught some movement along the track. Two Indians were slowly moving down the center of the track. They stopped about halfway between the advance scout and Fogg's group and held a muffled conversation accompanied by many gestures. Shortly they got up and turned back up the track, walking upright without any attempt to conceal themselves or to be cautious. No sooner had they disappeared around the bend than the two advance scouts appeared on the track and came running back to Fogg. They briefly said something to the other Stockbridge who in turn said something to the Ranger Sergeant and the three of them started back down the track to Gris.

The Ranger Sergeant said in a loud whisper to Fogg and his men, "Quickly lads, move back down the track. They have discovered that they are being followed." With that, he bolted out of the brush and headed down the road. Fogg, giving way to the Sergeant's experience, followed him. Two rangers grabbed some brush and wiped out footprints as they moved backward down the track. This continued for about a hundred or so yards and then they got off the track to the land side. There was a little knoll covered with hardwoods and the Sergeant said that they should get up on it and hunker down. Instead of running directly up the hill, he led them across the front and then cut back along the side slope to the top. The men got down and took up position among the trees in groups of three. Fogg ordered that none should fire until the Sergeant fired. The Stockbridge had completely skirted around the back of the hill and had come up on the left flank of the knoll. The minutes seemed to crawl by as they waited to see if the enemy had discovered their trail and had followed them. Shortly there was some movement just beyond the foot of the knoll where the forest changed into hardwoods. Like a pack of hounds the French Indians appeared out into the stand of beeches, one in front moving slowly along the trail that they had left when passing through the leaves, the rest following. There appeared to be no Frenchmen with them. Perhaps they only sent some Indians to deal with whomever was following them. One of the

Indians appeared to be in charge and he also looked lighter than the rest, his hair appearing brown instead of black. There were only eight of them and they were semi bunched up where the lead one had stopped, just at the foot of the knoll where the path veered off to the south. They seemed to be discussing the merits of continuing on or turning back.

It was at this point that the Stockbridge rangers opened fire. They had not been present when Fogg gave his order not to fire until the Ranger Sergeant did. Two of the French Indians went down while the rest turned to the right to see from where the fire had come. One of the Indians pointed toward the smoke and started to run in that direction, tomahawk drawn. The third Stockbridge took him out with one shot. At the same time the Sergeant opened fire on the remainder of the group and was quickly followed by the rest of the three man sections, each firing only two shots per section. Three of the five remaining French Indians went down, the other two turned to flee in the direction from which they had come. This was a mistake because it put them running straight away from the remaining English who had not fired and at an angle to the Stockbridge. The two who had fired first were up and running toward the French Indians, cutting down the distance. Before the French Indians could disappear into the mixed woods where they would be able to more easily evade their pursuers, the two fired, knocking down both of the fleeing Indians. Both were still alive when the Stockbridge got up to them and were quickly subdued.

Fogg and the Rangers were quickly down the knoll to check on the others, Gris holding his sections in readiness to cover their retreat. Three of the Rangers ran over to where the Stockbridge were and relieved them of their prisoners. The Stockbridge rangers moved slowly back up the trail that the French Indians had come down to set up a screen. There was one other Indian who was alive, the one with the brown hair and lighter skin. The Ranger Sergeant took him by the hair and held his head up for Fogg to see.

"Do you parlez, Major?" he asked. Fogg moved over to the man and asked in French his name. The man just looked coldly at Fogg saying nothing. Fogg asked him again and still nothing. Fogg's hand shot out and grabbed the man by his windpipe. This time Fogg said that if the man understood him to nod his head and if he failed to do so, he would crush his windpipe as he was useless if he didn't understand. The man, whose eyes were already big from surprise, grew bigger as he stared into the Fogg's unblinking stare, nodded his head as much as possible under the circumstance.

124

"Bien," replied Fogg letting go. The man coughed wildly trying to catch his breath. Fogg took the man's French-issue canteen and offered it to him. After he had gained control of his throat from the chocking he sat there silently. Finally, Fogg asked him how many were in the French party and he lied saying there were thirty-six. Fogg did not let on that he knew there were no more than eighteen or twenty. He instructed the Sergeant to bind up the wounds and then they would be on their way. The Sergeant ordered a couple of the Rangers to take care of the Frenchman and the two Indians, making sure that they were bound up tightly and gagged. Fogg took the Sergeant and Gris aside and laid out his plan. He intended to remain off of the track and move north parallel to it. At the next stream they would move down the stream and back onto the track. By then the remaining French would have moved on up the track as they realized that they had lost almost half of their force, including one of their Indian Department officers. They agreed that it was a plausible plan and gathered up their men to move out. One of the Rangers went down the trail to gather up the Stockbridge. In a few minutes, they returned and Fogg and company moved out toward the north.

When they hit the first stream, they turned east and walked down it until they cut the track once more. Sure enough there were footprints heading north with no attempt to hide them. According to the Stockbridge, who thought it was amusing, they were doing so at the run. As Fogg and his party got a little further on the prints veered off to the west on a small trail that intersected the track. They were only a short distance below Fort Edward and the series of trails and roads that connected it to the Royal Block house and several smaller ones. Their plan was to get up opposite the Great Island and hail for a longboat to come across the river and pick them up. Just short of the lower island, they made contact with one of the Ranger patrols that constantly patrolled the huge military complex that Fort Edward was becoming. They were surprised to see a force coming up the west side of the river. Fogg inquired if Lord Howe's column had as yet arrived and was informed that it had.

Shortly they were up opposite the Great Island and within a few minutes, two longboats came over to carry them across the river. They parted company with the Rangers, who were now in their home base and went over the floating bridge with the remainder of the 80th. Gris instructed the men from the 80th to take the prisoners to the provost headquarters and leave them there with instructions for them to be held until further orders from Lord Howe. With that, he and Fogg went in search of His Lordship.

# Chapter 28

Fort Edward had become a large sprawling military base during the years since 1755. It was the assembly point and main supply depot for any campaign going north by way of either Lake George or South Bay. Where Fogg and Gris had first landed was the Great Island that sat opposite the fort. Their longboats had come ashore by the Quarter Guard post and in front of them lay the huts occupied by the Rangers, stretching off to the southern part of the island. In that area were located some store houses and the soldiers garden with some livestock pens. On the far southern end was the smallpox hospital. There were also guardhouses stretched along the western shore of the island. The northern end of the island was to be the camp for a large body of the provincials. As yet there were still very few come up from Albany.

The huts had been laid out according to regular castrametation procedure for a short front camp. The hut lines ran perpendicular to the officers huts. The sergeants occupied the huts next to the parade and so forth. Major Rogers' hut was in the center of the staff line. Arrayed behind this line were the kitchens and the petty sutlers for the rangers. The Rear Guard post sat behind the sutlers and there was a bridge guard post near the floating bridge on both ends. Located just east of the storehouse area between and halfway between the hut rows and the garden was a block house. The officers necessaries line the east bank of the island and the soldiers lined the west bank just past the Quarter Guard. All along both shores there were bateaux and longboats tied up with a constant guard on them.

The fort itself had grown from the fort proper to several sets of earthworks that encompassed the various stages of the regulars' camps. The first set had been constructed to the east and then had been continued on around to the north to enclose the north ravelins. Outside of this ravelin another set of earthworks had been built to protect the main regular camp that was also set up short front. Fogg estimated the area between the outer works and the inner works to be at least seventy-five yards. The side toward the river, being covered by the island was only stockaded with no ditch. The other parts were ditched on the front and built up with a fire-step. There were bastions

126

set on the ends to cover the two gates set into each platform wall. The gates had stockaded mazes in front of them that limited the amount of people who could come through at one time. The road north to Lake George went through this northern works. There was a wide level plain between the fort and the forest to the north. The east approach was through a drowned lands that had a stream running through the center of it. Just south of this stream and next to the fort was the trading post of the Sutler Best. There was a small foot bridge that connected it to the land on which the fort sat. Off to the east was another blockhouse that guarded a bridge crossing the stream that ran through the swamp or drowned lands. The road from Albany came across this bridge and around to the north wall of the outer works. A little south of Best's was located the Officers Gardens.

There were soldiers everywhere. Out on the plain there were units drilling while other units were working on fatigue details. There were parties cutting wood on the far side of the plain with ranger covering parties out beyond them. There were soldiers from the 80th drilling in irregular tactics along side ranger units. They were learning how to equalize their movements so as to enable them to operate together in the up coming campaign. The camps were a bustle with activity as the men that Lord Howe had just brought up were setting up their tents. There were soldiers from the Quartermasters work detail who were unloading wagons and moving supplies to the various warehouses. Everywhere one could see patrols on the outer perimeter of the complex. Across the river on the west side you could see the Royal Blockhouse that sat up on the bluff. This was garrisoned with a force large enough to hold its own until relieved from the fort. For the most part, all of the Ranger patrols and other activity kept the French and their native allies a good distance from the fort, especially now that the English were staging a major campaign. One of the most recent orders to Major Rogers was to endeavor to take as many prisoners as possible for intelligence purposes.

When Fogg and Gris finally found Lord Howe, he had been in the fort proper but was now on his way out. They met him as he was coming on to the ravelin, where the road crossed the ditch and went out onto the area between the curtain wall and the outer works.

He greeted them with, "Gentlemen! Glad to see that you made it up the west track. How was the trip? Any of our friends and their dusky minions lurking about?" Fogg, as the senior officer gave the report of their encounter as they continued walking toward the 55th ground. Howe stopped him only for more particulars and then simply would say, " And then?" He seemed particularly interested in how they handled the ambush. His comment about that was that perhaps from now on they might develop a standing order for that type of an affair.

His final comment was, "Well done, gentlemen, well done. What do you suggest we do with the native prisoners? Obviously they will be of very little intelligence use to us as they are prone to remain silent even when being dealt with by other Indians."

Gris gave the most plausible answer, "I would send them down river to Albany and thence to New York, there to hold them until the end of this campaign season. I would then bring them back up to Albany and release them into the western Mohawk Valley where they can make their way back home."

"Why not do that now?" asked Lord Howe.

"My Lord, these people can cover the distance from German Flatts in the western Mohawk to Frontenac or Niagara in less than a weeks time. That would mean that they could be back on Lake Champlain in anywhere from three to four weeks. They are a formidable enemy and one of the greatest assets that the French have, the same as the natives who fight for us. The secret is in motivating them, which Sir William does quite well. The French have no one person like Sir William but unfortunately have several smaller versions who, in the long run, influence more than he does." Lord Howe stopped walking and thought for a minute.

"Very good, Captain Gris. I will follow your advice and have the devils shipped down river. We will see what we can learn from the Frenchman. I would think most likely he is a Canadian and not a troope du terre. What chance do you think we have of corrupting him?"

Again, Gris answered, "I would think very little, Sir. He is as hard as the people he was leading. He is most likely a la Marine officer or sous officer and has been living with les sauvages for a long time. You will be lucky to get him to admit that he speaks French as it is much easier to hide behind ignorance."

Lord Howe shook his head in disbelief, "God what a savage country this is." and then with great glee, "I love it! Carry on, gentlemen, carry on. I have had a tent set up for you here on the 55th ground. There, just on the far end of the staff row. Your baggage was already delivered to it. I have notified the Mess Sergeant that, like all of the 55th officers, you will be dining out of the regimental kitchen. We are a Spartan group, the 55th, but we share and share alike." With that, he walked off to his own soldiers' tent.

Gris turned to Fogg and asked, jokingly, "Are you sure he is related to the rest of the Royal family?"

128

Fogg's reply was, "At times I find it hard to believe myself but then wait until you meet Brother Dickey." They reached their tent and stowed their arms and gear, pulled off their shoes and flopped down on their bear skins. It had been another long day.

# Chapter 29

Saturday, the third of June was another very busy day. The Rangers were ordered to move from their cozy huts sites on the island to encamp with the major portion of the army on the main land outside the fort. This was all accomplished with much grumbling, bitching and moaning. The regiments who had been encamped there the longest were also ordered to move their camps, which was received with the same grumbling, bitching and moaning as the Rangers. Security around the encampment was increased. A standing order for out-sentries was issued to not pay complements to officers. Also no man was to pass beyond them except parties under arms accompanied by a proper officer with specific orders to do so. The order for no discharging of arms or causing false alarms was evoked under the Articles of War, which were read in all the companies.

In the ensuing days all sorts of activity was happening through out the camp. On Sunday the entire Ranger companies were ordered to have their arms inspected by Captain Stevens of the Royal Artillery for the purpose of determining how many needed replacement or repair. As usual, this was received by the Rangers in the usual manner that all activities that were "regular" were received. The Rangers were an Independent Company as such were subject to all of the same rules as regular foot companies. This did not mean that they liked it but is was just the way things were. Another activity that induced much of the soldierly attitude of grumbling about useless work was the order for all the regiments to turn in their tools to the Quartermaster. It seemed that every time they needed tools they would go to the Quartermaster and draw additional ones instead of finding the ones that had been used previously. From this day forward each regiment was to receive fifteen spades and five mattocks only. All were to be turned back to the Quartermaster when a regiment or any major part of it marched. The Quartermaster was to confiscate and report any tools to the headquarters that they found lying about the camp. The regiment in whose camp or vicinity they were found was to give an accounting of their tools. Each regiment was ordered to send its Surgeons and Quartermasters to secure huts on the island for use as hospitals. All parties going to the island for wood or vegetables were to have a junior officer and non-

130

commissioned officer in charge. No individual man was allowed to the island without a written pass from the Officer of the Day. Single men had a tendency to disappear off the island as it was a short swim to the other side. There were also many boats and canoes on the west shore.

Two large parties were formed to go north. On the 5th of June a party of twenty-five officers and eight hundred men with a small party of Rangers departed for the Lake. They took no tents and carried all their provisions and tools due to no wagons being available. Another party of one hundred men with officers were dispatched to escort bateaux from Fort Miller. The following Wednesday, a large scout was sent out to scour the forest between Fort Edward and the Lake. They were to move up parallel to the road on its west side. Spread out in two offset skirmish lines, they would cover a swath almost three-hundred fifty yards wide. At given intervals, they were to change directions moving in a zig-zag pattern. One smaller party would move directly forward on the road side following the larger party. The party was provided with eight days' provisions and consisted of one hundred regulars that were mostly volunteers, forty men from the Light Infantry Regiment, twenty Rangers and ten Stockbridge Rangers. There were two officers from the 55th, one each from the 44th and 42nd , two from Gage's and the same from the Rangers. The party was to eventually report to the camp at the Lake.

On Monday, June 12th, a detachment was sent to finish the repairs to the road to Lake George. It consisted of Colonel Bever and twelve other officers, along with the men from the 46th and the additional companies of the 42nd plus all of the New York troops in camp. In all the strength of the party was close to twelve-hundred. It was capable of providing its own covering party.

Fogg and Gris were ordered to form a detail of no more than fifty picked men to shadow this work detail. Their job was to search for any French that moved into the void caused by the scout sent to sweep the woods along the road. They went in search of the Ranger Sergeant who had come up the river with them. They found him out training a group of newly recruited Rangers. When offered the chance to get away from his baby-tending assignment he jumped at the chance. Fogg told him he wanted twenty Rangers including himself plus ten Stockbridge Rangers. They were to report tomorrow morning at the Quarter Guard. Next, they went to the 80th and secured twenty Light Infantrymen to include a senior Sergeant and two corporals to meet the same as the Rangers tomorrow.

Their next task was to find Israel Putnam. They wanted to learn more about the country between Fort Edward and the Lake. They found Putt over in the officer country of the Ranger camp. He was overjoyed to see them.

"Lads, you caught me just in time. I am about to go up to the Lake and lead a scout out on the Lake as far north as a mile or two past the narrows. It is a four longboat party. Care to come along? We will have plenty of room." They explained that they had an operation of their own to conduct and they needed his expert advice. He allowed as he could spare an hour of his time before departing. They asked all of the questions that they could think of and Putnam added whatever advice he thought would be useful. He warned them that on a fifty-man scout they should never divide their party, except in dire circumstances. If ambushed and pinned down then they should disperse at night to a pre-arranged rally point. It should always be set first thing in the morning. They should also listen to the Sergeant they were taking with them. He was an experienced non-commissioned officer who had been through many scrapes and perhaps one of the best choices they could have made, except maybe for himself. All too soon the hour passed and Putnam had to depart to muster his men. He was taking both Rangers and Light Infantry of the Regiments with him. For most of the Lights, it would be their first time out on a Lake scout.

The next stop was headquarters to see if there were any maps available for them to look at. There were a few but none of them agreed on anything including the road. They decided that they would have to rely upon the knowledge of the senior Rangers and the Stockbridge in their party.

They stopped by the 55th kitchen to get something to eat and draw rations for a week long scout. Their plan was to keep pace with the work detail and to re-supply at Halfway Brook if necessary. After eating, they returned to the headquarters tent to either leave a message or inform Lord Howe that they were ready to depart just before first light in the morning. They were surprised to see Moneypenny who had returned from Albany a couple of days before, unbeknownst to them. He took the message for Lord Howe, who was out on the island and wished them good hunting. On their return to camp Fogg spied a Sergeant from the 55th Foot.

He said to Gris, "Isn't that the Sergeant who was in the barn?"

Gris studied him over closely, "By God, it is!" They agreed that the best course of action would to be to find out his name and company. On return from the Lake they would inform Lord Howe.

After he had passed they approached one of the privates and Fogg said to him, "Private, was not that Sergeant Jones of the 3rd Captains Company?"

"Him Sir? No Sir, that be Sergeant O'Leary of the Major's Company."

"Are you positive, he looks like Sergeant Jones," replied Fogg.

"Oh yes Sir, to be sure that be Sergeant O'Leary. He be the senior Sergeant in the whole of the 55th. I knows him well I does." Fogg dismissed the Private and they walked away toward their tent.

"Sergeant O'Leary, and would that not sound Irish to you, Mr. Gris?"

"That it would Mr. Fogg, that it would." With that they turned in for the night. This was the first night in a couple of days that they would be able to not have to sleep completely dressed. Of course. it would also be the last night for at least the next two weeks that they would get to sleep, let alone in a tent.

## Chapter 30

It seemed that they had just dropped off to sleep when the orderly was scratching on their tent telling them that it was time to wake up.

He presented them with two mugs of strong tea according to him, "This, Sirs, is just to start your hearts pumping." Gris threw his shoe at him. The orderly stuck his head back in to return Captain Gris' shoe and hand them a package. "This is from His Lordship," ducking as Gris picked up the other shoe. Fogg picked up the package and opened it. It contained four pair of moose-hide moccasins with a note that said simply, "Don't leave your shoes behind." They had been double soled with the extra sole sewed into the inside of the moccasin. With a heavy pair of socks they were quite comfortable. They put their shoes into their packs, finished drinking tea and getting dressed.

Within twenty minutes they were out and on their way to meet their party at the Quarter Guard. The camp was quiet with few people up and stirring due to the Sergeants who habitually arose before their men. The most activity was in the Ranger camp where they were mostly all up. The Rangers were in the habit of being up before first light and on the move so they were already at the Quarter Guard and the detachment from the 80th was crossing the Parade as Fogg and Gris came up.

"Been here long, Sergeant?" asked Fogg.

"No Sir, only a few minutes. We have one of our officers with us. Major Rogers ordered him out last night. Ensign Purdy. He's over there Major." He pointed toward a young Ranger distinguished by his castor hat and hunting bag.

"Would you request the young gentleman's presence over here, Sergeant?" The Sergeant went over to where Ensign Purdy was conversing with the Officer of the Quarter Guard. As Fogg outranked both of them the Sergeant interrupted them to inform the Ensign of the Major's wish. Purdy looked nervously in Fogg's direction and said a couple of more words to the other officer then turned and approached them. He came to the position of attention in front of Fogg, waiting for Fogg to speak.

"Report Ensign."

"Ensign Purdy, on temporary duty to Major Rogers Cadet Company reporting, Sir! I have two Sergeants, two Corporals and fifteen Privates plus ten Stockbridge rangers, commanded by a native officer, Sir."

"Thank you Ensign Purdy. What regiment are you from?"

"The Royals, Sir."

"Quite. From now on you are not to come to the position of most attention when addressing Captain Gris or myself. If we were out in the bush and being observed by the French or their natives, you just marked me as the officer in charge. You watch the Sergeant here and see how he acts when he speaks to us. Understood?"

Looking slightly rebuked, he returned a very subdued, "Yes Sir."

"Alright then, quietly look to your men and drop that gorget inside your waistcoat so you do not mark yourself as an officer. Sergeant, a moment please." The Sergeant followed Fogg away from the group. "What in hell was Major Rogers thinking of? Sending a cadet out with us? He is still wet behind the ears. Are there any more baby rangers in this batch?" inquired Fogg, more calmly as he was over his irritation of having to babysit.

"No Sir, the Ensign is the only new ranger. I picked the rest myself. As to why, well I don't pretend to know what Major Rogers thinks. Perhaps Major Rogers was thinking this would be a fairly easy scout where the lad, I mean Ensign Purdy, could gain some experience, Sir."

"Alright Sergeant. You are most likely correct in Major Rogers reasons." *I'll give Major Rogers my reasons for not wanting to take babies out on my patrols when we get back.* "What about the other Sergeant, can he take Ensign Purdy under his wing and keep him alive so that some of the valuable experience he gains on this scout will be of future use to His Majesty?"

"Aye Sir. That he can. We've both been at this since the beginning and beyond."

"Good. By the way what is your last name?"

"Sergeant will do fine, Sir. My last name is Surgent and Sergeant Surgent sounds like you're repeating yourself." He said with a large grin.

Gris came over followed by two men from the 80th. He introduced the younger as Lieutenant Frome and the other as Sergeant Burke. They would each command a nine man section that included a corporal.

"Very well, Lieutenant, Sergeant. See to your men. We are moving out in five minutes. Captain Gris are we clear with the Officer of the Quarter Guard?"

"All clear, Major."

Both he and Fogg shouldered their packs and gave the signal to follow on the officers' lead. The detachment moved out in single file. They still had plenty of half light left to clear the works and the Plain, as the cleared land around the fort to the north and east was called. By the time the sun poked its head over the eastern horizon they were well clear of the Plain. After a half hour, Fogg signaled for a halt. They had already moved off to the west of the road. The men had halted along the small animal path they were following. They squatted down. Then they alternated facing outward. Fogg gave the signal for all officers and NCO's to him.

He explained the purpose of their mission. It was to search out any parties of the enemy that might have filtered in behind the scout sent out earlier. They were to move with the utmost caution, maintaining silence. They were to issue orders only with hand signals and would only speak in whispers, when necessary, in clusters as they were doing now. Only the Stockbridge were allowed out of sight at any time. Everyone else was to maintain visual contact with the rest of the detachment. They were to move in two files with each file having two flankers on its outside. This would make the appearance to any trackers that there were four columns moving through the woods, making it difficult to determine how many were in the party. They would move no faster than the Stockbridge rangers could determine what lay in front of them

In this manner they resumed their march, slowly working their way north parallel to the road to the Lake. The remainder of the day went by in this fashion. At dusk, they moved the columns closer together and pulled in the flankers. The Stockbridge took up positions about twenty yards out from both ends of the column. Each man ate his rations in silence, pulled his blanket around him and went to sleep. Every fourth man stayed awake for two hours, woke up the man to his left and so on for the remainder of the night. With the exception of Ensign Purdy and a couple of the 80th men, they all were seasoned campaigners. It was arranged so that either an officer or a sergeant was awake for each watch.

A half hour before false light, the Sergeant woke Fogg. Fogg nodded his head and poked Gris who did the same until the signal had gone around the detachment. Without any noise, the columns split slightly apart and moved on up the trail. As the light increased, they moved out to their marching distance and put out the flankers. All but three of the Stockbridge had moved back up to the front of the columns. The three, being the rear guard, stationed themselves about fifty yards to the rear. The ones in front were divided into two groups. The lead group about one hundred yards and the other half way between them and the main party. The men ate their morning ration on the move.

They traveled like this for about two hours when the advance guard gave the signal to halt. At this, everyone instantly went to the kneeling position, both columns facing out with the exception of the first and last man in each. They faced one forward and one to the rear. Fogg and Gris remained in place, waiting for one of the Stockbridge who was making his way back to them. He indicated that the leader wanted Fogg to come up. Fogg signaled for Sergeant to follow him and moved forward with the Stockbridge Ranger. Fogg had forgotten how far one hundred yards was when you were moving half-crouched and half-squatting.

When they got up to the advance guard, the native officer showed them a set of human tracks that had cut out across the animal path that they were following. The other humans were following a deer runway. The Stockbridge pointed to one of the moccasin prints and gave the sign for Huron and another set of shoe prints, indicating it was soldiers and French. Fogg looked at the Sergeant and mouthed "How many?" The Sergeant signed to the Stockbridge who indicated that there were about half as many as Fogg's detachment and they had passed through here about an hour ago.

The French were headed for the road and were between the work detail and the Fort. Perhaps they were going to cross the road and move along the east side in hopes of picking up a prisoner or two from the fatigue detail. They would be unexpected from the east. Fogg sent one of the Stockbridge back for Gris. When Gris came up he and Fogg and the Sergeant huddled together and in very low whispers held a council of war. They decided to take a chance and follow the French, at least to the Lake George Road. When they reached it, they would make the next decision depending on what they found. The Sergeant went back on the path until he could signal for the remainder of the party to come up. He indicated that everyone should look to his priming. They moved cautiously along the deer runway that skirted along part of the swamp that lay between them and the road. The two columns had become two sections of the same column and in turn both sections were moving on both sides of the runway.

The Stockbridge Rangers cautiously made their way, literally one tree at a time, down the deer path, silently floating from one tree to the next. They had stowed their shirts and were wearing only mitasses and breechcloths. They blended in with the shadows as if thousands of years of forest warfare had made them a part of the forest itself. In this manner the whole detachment made its way to the roadway. About fifty yards from the clearing that ran along the side of the road, the lead Stockbridge held up the signal to stop. Everyone went down and silent, hardly breathing. They held this position for a long time while the Stockbridge determined if there were any of the enemy rear guard watching the crossing. Shortly he gave a signal for the detachment to move toward the south, slowly. Silently as possible they did as he indicated. After what seemed a long time to Fogg, he gave the signal to stop. They held their position for a few minutes while the Stockbridge observed the roadway. Fogg saw one of them dart across the clearing and the roadway and then disappear into the trees. Again, they held their position for what seemed like an eternity.

Fogg saw a movement on the other side of the roadway and the Stockbridge reappeared, holding up something in his hand. The lead Stockbridge signaled for them to move forward and cross the road at the trot. With in a couple of minutes all of the party was on the other side of the roadway and into the trees. When Fogg got to the other side, he saw what the Stockbridge had been holding up. It was a fresh scalp, most likely from another Indian. The Stockbridge indicated that the former owner had been watching the road crossing. When they got up to where he had been watching, two of the other Stockbridge picked him up and carried him down to the clearing and propped him up against a stump. One had a wolverine paw with the claws on it. He took the paw and with a quick stroke swiped across the dead Indians throat. They left his gun, ammunition bag and everything in place. When they came back, he smiled at Fogg and said one word, "Carcajou!" Fogg looked at Gris and the Sergeant and shrugged his shoulders, questioningly. Gris leaned over and whispered that the Hurons and most Algonquins believed that the wolverine was an evil forest spirit called Carcajou. The Stockbridge were making them think that the Carcajou was fighting for the Anglais and Yangees. *Damn good idea. I need to get me one of those sets of claws.*

The column moved out at its slow pace, following the tracks leading north.

## Chapter 31

The French had left the deer run and were moving in two, single-file lines parallel to the road. Fogg's detachment maintained its regular formation and followed them for another two hours before the Stockbridge in the lead signaled that they saw something. They all knelt and waited, thankful for the brief rest but anxious as to what was ahead. It took one of the Stockbridge five minutes to crawl back to where they were. Fogg could see that the remaining Stockbridge had gone prone and also had moved back a few yards.

When the messenger got back to them he spoke to the Sergeant who, in turn ,relayed the information to Fogg and Gris. It seemed that the French had halted to set up an ambush along the road, in hopes that another work party or small detachment would pass by. Fogg inquired as to how long they thought that the French would wait. They were discussing their choices when one of the advance Stockbridge signaled for Fogg to come up. He and the messenger crawled their way up to the front.

The Frenchman, who appeared to be in charge, was getting his men ready to move. Apparently he did not like the site for an ambush and was going to move on. This suited Fogg as he had wanted to be able to hit the French when they were caught between him and the cover party for the work detail. He moved back and returned to the main party. Gris and the Sergeant agreed with his decision to wait. They passed along the word for everyone to relax while they waited for the French to move on. They had lain for about a half-hour when they heard shouting over on the road and then some sporadic fire. The Sergeant sent two Rangers back to take a look at the cause.

Shortly they came back and reported that there was a small party of regulars, 46th maybe, with a wagon. The French had sent back one of their party to get the Indian who was watching the trail and they had surprised him and shot him dead along with the already dead one. They then loaded both corpses up on the wagon, turned around and headed back for Fort Edward, probably convinced that the road to Halfway Brook was full of Indians and Frenchmen just waiting to kill, scalp and eat them. The French would have heard the firing and would either send back a small scout or leave the two

Indians to their own devices and move on up the roadway, hoping to set another ambush. They waited for another half hour and when no sign of the French showed they moved on out in their slow but steady pursuit.

Fogg's party moved steadily along, halting whenever the advance guard signaled and then moved on again. Along about mid-afternoon, they could start to hear the sounds of people cutting trees and soon the sounds of people working. The party working on the road was large enough so that they made a great deal of noise and could be heard for at least a couple of miles in the silence of the forest. The work party had no reason to be quiet. Being well over a thousand men, they were larger than any enemy force operating as a scout. Fogg's advance party sighted the French within another fifteen minutes.

The lead Stockbridge came back himself this time. He told Fogg that the French were spread out in a line just parallel to the southern wing of the fatigue party. The construction of the road had let in sufficient sunlight to have caused some brush to grow in an otherwise primeval forest devoid of much ground scrabble. It appeared that they were waiting for some poor soul to wander a little too far off from the rest. There were several of the French Indians concealed in closer to the roadway. These would be able to cut off anyone who ventured past them. The cover party was situated just along the edge of the tree line in extended order with small support parties stationed along the line.

Fogg, Gris and the Sergeant decided to move on an angle away and up toward the center of the French line. They would then turn and move into a crescent position to open fire behind the French, hopefully driving them into the cover party.

It took another fifteen or twenty minutes to get everyone in position to the east of the French and then turn to move west and in behind them. They had one close call when one of the 80th made some detectable noise. A couple of the French turned around and looked back into the forest. One of the Rangers made a couple of strange blowing noises and the Frenchmen looked at each other and shrugged, one putting his hands up to his head like a set of antlers. Fogg looked over to the Ranger who had acted so quickly and nodded his head laying two fingers on his own right shoulder like a corporal's knot. The Ranger just grinned back, shook his head no, pointed to his chest and laid three fingers on his own shoulder. It was the other Sergeant. Fogg looked at the senior Sergeant and nodded his head yes. The Sergeant, who already had his musket lined up on a Frenchman, nodded back and pulled the trigger. The forest erupted

140

with a silence-shattering explosion of musketry as a third of Fogg's detachment fired into the French. For a moment, the French seemed frozen in time but rapidly they realized from where the fire had come. Some turned around and fired back at the smoke, which was all that was visible. One of the 80th men lost his leather cap, but that was all the casualties from the first volley. The French and their allies had fared much worse. They had lost almost a third of their men in that first exchange as the English had time to sight upon a target.

The second firing of the English only reduced that number by two or three more. By now the French leader, who had been grazed by a ball, realized that he was in a very bad position. The covering party down on the road was now firing wildly into the woods at puffs of smoke. His party was close enough to the road to be in danger from even poorly aimed shots, the English behind him were well out of the other English musket range. His only choice was to cut and run with the biggest decision being in which direction. He had heard the firing to the south earlier and decided that perhaps there was another party coming up the road. This left only north and he called to his men to flee north, hoping that the English who ambushed him did not have enough men to set up a blocking party. Six or eight Frenchmen ran, in a crouch to the north between the two lines firing at them. One of them went down hit in the legs or lower part of his body, the rest made it clear of the end of Fogg's lines only to run into a party of New York Provincials who had grabbed their muskets and dashed into the woods when the firing had started. They realized that the French were caught between two lines of fire and had no place to go but out the ends. They just hoped it was their end.

As the remainder of the French came into range, the Yorkers sprang up and fired almost point- blank. The effect was devastating. All of the French went down either dead or badly wounded. One of the Yorkers was hit by accident in the side when one of the Frenchman dropped his musket and it went off. Fogg called for cease fire but the troops on the roadway kept firing. It was then that Fogg realized that they were firing at the Indians who had been in closer to the roadway, out of Fogg's line of sight. He called to the second Sergeant of the Rangers who immediately took his section and closed in on the trapped Indians. The remaining Indians decided it was better to attempt to make the woods on the other side of the road and bolted from their  location, taking the regulars on the roadway by surprise. Two of the regulars went down under the tomahawks of the Indians and one regular was shot by another as two Indians ran between them. It was all over in a few seconds as the remaining Indians made the other side of the road. The Rangers pursued them to the other side and into the skirt of the woods for a few yards but halted from going to far. A group of Scots from the 42nd had joined them by now and they set up a screen along that side of the road.

Fogg and his detachment had moved in closer to where the French had been. They checked the bodies. All in all, there were sixteen Frenchmen of which ten were wounded and probably only two of them would live. The Rangers were able to find eight Indians and they had counted four who made it across the road. In a few minutes, the Stockbridge came in with two more wounded Indians and one more Frenchman that they had found hiding in the brush along the road. The Frenchman was unscathed and only a teenager. Fogg inquired of his age and he answered that he was eighteen years. The Ranger Sergeant grabbed him by the face and turned his head back and forth, declaring that he didn't look like he had ever shaved as he still had peach fuzz on his face. With that, two of the Rangers grabbed him and the Sergeant pulled aside the terrified Frenchman's breechclout.

He exclaimed to Fogg, "Hell Major, he's just a kid. He ain't barely started to hair over."

The other Rangers let him go and he sank to the ground covering himself back up, glad that they had not done either one of the two terrifying things that he thought they were going to do. Fogg called to the 46th covering party and told them to take the boy into custody and either turn him in at Halfway Brook or, if a party went back to Fort Edward, send him back there. He quickly wrote out a report to Colonel Bever of the 46th and gave it to a Lieutenant signifying that it was for Lord Howe. He gathered up his detachment and, after thanking the Yorkers for their quick action , moved his men back off into the woods on the west side of the roadway. He did not want anyone coming back to observe that there was a detachment loose in the forest, hunting for the French. He hoped that the Indians who escaped would think that they were just a part of the covering party who had worked around behind them.

After a short council of war with all of the officers and NCO's to discuss the feasibility of following the fleeing Indians to see if they would led them to an other French party, they decided against it. The Sergeants agreed that if they were the Indians and they met up with another French body that they would want to double back and ambush anyone following their trail. Together, they decided that the best course of action would be to move back away from the roadway and keep within listening distance of the work detail, moving north as they did. Up to this point, Fogg had lost none of his men, either dead or wounded and he intended to keep it that way.

Except for the one incidence of the 80th man stumbling, all of the new men were coming along well. They had all paired up with a veteran and were learning their lessons well, even Ensign Purdy who did exactly as the other Ranger Sergeant instructed him. When they were somewhere even with the center of the detail working on the road, they halted and settled in for the remainder of the day.

*We have been out two days and have had two encounters with the French. I wonder if we are as active as close to the French main base as they are to ours? If we were it would seem that they would be less active here. Something else to discuss with Gris and speak to Lord Howe about.*

The rest of the day was quiet with the exception of the fatigue parties working on the road. Along about six o'clock the sounds of the work began to subside and they could hear the changing of the sentries as the work parties started to get settled in to cook their evening meals. Within a half hour or so, they could smell the mixture of wood smoke and boiling beef. Soon the men were digging into their packs for their own rations, hoping that eating would make the smell go away.

The work party had bivouacked in a large open area at a place called Meadow Run. Fogg moved his men back another one hundred yards or so from their previous position near the clearing. They took up a position in a stand of hardwoods that gave them a good command of the surrounding area. At night and in the dark it was a better position. They all set up with the two columns back to back and the Stockbridge out forming a crescent at both ends of the columns. The watch arrangements were the same as the night before, every fourth man awake for two hours. Tonight, Gris took the first watch and Fogg took the last with the two Ranger Sergeants taking the two middle watches.

Just before he dozed off, Fogg made a mental note that tomorrow night they would change how they set up their night position. It did not pay to be too repetitive, a lesson he had almost learned the hard way during his short career as a highwayman. Maybe he would take up that life-style again someday.

## Chapter 32

The next two days were spent doing a lot of sitting. Fogg sent out small patrols of one each a Stockbridge, a Ranger and a Light Infantryman. They were mainly for the soldiers to gain experience from the Stockbridge as trackers. They were to range only so far and then only in an elliptical path. Upon returning to the main party they were to cross in front of it and then loop back on the opposite side. This action would draw anyone following them across the field of fire of the main detachment.

On Friday, June 16$^{th}$, this method paid off. A patrol with Ensign Purdy as the Ranger had cut across a set of tracks that the Stockbridge estimated to be four or five Frenchmen and one Indian. The tracks were leading north, so they decided to cut short the patrol and move back toward the main party. They held to the operating plan and crossed in front of the main party but to the outside of the Stockbridge screen on the west of Fogg's main force. As Purdy's patrol moved off to the left of the Stockbridge to make a wide swing before coming back, one of the Stockbridge detected a slight movement off to the far right on the track that Purdy was following. He tossed a small clump of dirt over to where the main party was sitting, hitting the senior Ranger Sergeant on the shoulder. Sergeant turned and the Stockbridge signed that he saw enemy approaching. Sergeant nudged the man next to him and passed on the message to Fogg. Fogg signaled that everyone move closer in that direction, crawling. This was accomplished with very little noise as the signal was preceded by the sign for enemy. He left one man to caution Purdy that he had been followed and to remain there as the rear guard.

As Fogg and his men lie there concealed, the French party slowly moved into view. They were going very cautiously. The Indian, a French Cagnawaga Mohawk, crouched over studying the trail. He stopped and talked briefly with the Frenchmen who seemed to be in charge. They fanned out and started to move forward again, all of them studying the ground. Fogg suddenly realized that they had found signs of a previous patrol and were now perhaps thinking that there was a larger party at work here. As he had moved his bivouac every day the most that they might find was tracks from a much earlier patrol that had crossed in front of Purdy. One of the

144

Frenchmen gave a low crow call and the others looked to him. He pointed down on the ground and held up three fingers and made a motion pointing toward the south. The one in charge motioned for him to come back to where the rest were and they held a short parley, squatting in a small clearing as the Mohawk kept watch. Within a few minutes, they got up and, instead of moving along Purdy's trail, they started toward Fogg's party. Fogg looked along his line in both directions. Everyman was looking toward him, waiting for the command. He held his hand out in front of his face and closed it like grabbing something. It was the signal for hold but he repeated it again, this time pointing at the party moving toward them. He got a nod from all of them. They waited until the French were within a few yards from them and they all sprang up to their knees, muskets pointed at the French party. Fogg said one word, "Arretez!"

For a moment it was a frozen scene, fifty English Rangers, Light Infantrymen and Stockbridge, all with muskets leveled at five French Partazans and one Mohawk, all carrying their weapons at the ready. Fogg could see the eyes of the French leader, going from side to side assessing the situation. At this range his party were all dead men. They would never be able to bring their weapons to fire. Slowly he held out his musket and with one hand held out in a stop position, he laid it on the ground and said something to his men. They all followed suite. Only the Mohawk remained unmoving. Fogg could see his hands tighten on his musket and before he could say anything the Mohawk spun and started to run down the slope. Two Rangers sprang up but before they could fire the Mohawk stopped in his tracks. He turned around toward the Frenchmen trying to say something but was unable to utter a sound. There was an arrow sticking out of his throat. He tried to raise his musket to fire but lurched forward and fell to his face. No one had even noticed that the Stockbridge who were acting as the screen for the ends of the line had moved to cutoff any of the French who made it out of the ambush. The one who shot him was kneeling behind a tree not ten feet from where the Mohawk fell.

Fogg's men had quickly disarmed the Frenchmen and had bound and gagged them up, moving them down to the road-ward slope of the ridge. One third of the detachment remained in place to watch the trail in case this was only an advance scout. Fogg and Gris went through all of the papers that the French were carrying. There was a commission paper for a sous-lieutenant of La Marine, some letters from a couple of women, a very crude map of the area west of Fort Edward and some numbers that could have been a troop count from some point in time. Most interesting of all was a letter that stated that Lord Howe's army was moving up to Fort Edward and thence to Lake George to attack St. Frederick by way of Carillon. It also stated that the army numbered only five or six thousand regulars and only half the expected Provincials. When they read this, they knew from where the information had come. However they said nothing as one of the Frenchmen might understand English.

Fogg detailed a party of six mixed Rangers and the 80th under the command of Sergeant Burke to take the prisoners onto the roadway and turn them over to Colonel Bever. He gave them another written order that they were to be sent immediately to Fort Edward and turned over to Lord Howe and no other officer. He told Sergeant Burke that they would be moving the bivouac another mile further north and to meet them there as soon as possible. As soon as they finished burying the Mohawk, Fogg told Gris to move the detachment another mile north. Fogg took a Stockbridge and a Ranger and a Light Infantryman and started out to make a sweep in a semi-circle to the west, planning on coming back onto their main track at the rendezvous point. After a half hour, Fogg and his scout started to swing back toward the rendezvous point. They had found no additional track or indication that there was a larger French force in the immediate area. In spite of this, Fogg had a feeling that all was not quite as it would seem to be. He formulated a plan to execute immediately upon joining the remainder of his detachment. The Stockbridge felt it also as he kept looking back along their trail.

## Chapter 33

Fogg and his scouting party joined up with Gris and the main force of the detachment at the point that they had designated earlier. Sergeant Burke had came in with his men only a few minutes before. Fogg drew Gris and all of the officers and NCOs together to hold a council of war. He explained his premonitions that while on the scout he felt like they were being watched. He also said that the Stockbridge acted like he felt the same thing. The Sergeant signaled for the Stockbridge who was with Fogg to come over to the meeting. The Sergeant asked the man if he felt something was wrong when on the scout. The Stockbridge nodded his head and replied in a short statement. The Sergeant translated it.

"He says that he felt that you were being watched and followed but he could never quite catch sight of who it was." Fogg signed "good" to the Indian who returned to where he had been sitting with the others of his people.

Fogg explained, "Here is my plan, we will wait until dusk and then move the detachment in two columns from the ends. I will take one column, Captain Gris the other, using the Stockbridge on the ends as a rear guard as they will be the most silent. We will do this at about one hundred yards apart. I want every man to hold on to the haversack of the man in front and do not let go under any circumstances. Once onto the road way, we will rejoin by first crossing the road and then moving toward the center along the skirt of the woods. We will then move on up the road to confuse our tracks and at sometime before false light move into a new position on the east side of the road. Agreed?" Everyone indicated that they understood and agreed and returned to his section and passed the plan along, signaling when they had finished. The two groups of Stockbridge on the ends of the line were the last to indicate that they had the plan. The men settled down to wait for the order to move out. Some napping and some taking the time to grab some rations or rearrange their gear for the move.

As soon as it was dark enough, Fogg and Gris moved down the line toward the ends, telling the men it was time to move. When they got to the ends, they turned in the direction of the road and when the man behind them had a hold of their haversack they started forward taking careful small, slow steps. It was rough going as the man holding on to the haversack had a tendency to pull the other fellow backwards. It was necessary to hold your hand with the musket up in front of you to stop from getting slapped in the face with twigs and branches. Even with that precaution it was unavoidable but it outweighed the alternative. Fortunately or unfortunately it was a dark night, due to the clouds. The moon was in its first quarter and would have been a little help but would also have revealed to anyone watching that they were on the move.

It took almost an hour for both columns to reach the western edge of the roadway. Fogg had expected to run into sentries posted along the work detail but there were none in this area. Once having crossed the road they were able to let go of their file leader and make better progress. Within fifteen minutes the two columns had rejoined.

Fogg whispered in to Gris' ear, "Did you come across any sentries?"

"None and I thought it a little strange."

"As did I. I think I will pull in the Stockbridge on our way up the road. Put a Ranger advance guard out with only one Stockbridge. Have Sergeant lead it. I am hoping that they have only pulled in all of the sentries to a consolidated camp, somewhere along the road." Within minutes, they had reorganized and were moving cautiously up the roadway. Fogg wanted to spot the sentries before they spotted his detachment and opened fire thinking that they were French. A party from Fort Edward ought not to be moving at night, except Rangers, which is why he had placed the senior Sergeant in charge of the advance guard.

The senior Sergeant and his party moved cautiously up along the east side of the road. Fogg had figured that staying directly on the roadway was perhaps the safest way, hoping that the sentries would not fire at a party that was coming from the direction of Fort Edward using the road. They had proceeded approximately a half mile up the road when a voice rang out challenging them. The Sergeant answered back and was told to advance slowly and be recognized. The sentries were from the 42nd and just happened to be the same ones who had relieved them the other afternoon after the ambush. The Sergeant sent one of the Rangers back to tell Major Fogg to bring on the rest of the detachment. When Fogg arrived at the point where the sentries were, the Sergeant of the Guard was already there. Fogg inquired as to where the rest of the work party was. When Sergeant Burke had delivered the prisoners, Colonel Bever had decided to move his work party a little north and compress it for the night. He had formed a square in the roadway about one hundred yards north of where they were. The fatigue party were all laying under arms for the night without their tents.

Fogg thanked Sergeant and took his party on through the sentry line to where the main party was. As they approached the square, they heard a very loud whisper say that a party was approaching the line. At about ten yards, they were told to halt and an officer came forward to identify them. He took Fogg directly to Colonel Bever, the rest of the party being left outside the square.

Bever's first comment was, "Who the devil are you and what are you doing thrashing about on the roadway at night?"

"I am Major Fogg, Lord Howe's staff. Would you care to see my orders, Sir?"

"Hummm. Lord Howe's staff, you say. Then you are the fellow who sent in the prisoners this afternoon. Good show, been bird-dogging us for the past few days, I believe."

"Yes Sir, I would be that fellow. I am glad to see that you have pulled into a defensive position. I have a very strong feeling that there is a French force in the immediate area but have not as yet been able to spot them. We will be moving out into a position parallel to you on the east side of the road where we can cover you. I would suggest perhaps doubling your cover party and leaving a good space between your details and the west side of the roadway. We will be with you until you reach Halfway Brook. At that point we are to reassess our mission and adjust it accordingly."

With that he bid the colonel good luck and moved on back to his men. Gris had been able to move the detachment into the square and had let the men relax in its relative safety. They had been able to light their pipes, which they had not been able to do since leaving Fort Edward and were basking in the luxury of it. The Scots had even shared some of their cold, cooked beef with them and a chunk of bread, baked only a day ago. To Fogg's men it was a feast. Fogg gave them an extra half hour and then had them move out. They needed to be in place before false light and it appeared that some of the cloud-cover was disappearing, taking with it the darkness that he wanted to use to get in place.

It was well after mid-night when he and Gris made their final round of the men. It had been difficult moving into place in the dark and maintaining a line. They would probably have to adjust it in the morning when they could see but for now, it was sufficient. They had moved in two single file lines, close enough to see each other. When they had reached what Fogg thought was about fifty yards, he and Gris had turned ninety degrees to their outside and then proceeded another fifty yards in that direction. They had then moved back along the line to the center counting the men as they proceeded. The operation had worked well as they still had everybody. The Stockbridge, who seemed to have amazing night vision had filtered through the line and were spread out in a crescent east of the line with enough space to give an adequate warning should anyone approach from the east. They all settled in using the same procedure as before with every fourth man on watch.

The night passed without incident. Fogg could hear an occasional sound from down below but the fatigue detail, for its size, was amazingly quiet. The majority of the sounds were just forest night sounds. The usual animals that moved around at night, trees creaking in the slight breeze and the occasional rustle of some ground nocturnal in the leaves. The only thing missing were the night birds and that made Fogg uneasy. He did not expect to hear any in their immediate area but he did expect to hear them from across the roadway and there were none. When he awoke the Sergeant, he made a point of it.

"Aye, I know Sir. The silence has kept me waking up frequently. I think that there may be French night birds out there tonight. I hope they don't notice that there ain't any signing on this side." Fogg checked his priming and drew his dirk, laying it next to his hand. He pulled his maud closer around him and closed his eyes.

## Chapter 34

Fogg had been dreaming of London and several ladies with whom he was well acquainted, when one of them shook him by the hand. He opened his eyes and was staring into the face of the Sergeant. Fogg started to say something but the Sergeant held his finger up to his lips and motioned back over his shoulder toward the roadway. Fogg got up very slowly and let his eyes focus in the direction that the Sergeant had been pointing. He could see that Gris had moved forward a couple of yards to get a better view. Slowly, Fogg moved to join him. One of the Stockbridge was beside Gris and he slowly pointed to a spot just above the skirt of the woods. At first, Fogg could not see what he was pointing to but then he caught the flash of the sun on either a piece of metal or perhaps a spy glass. The sun was barely breaking the horizon and was behind Fogg and his detachment. Gris handed him his spy glass. It was completely covered in leather and had a very deep guard ring around the lens. Fogg slowly moved it up to his eye and focused it on the spot where he had seen the glint. At first he thought that who ever was there had left but then he made out a slight movement. There they were, two white men wearing brown-dyed hunting smocks and neckerchiefs tied about their heads. He could not make out what they were wearing on the lower part of their bodies but he would bet that they were dressed as Indians from the waist down. The one with the glass raised it to his eye and Fogg could see that he was scanning the tree-line on Fogg's side of the road. He was looking too far down and from that distance he would probably not be able to see where they had entered the woods. He might even think that they had gone down to the road and were either in the fatigue camp or more likely headed back to Fort Edward. If he saw the Rangers in Bevers' work party he would possibly think that they were the same ones who had ambushed his scout the day before.

Fogg moved the glass slowly along just beyond where the two were concealed. He was able to spot three or four more without making any great motion on his own part. He whispered what he saw to Gris, who rolled over carefully on his back and signed to the Sergeant what they saw, giving the signal to hold tight and silent. Fogg handed him back the glass and Gris continued to watch the other side. Shortly, he put the glass down and whispered that the two had moved back to where their main body was concealed. He also indicated that he had spotted several more, both French and Indians, concealed further back from the road. Depending upon how they were arraigned, there could be anywhere from fifty to one hundred fifty and that was a wild guess. The French were known to send parties of two to three hundred out on a scout this far south.

Fogg thought for a moment and then took the glass. There was no movement in the square except for the sentries. The majority of them were still asleep or at least rolled up in their blankets. If the French attacked now, they would have a large advantage and might possibly even capture one or two of the out-sentries. They would probably think that they could strike quick and get away without anyone following as there were so few Rangers with the work detail. He leaned over to Gris and asked if he had ever seen a bonxie in this country. Gris looked at him puzzled and then realized what Fogg was planning to do.

"Never. Do you think it will work?" Fogg shrugged, rolled over on his back and cupping his hands made a shrill bird sound that kind of trailed off. All of his own men looked at him and he shook his head no. He called one more time and then rolled back over to look down on the roadway. A couple of the Scot sentries looked up toward the east slope and then turned back to their rounds. Fogg saw one of the 42nd NCO's sit up in his plaid and look around and then shook himself and got up. As he was arranging his plaid he walked slowly along his line of men, kicking one every so often. None of them seemed to move too fast but Fogg could see that they were waking their mates on either side and all were slowly gathering their arms but none were getting up. They all lay where they were, appearing to still be slumbering. The Sergeant had now completed the walk of his line and was coming back to his original position. When he got back he squatted down and lit his pipe from the embers of one of the small fires that were spread around the camp smoldering.

For what seemed a very long time the sounds of morning moved uninterrupted toward the world awakening. Most of the birds had become used to the humans both in the roadway and in the woods and were starting to sing their morning songs. Even the jays seemed to be ignoring the "thieves" who were intruding upon their forest. Fogg and his men saw the smoke before they heard the reports of the French muskets. The French had moved to just within the skirt of the woods. As they fired they burst out of the woods, charging toward the apparently slumbering Scots in an attempt to surprise and kill as many as possible and take prisoners for intelligence.

As the French and their Indian allies cleared the woods they were fifty to seventy-five feet from the English line. Instead of jumping up in panic, as the French expected them to do, the Scots all rose to one knee and fired a volley directly into their would be ambushers. The French faltered, hesitated. Confused for a moment and realizing that they had been duped, they turned as a body and disappeared into the woods. The Scots quickly formed into two ranks, all three sides of their square coming to face the west side of the road. By sections, the officers had them wheel right about and move to the east side of the roadway, increasing the amount of clearing between them and the French. Within a minute, the whole were now on the east side of the road. The only way that the French could now reach them was to cross the entire cleared area of the roadway or to circle around. If this happened, the Scots were confident that Fogg's party had their rear and flank covered. Both they and the French could hear the drums at the other encampments, just north on the road, beating the General, which meant that within a few minutes they would be reinforced. The French were aware that there were at least twelve hundred English in this working detail. They knew that the English outnumbered them ten to one and that they had completely lost their element of surprise. They also were aware of Fogg's detachment being somewhere in the area. They had lost track of him because of his night move and had not been able to locate him or where he had moved through. Obviously, none of the Frenchman had ever heard a bonxie or knew that it was not found in at least this part of North America. Fortunately, to the Scots it was a familiar bird that would not have followed them to North America and its call could only have been made as a warning by another Scot.

Fogg got his men up and they moved to the edge of the roadway where they could deploy concealed from the view French by the 42nd who were in two ranks deep. His men moved in close behind the Highlanders and knelt. Fogg went to the center where the officers were stationed.

"There is no movement on the other side of the roadway. I believe that they have withdrawn completely. I would propose to send my detachment to confirm this. I would also suggest that perhaps it would be a good idea to put your Rangers in a screen to the south. Your north is covered by the remainder of the work detail." The Captain in command of the Highlanders just nodded his head yes, as he did not know quite what to make of this English officer who commanded such a mixed detachment and spoke with such confidence. He was more than happy to allow him to chase after the French as his men had just narrowly escaped an ambush. His casualties were only a few men with minor wounds as the French had mostly fired too high. It was apparent from the bodies lying at the edge of the road that the French and their allies had not been quite so lucky. He could see at least a dozen from where he was standing and was sure that there were more as his men had been able to get off two volleys. Fogg had the Scots open two files in the center of their line and he led his men through in two files from the center. As they passed the center of the road, he gave the signal for them to form two ranks offset, front and then to extended order. The Stockbridge split and took the two flanks. When the whole hit the woods, they stopped just inside of the trees and went to a kneeling position. Fogg signaled for every fourth man to move forward in a skirmish line and to search the ground. It appeared that the French simply had run away as a disorganized mob. Fogg gave the signal to move forward and his men swept slowly through the woods. At a point somewhere around three hundred yards, it appeared that the French had started to become more organized and had moved off toward the north. Fogg halted his detachment and sent four of the Stockbridge out to make sure that this was the way that they had gone. The Stockbridge returned in less than twenty minutes, reporting that the French were still moving northwest. They had found signs of a lot of blood so that the French had sustained enough casualties to probably withdraw. The trail signs also indicated that their Indian allies had decided to not stay with them and had moved off by themselves. If they were Cagnawaga Mohawks they might even be headed toward Mohawk River Valley where they would be welcomed as brothers and re-supplied so they could return home.

Fogg decided that it was time to pull his detachment from their mission for a brief rest. They would return to the road and make for Halfway Brook. They would be able to get hot food, rest and repair clothing and equipment. There might also be messages or further orders for him there. Fogg rubbed his chin and decided he might even shave and take a cold bath in the brook. He had forgotten what a hot bath felt like. He gave the order to withdraw. When they came to the road he reported to Colonel Bever who had arrived on the scene. Then he told his men of his decision. They all gave a hearty Huzzah and headed in the direction of Halfway Brook.

In a little over an hour, they arrived at Halfway Brook. Fogg left his men on the side of the roadway and crossed over to the east where the new works were not quite complete. Fogg located the Officer in Charge and reported that his unit was going to encamp across the road and that they would only be there for a day.  The Officer informed him that he could re-supply him with only two days rations that would get them to the Lake.  Fogg thanked him and calculated that added with what they were still carrying they could remain out for another nine days, if necessary.

Fogg returned to his men and moved them to the site he had selected.   They had just settled in when they heard the drums approaching from the south.   Within a short time the column appeared.  It was Lord Howe with the 55th, 42nd, 44th, New Jersey Regiment all of the Rangers, including the Indian companies.  Fogg and Gris left the men in the charge of the other officers and walked over to the road to pay their respects to Lord Howe.

# Chapter 35

Howe saw Fogg and Gris approaching and walked over to meet them, leaving Major Eyre in charge of the column.

"Gentlemen! How good to see you have made it this far. I heard about your little tussles with the French from Colonel Bever when we came past his post. I would have hoped he would be further along by now. I have told him to move his party up and to only repair the bridges between here and the Lake. What more do you have for me?"

Fogg reported, "Firstly Sir, we have only come up to this post today and I need to let my men rest at least until tomorrow. Sleeping out, sitting up for the last several nights has somewhat worn them down a little. If we can get a full night tonight ,without having to put out our own security, it would help. Secondly, we would like to be able to move on up to the Lake in advance of your column. Someplace out there is a very large French force, perhaps two hundred with more in reserve. We lost track of them back down by Colonel Bever and would like to make sure that they are not still in the area. Our senior Ranger Sergeant says that with any luck, if they are still out there to the west, we just might drive them into one of the Ranger detachment patrolling to the west."

Lord Howe thought for a moment and replied, "Very well Major Fogg. Where are your men now?" Fogg pointed them out. "Bring them down from the rise and we will put the Jersey boys up there. Have your men encamp down here near the roadway, perhaps over there." He pointed toward a small clearing just aside the new works. "Would you like to reinforce your detachment? I can let you have some additional Rangers."

"Yes Sir, if I can have another two sections of Rangers and some additional Stockbridge it would increase our chances," replied Fogg.

Lord Howe turned to Major Moneypenny. "Alexander, write out an order for an additional thirty Rangers and ten more Stockbridge to join Major Fogg's detachment. They are to fall out immediately and encamp with his unit. Write it for a Captain, two Lieutenants and an appropriate number of NCOs. Do you have an Indian officer?" Fogg indicated yes. "Good, just the ten Stockbridge then. Do you have enough supplies and if not an order to complete up to two weeks. Good enough gentlemen. I'll see you at the Lake in a week or so." With that he turned and went off to get his column settled in and make sure that the additional supplies coming up with the one hundred seventy-three ox teams, ninety wagons and thirty-eight longboats on trucks were taken care of. There was a large meadow just to the east and north side of the works that would accommodate the majority of the almost seven hundred oxen and horses necessary to move the supplies. There were several other small clearings where the remainder could graze. They would be moving on to the Lake on Monday.

Fogg signaled for his men to come down to where he was. This was accomplished with much complaining until they found out that they would not be standing any guards this night.

They settled in once more just to the west of the works and were joined by the additional Rangers and Stockbridge. These additional Rangers were glad to be free of the column. It would be good to get back to Ranging instead of playing toy soldier at Fort Edward. It also meant that they would miss a lot of the necessary fatigue details that went with a large army encamped. The excitement was either out on the Lake or in the long-range patrols such as this one. The perimeter patrols around the camp at the Lake were too humdrum to suit them. Better a few nights in the woods than the noise and smell of the main camp.

Fogg took the opportunity to go over to the brook and get cleaned up. When he got back to the camp the Sergeant had some water boiled for them and he actually got to shave with hot water. Fogg's officers and senior NCOs also had a hot meal as one of the more resourceful Sergeants had come up with the ingredients for making a stew. It consisted mostly of beef, pork, potatoes and onions with a little pickled cabbage thrown in plus some turnips. No one asked from where he had procured them and it did not take long to make sure there was no evidence left that the stew ever existed.

When they had finished, and everyone had a chance to savor the luxury of a hot meal, Fogg called all of the officers and senior NCOs to the side for a council of war. He explained what, in general, the mission was and then asked for opinions on how best to accomplish it. He went around the circle asking each man individually what he might have for suggestions to best accomplish it. He saved the officers till last, letting the NCOs state their opinions and ideas. Most were of the opinion that because their detachment was now up to ninety that they might stand a chance of ambushing the French, if they could find them. It would be best to ambush them in two stages. Half the party for the initial ambush and then withdraw to the second rally point, hit them again and then withdraw. If the French continued to follow to repeat the process as many times as was necessary, all the time moving toward the road and the Lake. They all agreed it was risky but might work. The trick would be to avoid getting ambushed themselves by a party of two hundred plus French and Indians.

Fogg and his detachment were up and out at first light. Their course of action was to march south, back down the road so as to look like a party returning to Fort Edward. About two miles down the road they approached the good sized swamp that the road cut through. Fogg halted his men and gave the order to check their priming. This was an excellent spot to be ambushed as the swamp was a natural choke point. It did not provide the open spaces on both sides as did most of the rest of the road. He split his column into two and they proceeded down the corduroyed road one half on one side and one half on the other. This way if attacked from only one side they had a short fall back point. It was quiet as they proceeded through the swamp, no birds, just the sound of their walking. At a point about halfway through, one of the lead Stockbridge held up his hand to halt. Both columns went to the knee, muskets partially drawn up to the ready, everyone facing out, their eyes straining to catch any kind of movement.

They held this position for a few minutes, no one moving. Suddenly a swamp deer burst out of the swamp, started across the road and seeing the humans all staring at her stopped, looked at them, flicked her flag and bounded off the road in the same direction she came from. The Stockbridge signaled forward again. She had not been driven out of the swamp by any other human party as she returned along the same path. Everybody gave a sigh of relief and the men looked at each other with that "I wasn't scared. I knew it was a deer." look. There was also a slight murmuring and the officers and NCOs had to caution them about the noise. The slightest sound in some swamps carrys a long way but the biggest part of the problem is that it is difficult to figure out which way it is coming from. Fogg gave a little shudder, he did not like swamps, they reminded him too much of the moors in England and Scotland where he had hidden out on more than a couple of occasions.

Their passage through the rest of the swamp was without incidence and once south of it they followed along its edge to swing west around it. A little beyond the swamp they came to another creek that flowed out of the swamp and followed it toward the west for about two and a half miles to the mountains out of which it rose.

158

There they turned north west between the two peaks and followed a trail that ran another four miles to a string of small lakes or ponds.

All of this time they had been traveling in their two column formation. Fogg called a halt and let the men take a break to eat something and tighten up their gear. He called the officers and the senior Sergeant of Rangers in and gave the order to split each column into two sections and proceed as four shorter columns, each keeping its neighbors in sight. Under no circumstances were they to be further apart than where they could see each other.

They started out again after a half hour and followed a track that led toward the northern leg of the Hudson River. The track showed signs of having been heavily traveled of late. The Sergeant said that this was the route used by the French to come from the Lake down to the Hudson or perhaps they had even found a way to go from Crown Point over to the Hudson and down into the Lower Hudson and Mohawk Valley. He pointed out that it was not that far to the Sacandaga, which ran into the Mohawk. He also pointed out that the woods were only a deterrent and hardship to the European-style armies. To the Indians, and the men like the Canadian Partisans or the English Rangers who traveled with them, the forest with all of its lakes, ponds, creeks and streams was a vast network of communication. Even the large range of mountains that lay between Lake Champlain and the southern St. Lawrence was not a barrier to the Indians. They had been fighting for centuries and the mountains were laced with war trails.

When they reached a point just shy of the Hudson, he pointed out a mountain that was to their north. This mountain overlooked the camp at Lake George and if there were to be any French in this area, that is where they would most likely to be found. Fogg decided to settle in for a while and observe the mountain and its approaches. They put out a screen using every fourth man and half of the Stockbridge. Once more the men were cautioned to be silent, no talking except in a whisper. For the remainder of the morning they watched the mountain and the areas where there appeared to be trails leading to it. There was no movement detected. Shortly after noon, Fogg had the NCOs call in the screen. He and Gris had decided to approach the mountain from the northwest trail. This might give them some assistance, as it is the direction from which any French would be coming.

They set the men into the four-column formation and put a third of the Stockbridge out in front, the remainder bringing up the rear guard and flankers. It was about a half-hour march at the rate they dared move to where they cut the trail that led up the northwest slope of the mountain. This trail was full of signs of a great deal of use. There were both shoe and moccasin prints. The leaves in the trail were almost completely gone, ground into the underlying layer of loam. Fogg went forward to the lead Stockbridge, who told him that some of the tracks were fresh as of last night. Perhaps the same party they had run across down below on the road. Fogg decided to keep to the present plan although it would be more difficult to withdraw toward the camp. As they got closer to the top they slowed their pace to a crawl, stopping every few yards to listen and observe everything in front of them as closely as possible.

When they were within a couple of hundred yards of the top, the wind shifted to the south and there was a faint tinge of wood smoke in the wind. This puzzled Fogg as a fire would give off smoke that was visible from the camp at the head of the Lake. He turned to Gris and the senior Sergeant giving a shrug of his shoulders and wafting his hand under his nose. He could see them sniffing the air and they gave the same indication. He once more worked his way forward up to the lead Stockbridge. The Stockbridge looked as puzzled as he did. *Well, there is nothing for it but to press on.* Fogg motioned to the Stockbridge to continue forward. Fogg waited for the rest of the column to come up to him and they crept forward a few yards at a time. The forest was silent except for the sounds of a few far off birds. The only different sound that they heard was what sounded like a small rockslide from the east side of the mountain. Shortly, they were on the fringe of the brush on the top of the mountain and the Stockbridge was pointing toward a couple of lean-tos and a windbreak that had a small fire burning in it. Cautiously, the Stockbridge searched around the camp and its perimeter. Two of them motioned for Fogg to come over to where they were on the eastside. They pointed to the ground, indicating a fresh trail that led down that slope.

One of them said to Fogg, "The Frenchmen, they go just now. Boats or canoes down on lake."

Fogg called Gris over to where they were and asked. "What do you think Gris? Should we go after them or hold here on the mountain?"

"Let's stay with our original plan. Send half of the force down after them and the remainder follow fifty yards behind. Leave a couple of the Stockbridge up here on the top to watch our backs although I could not find any other sign that they went down anywhere else."

"Right you are Captain," answered Fogg. "You take the lead party, I'll take the fall back party. If you catch up with them, fire one volley and get the hell back up to us and we'll take them on together. We should have an advantage being uphill on them."

"Agreed. I would like to have Sergeant with me, if you don't mind?"

Fogg nodded his head indicating yes and they set about getting ready. Gris told Sergeant the plan and he got his section ready to move along with the main body of the Stockbridge. Gris spread his men out in a line two deep and they started down the hill with Gris and Sergeant in the center, both wings dressing on them as best they could. Fogg waited until they had disappeared and he followed them down in the same type formation.

Gris' detachment was about halfway down the mountain when the silence of the woods was disturbed by musket fire. His men dropped to their knees at the ready and then realized that they were not the object of the firing. It was coming from the bottom of the mountain. Fogg also realized that it was not coming from the area where Gris was. He signaled for his detachment to move down the slope until they joined up with Gris'.

"What do you think Captain?"

"It sounds like our elusive Frenchies have either run into an English party or perhaps have ambushed them. Maybe they spotted them from the top and came down here for that purpose. What do we want to do?"

Fogg thought briefly and said, "Let's go get them. I'm tired of chasing them around in the woods. Perhaps between our detachment and who ever they are mixing it up with now, we can give them a good drubbing!" With that, they moved back into their two-lines formation, the Stockbridge on the wings.

# Chapter 36

The firing to their front grew louder as the distance decreased between them and the enemy. Fogg still had the advantage of being up hill from the French and, within a few moments, the smoke from their muskets became visible. He could barely make out flashes from the other side of the French because of the smoke but it indicated that who ever was over there was putting up a good fight. From the sound of it, the English under fire were equal to their French opponents.

Fogg and Gris looked around but saw no French rear guard. They had been confident that they were the only ones on the mountain. Fogg gave the signal for the lines to fire fours. This made them able to sustain a steady fire on the enemy. At the first crash of the muskets, the whole French line seemed to go silent. It took them a moment to realize that the firing had come from behind them. When the second section fired, some of the French took cover and tried to return the fire. The advantage of being uphill made most of the French fire fall short. Who ever was in charge of the English on the other side was instantly aware that they had been joined by another English unit and redoubled their fire.

The French were now caught in a cross fire that took way any advantage they might have had previously. The French leader once more opted to withdraw and his men all shifted toward the lake end of the line, firing and loading as they ran. Any of the Natives who were with the French had already realized that this was a bad position and had departed for the lake and perhaps their canoes. Fogg held his men where they were. They had accomplished their mission, to show the French that they, the English, were in control of this end of Lake George. Fogg had one of the Rangers hold up a white rag on his ramrod to call for a cease fire from the other English party. Gris put a mixed party of Stockbridge, Rangers and 80th out as a screen toward the direction where the French had recently departed.

The other English party proved to be a wood cutting detail looking for suitable trees to make large planks for one of the vessels being built. They were from the New Jersey Regiment along with a small party of Rangers as guides. The party consisted of three companies. This wood-cutting party was numerically a match for the French who had made the mistake of thinking that they were militia.

The majority of the Blues were wearing only their shirt sleeves, to keep their waistcoats and coats clean.

The officer in charge greeted Fogg like a long-lost brother. His men had been complaining because they were being used mostly for fatigue and were semi-glad when they were attacked. The "Jersey Blues" were even more overjoyed as they had not only cut the required timber but had taken on the French, had driven them off and had witnesses to prove it. Of course, they acknowledged that Fogg's detachment helped a little.

Fogg's men had been busy locating any dead or wounded among the French. The French had lost at least twenty-one killed and another three dozen wounded and of these probably half would die. Among the dead were a half dozen Indian, French Mohawks according to the Stockbridge. None of the French were troupe de terre, regulars. They all were most likely native-born Canadians. None would speak when asked a question.

The Blues had one man killed and a dozen wounded, but none seriously. Once more, Fogg's detachment had escaped virtually unscathed. One of the Rangers was grazed in the head by a musket ball and knocked unconscious but his messmates said his being hit in the head would probably not hurt him. Everyone present had a good laugh. A man from the 80th got hit in the haversack. The ball penetrated the outer layer of the bag and lodged in a rawhide envelope that held parched corn. It had knocked the wind out of him and left a large bruise that would probably turn ugly but otherwise he was hale and hearty.

The senior Sergeant suggested that they turn over one of the youngest looking ones to the Stockbridge and see if that might change his mind. Fogg discussed it with Gris for a few moments. They called over the officer of the work detail who also agreed with their plan. A couple of the Stockbridge disappeared and soon the smell of wood smoke drifted upwind toward the work party and the French prisoners. One of the Stockbridge who went to start the fire came back, said something to the others and they grabbed one of the older Frenchmen and dragged him off amid a great deal of cursing and kicking.

Gris had gone with them and soon there was a great deal of shouting in French as Gris began to interrogate the prisoner who only cursed him. All was quiet for a moment and then the Frenchman was heard cursing "les sauvage", "les anglais" and the word fire. The next sound that was heard was a horrible screaming, incoherent French and the smell of burning flesh. This went on for about ten minutes and then there was nothing. Gris and four of the Stockbridge came back

163

and Gris said only, "Il est mort. Un autré," pointing to youngest looking partisan. The Stockbrdige grabbed him and he began to scream and struggle. The other Canadians began shouting in protest offering to be taken instead as he was so young. Gris shrugged and the Stockbridge threw him back onto the ground and grabbed the Frenchman who had protested the loudest who instantly began to regret being noble. He cursed and kicked and struggled to no avail as the Stockbridge easily carried him off to the party.

Once more, Gris was heard to question the man but received only a barrage of curses. Gris was heard to ask again and the man started to curse but it ended in a cry of extreme pain. This went on for ten to fifteen minutes with the same results. Suddenly the man began to scream and issue half-comprehensible curses and soon the smell of burning flesh once more drifted toward the French prisoners and their captors who seemed to be enjoying the whole experience.

The majority of the Blues had gone back to their timber detail and others were starting to clear a path back toward the camp. Ox teams had appeared and were starting to skid the timbers from the area. Fogg's men, who were not on screen, were using the opportunity to smoke their pipes and have something to eat.

Once more Gris came back, shaking his head. He spoke to Fogg in French for the benefit of the "captive" audience.

"That one died also. These Frenchmen do not seem to last long in the fire. I told the Stockbridge that maybe they needed a smaller fire. They have started to gather some pine to make wooden skewers out of. They tell me that they stick it under the skin in the genitals and set it on fire. They claim it will make the most resolute man cry like a little girl and beg for death." The four Stockbridge had returned and Gris pointed to the youth once more. The other Frenchmen started their protest until one of the Stockbridge struck one in the head with his musket butt, knocking him out. The others seemed to lose their appetite for protest and remained silent. The youth was still screaming and sobbing when the Stockbridge carried him away. Gris followed them out of sight of the remaining French.

When they arrived at the spot where the Stockbridge had built the fire, they stripped the youth naked and tied him to the tree nearest the fire so he could feel the heat of it. One of the Stockbridge came up with a hand full of pine splinters. The young man started to struggle and twist in his bonds, now crying and screaming constantly. Gris stepped up to him, struck him in the face grabbed his chin.

Loudly in French, "How many in your party, the leader and where are your boats?" and softly, "Tell me and I will not let them stick the splinters in to your, well, you know what I mean." The boy

164

had stopped sobbing long enough to comprehend what Gris had said. The Stockbridge with the splinters moved toward the boy, who screamed and struggled to slide around the tree. Two others held him tight and when the one with the splinters reached for his genitals, he fainted. The Stockbridge thought this was amusing and all started to laugh.

One of them said in broken French, "He is like a little girl, this Frenchman!" They all laughed again. Gris took his canteen and poured water in the boys face to bring him around. Slowly he opened his eyes and started to open his mouth to scream. Gris clamped his hand over the youth's mouth and repeated his question. The youth's eyes were wide open, staring at the Stockbridge with the splinters who was still standing in front of him with a big grin. He kept glancing at the boy's crotch. The young man caught his breath and was able to blurt out the answers to Gris' questions.

"There are one hundred sixty of us...under the command...of Captain Marin, De la Malgue. Our boats are at the big bay on the west side of the lake." Gris motioned to the Stockbridge to take him down from the tree and give him back his clothes. They did this and when he was dressed, they brought him back to the main body of prisoners. The youth was ashamed that he had told the English what they wanted and sat silently by himself. The rest of the party sat, just staring at him. They were all surprised when the first "victims" appeared from the direction of the fire, bound and gagged but none the worse for their ordeal. Two of the Stockbridge were carrying several pieces of charred salt pork, borrowed from the Blues, which they dangled tauntingly in front of the French prisoners. The French were slow to comprehend that the Englishmen and their Natives had played them for the fool. It was the salt pork that they had smelled burning and not their compatriots. When the Englishmen and Stockbridge began to laugh at them, they were furious, cursing them for dogs, and pigs of every kind and color of which they could think.

Fogg and his detachment bid farewell to the Jersey Blues and headed for the English camp with their prisoners, strung together and in the capable hands of the Stockbridge who decided that they would go at their favorite trot to the encampment, about three and a half miles away. Fogg would tell whoever was in charge about the French boats and they could dispatch a party of Rangers to see if they could find and retrieve them. He had not been planning upon arriving at the camp on the Lake until a few days from now. He and Gris would have to go down to Halfway Brook tomorrow and report to Lord Howe. At least, maybe tonight, he would get a chance to take off his footwear when he went to bed.

## Chapter 37

Fogg and Gris were up just before dawn on Monday the 19th. Several of the Rangers had been up before first light, a habit hard to break. Fogg could smell the aroma of coffee and what seemed to be bacon coming from the area of the field kitchen pit. He put on his shoes and Light-Infantry gaiters, pulled on his waistcoat and, took his cup, walked over to the fire.

"Good morning Major. Coffee?" was the greeting he received from the Sergeant. "Have a pleasant sleep?"

"Yes, Sergeant. It was indeed good to be able to take off my moccasins and stockings. My feet thought they had grown another skin. And yourself?" replied Fogg.

"Like a baby , Sir, like a baby."

"Captain Gris and I will be going down to the Halfway Brook to report to Lord Howe this morning. I am leaving you in command. Ensign Purdy has returned to the Cadet Company and you are the Senior NCO. We will be discussing with Lord Howe the possibility of you and your handpicked men remaining with Captain Gris and I, to assist on special missions. Would that suit you?"

"That it would Sir. I find you and Captain Gris to be right and proper soldier's soldiers, if you don't mind my saying so, Sir. I don't believe that you will have to go down to the Halfway Brook as Lord Howe is marching up here this very morning. It wouldn't surprise me if they hadn't marched already."

"You can always rely on the Sergeant's message relay service to have any worthwhile information long before the headquarters gets it passed down to the officers," replied Fogg, laughing.

"Well that's because we don't have to rely on protocol, Sir. Just a simple, 'Did you hear…' does the trick. Now if you'll excuse me Sir, I've got to get these lazy buggers out of their blankets," nodding toward the Stockbridge fire. "If them Stockbridge was French Mohawks or Hurons, these boys would all wake up a little lighter on the top of their heads."

Good to the Sergeant's word, Lord Howe and all of the regiments that had been encamped at Halfway Brook, with the exception of the normal garrison number, came marching up to the Lake George camp. The Quartermaster had already laid out the

166

ground for the various regiments. The camp ran parallel along the small flats just next to the lake. They had laid out a short front, west facing camp with the regiments sitting in behind each other. The officers' tents were set in between each regiment. The camp was the very picture of what irregular castrametation should look like, adhering to the lay of the land. The Ranger camp lay somewhat above it, slightly to the south.

Fogg and Gris found Lord Howe, who had marched with his regiment. He had come on foot just the same as the lowest private in the 55th Foot. This is why his men respected him so much. Howe saw them standing by the roadway and motioned for them to join him. They fell in on both sides and he asked what they had to report. Fogg laid out all that had happened since they last saw him. He was most interested in the fact that the French had chosen one of their most famous partisans to keep tabs on the English. He was also keenly interested and pleased that his two chief agents had out tricked Marin at his own game. He inquired if they needed anything and if so they had only to inform Moneypenny and he would make it happen. This included additional men, different men, more supplies, whatever. They were also to have available at all times enough longboats to transport however many men they had. He would also see that Bradstreet assigned three men to each longboat that they had assigned to them. These bateaux-men would take charge of the boats when Fogg's party was ashore. Underway one would act as coxswain and the other two as bow-hooks and relief rowers.

"I want you to take your detachment, when it is fitted out with the boats, up into the large, northwest bay. Ganouski Bay I believe it is called, where the Canadian boy said that Marin had left his boats. See if there is any sign of this activity. You will also keep an eye out for Mr. Putnam who is, I believe, over due. This should give you a good feel for the boats and the Lake. I want you back here no later than next Monday, the 26th. Good hunting." With that Howe moved off to rejoin the troops who were being directed to their ground.

"Well, Captain Gris, let us find Alexander and get the required orders and such."

It took them a while to find Major Moneypenny who was set up in a temporary tarp shelter at the head of the camp. He now had four clerks working with him, plus people from the Quartermaster,s group. Fogg started to explain what Lord Howe had told him but Moneypenny just held up his hand to stop him. He went over to his dispatch box, opened it and drew out a handful of papers.

"It is all done. His Lordship explained what he wanted yesterday as far as additional equipment, men and supplies for your detachment. There is a draft here that will allow you to pick any men you want up to one hundred fifty, not including the bateaux-men or additional officers. This one will authorize you to draw ten longboats for your exclusive use. You may also complete your men up to sixty rounds per man plus an additional three hundred rounds per boat in pitched kegs. The longboats will come with a swivel and twenty grape rounds per boat. Good luck in your travails." They took their new set of paperwork and headed back to their camp. They found the Sergeant busy with getting his men and their gear back into shape. Some were repairing worn moccasins, and other leather equipment. He had a group who were inspecting, sorting and re-rolling cartridges. They were also making bundles of six cartridges, wrapped in a sheet of paper and tied together with linen thread. These would be stored in the bottom of their cartridge boxes and in their haversacks. Each man carried sixty rounds between his shoulder cartridge box, his belly box and the extras. Just the weight of the musket balls in the cartridges weighed a little under four pounds. In addition to this, each man carried a small bag of buck shot that weighed in at a third of a pound and all of this weight did not include the weight of the powder.

Fogg called the Sergeant over to him and explained Lord Howe's orders. He instructed him to get any men he did not want ready to go back to the Ranger Companies. He was to march them back there and to draw the additional men, as per Lord Howe's orders to complete the one hundred fifty. Fogg gave him the order that authorized him to do so.

"Do you think Major Rogers will object to this?" inquired Fogg.

"I don't believe so, Sir. I will explain to him my reasons for not wanting the men I am returning. He knows that I don't want no green Rangers if we're going out on the Lake. He may be upset that we're a-going in search of Marin, instead of himself, but likely as not he'll get over it, Sir."

"Good, Sergeant. You might offer to take one of his more experienced cadets along, providing it is understood that they know you are in charge of the Rangers ... and only if necessary to calm him down," he added the last as an after-thought. With that, the Sergeant went about getting the men he wanted to return ready to move back to the Ranger camp. Gris offered to go down to the boat landing and draw the required longboats. He knew Bradstreet and was familiar with many of the bateaux-men.

"I'll have them separated and pull them into the mouth of the east creek, if possible. That will put them closer to our camp."

"We may even be able to eventually change our camp, closer to the boats. However, His Lordship sounded like we might not be here that much longer as he wants us back by Monday next," Fogg replied. "Meet me back here when you are finished. The Sergeant may be back by then also."

Both Gris and the Sergeant were back in camp in less than two hours. Fogg had just returned from seeking Major Eyre who had made a rudimentary map of the south end of the lake, at least up as far as the Northwest Bay. Fogg would rely upon the Sergeant's knowledge of the lake and would start a map of his own in his journal. He was in the habit of keeping a detailed journal of all of his travels and experiences, including maps that he someday planned to piece together.

The Sergeant had his full compliment of picked men, one hundred and fifty in all. He either knew them himself or one of his choices had recommended them. They ranged from young men in their early twenties to a couple who were pushing sixty. They were all experienced both in the woods and on the lake. The Sergeant pointed out that the trick to surviving on the lake was to have good lookouts and to travel slow. Fogg's orders did not cover how many Stockbridge he could take so the Sergeant had adjusted his selections to include twenty of them. That would put two in a boat and, although they didn't like to row, they made excellent lookouts. If they treated every two boats as a section, it put four Stockbridge to a section in case they needed to operate separated. Fogg congratulated the Sergeant on his choices of men and reasoning. He told Captain Gris to explain to the men what they intended to do. He would return shortly as he had one thing that needed to be accomplished before they departed.

Captain Gris and the Sergeant had the men gather about and then they explained the up coming mission. They were going to go up to Northwest Bay and search for any evidence of Marin and his party's boats. Upon completion of that task, they were then going to search for any signs of Major Putnam's scout on the southern half of the lake. Gris gave the order for everyone to commence packing for the scout as they would be leaving this day or at first light tomorrow.

The men set about taking care of their gear. They would be taking only what they needed in the boats. Every man pared his kit down to the bare minimum. Arms and accoutrements, a blanket, spare moccasins and a haversack. In their haversacks most carried rations, a fire kit, a small auger with a ring mount and a short length of rope. All of their gear was well secured as loose metal objects were not conducive to silent movement.

Fogg was gone less than forty-five minutes. When he came back, he called Gris aside and showed him the paper he was carrying. Gris read it and whistled.

"How did you accomplish this?" he questioned.

Fogg just smiled, "Sergeant, have the men fall in and we'll set up the sections, as you suggested."

"Aye, Sir. All right, Rangers … close order … without arms … fall in!" In less than a minute, all one hundred fifty of them were standing in line, the Stockbridge taking up a position on the right of the line. Fogg and Gris took position in front-center facing the Rangers.

Fogg spoke, "Rangers, as Captain Gris and the Sergeant told you we are about to go on a mission. You have most of the details. We will be gone for no more than a week, most likely five days at the most. I have one important announcement to make before we set about establishing the boat crews. As of this day, Senior Sergeant Surgent is hereby promoted to Sergeant Major."

Fogg took a step to where the Sergeant was standing and handed him the warrant papers. "Congratulations Sergeant Major."

Sergeant Major Surgent saluted him and said, "Thank you Major Fogg, Sir! I'll do my best to deserve it."

"All right, Sergeant Major, get these men broken down to boat crews and we'll be on our way." When Fogg and Gris walked away, the men broke into a huzzah. Within another two hours they were at their boats and started out onto the lake.

## Chapter 38

They used almost the same formation with the longboats as they did when marching, the only exception being that instead of abreast they staggered the lines. In this manner it was possible for one longboat to help cover the ones opposite it by leaving an interval in-between. They left the mouth of the creek and headed across the lake to the west bank. As it was late in the afternoon this put them in the deep shadows of the west shore. The Sergeant Major suggested that they stay about one hundred yards off shore so as to give themselves a clear view of the shoreline, put them out of accurate musket range and give them a jump on any party intent of dashing out onto the lake for them.

They worked their way down the lake parallel to the west shore. Fogg estimated it was about three and a half maybe four miles to the island the Rangers called Diamond. They had avoided going between the small island just north of the head of the lake and the land side. He decided that this was a good practice when the islands were too close to the mainland. Much too easy to get caught in a crossfire. Just ahead to the north, he could see the tip of the Long Island. The Sergeant Major suggested that they remain on the west side of Diamond until dark and then steer for the Long Island. If they stood off, they would be able to see any fires on the island or hear anyone. They had muffled the oars with wool strips before they left the creek. Fogg had given the unnecessary order for no talking above a whisper. Their movement down lake so far had been silent except for the drip of water from the oars as they lifted out of the water and the gurgle of the bows cutting the water.

Fogg gave the signal to heave to and draw the boats in together. They put out the rope fenders and tied the little flotilla up together. There was a slight wind blowing from the south so they put out a small drag anchor from the last two boats. They held this position until the lake became dark with no hint of the sun left in the western sky so there was nothing to silhouette them. Fortunately, it was overcast with few breaks in the clouds, otherwise the approaching full moon would have made night passage in close to an island hazardous. Fogg and Gris had been studying the lake with their glasses since they tied up. Neither had seen a hint of any fires at any point on the lake, except for the occasional twinkle from the direction of the English camp. Fogg felt the Sergeant Major's hand on his shoulder and he leaned back. The Sergeant Major whispered into his ear that Captain Gris said to look about two hundred and ninety degrees and about twenty degrees above lake level. Fogg calculated where the two hundred and ninety was from the bow and about twenty above the lake. At first he did not see it but with a little searching movement he picked up the twinkle of a fire. It was probably from a French lookout camp, like the one they had raided. The fire was most likely built behind a break and could not be seen from the English camp. It was not a large fire and people moving back and forth between him and the fire could have caused part of the twinkle. He handed the glass to the Sergeant Major and pointed him in the right direction. When he found it, he looked for a minute and then handed the glass back to Fogg and leaned over and whispered.

"They know we're out on the lake, Sir. That's a signal fire. The reason it disappears is cause they're holding a blanket up to block the light then they drop it and pick it up again. It can only be seen from the direction of down lake from the lookout. There's probably French out on the Long Island."

Fogg leaned over to him, "All right Sergeant Major. Let's pull anchor and move down lake on the east side of the Long Island. If there are French on the island they should be looking for us to the west. If they come out on the lake, we might catch them off guard come daylight. Our swivels should give us an advantage. Pass the word to Captain Gris to pull anchor and proceed in marching formation." The Sergeant Major passed the word along and within a few minutes they were underway, moving around the north side of the Diamond Island toward the east side of the Long Island. It would be a tricky passage to navigate between the island and the long point that reached out toward it from the east shore. It was the outer tip of the piece of land that formed what the English called the South Arm. It was just over five hundred or so feet across the passage. The trick was to hold the center of the channel to avoid any French on the east point. When they approached the channel, they slowed down to a snail's pace. The only noise was the slight drip of the oars. It was pull and glide, then pull and glide again. This went on for about a quarter of a mile to insure that they were past the east point. Fogg then moved his boats out into the middle of the bay, slightly to the east. He signaled to stop and they held station for a quarter of an hour, listening for any indication of French on the island or of detection of their own presence.

Fogg was about to give the order to move on when they heard a splash from the direction of the island and a muttered, "Merde!" followed by a "ssshhhh!" The first voice protested, "Mais, c'est mon fusil," where upon the second voice said only "Idiot!" and then all was silent.

They held their station for another half hour before Fogg gave the signal to move on. They continued on southeast until they were clear of the north point of the Long Island. They then steered west until they were sure they were out in the broad lake. Once more they tied up into a nest to ride out the night. The wind had died down and when the sky started to light up they found themselves just north of the Long Island and a half mile from the mouth of a small bay northwest of it.

Fogg gave the order to untie the boats and they assumed a line abreast facing south. They held this position as the sky became lighter. Fogg had them step the mast in the lead boat and one of the Stockbridge went shinny up it with Fogg's glass. From his elevated perch, he could see further down the lake then they could from water level. Any French out on the lake would have a hard time seeing him as the mountains would help hide his outline. Shortly, the Stockbridge signed that he saw four canoes out on the lake making for the west shore. Fogg called him down and gave the order to get underway. They un-stepped the mast as they moved up the lake toward the canoes. The Rangers doubled the rowers without any orders. It was their regular operating procedure to increase the power of the boat. Fogg felt the boat leap through the water as they hit their rhythm. The French were mid-lake when they saw the longboats bearing down on them. It was too late to turn back toward the Long Island so they pressed on toward the west shore hoping to reach it before the English reached them. The French officer in charge knew that they were no match for what he perceived to be at least a half-dozen English longboats. He wished that he had the smaller canot du nord instead of these four canot du maitre. Even with everyone paddling, the canoes still moved too slowly for him. Now he could see the swivels mounted on the fore-posts and was sure that the English would be in range to use them long before he reached shore. He shouted the command to change course to the south west in hopes of increasing the distance between himself and his pursuers.

Fogg saw the maneuver and signaled to alter course obliquely so that his line was now headed in the same direction bringing the left wing of the line in. Within fifteen minutes the right of Fogg's line was within range of the two trailing canoes. They requested permission to fire, but Fogg held them up until the range was only seventy-five yards. He gave the command for a running fire from the right wing so that each gun could adjust based on the fire of the previous one. The first fired and sprayed just to the right and behind the closest canoe. The next boat in line adjusted and fired. They were at a slight angle to the canoe and had led the canoe a little too much. The grape hit the forward half of the canoe and everyone in that section plus tearing away the starboard front quarter of the canoe, causing it to pitch down and to the starboard, spilling all of those in it into the lake.

Boats three and four opened up on the next canoe simultaneously and the canoe simply disappeared, leaving nothing except floating paddles and gear where it used to be. Even the gun crews stared in awe. Apparently the grape shot hung together in a closer pattern than it should have at that range. They were now closing on the other two canoes. The paddlers in the middle of the canoes dropped their paddles and picked up their muskets. They managed to get off one volley before the other swivels could get off their rounds. Instead of concentrating on the lead or closest English boat they had seemed to just fire at whatever boat they thought presented the best target. Fogg wasn't sure how many rounds the French fired but it appeared to be seven or eight. One of the Rangers in his boat was hit and fell to the bottom of the boat and another round hit one of the oars close to the rower showering him with splinters in his hand and right arm.

Fogg also saw one of the Rangers in the boat to his right clutching his head. His attention was drawn back to the canoes when he heard the report of another swivel gun. This one raked the closest canoe, which was now only about fifty yards away and four of the men in it were thrown out of the canoe. The remaining men lifted their paddles above their heads in surrender. The lead canoe, seeing his companions surrender, decided to do the same as the longboats were now closing on him. Better to be a prisoner than to be wounded and thrown into the water to drown. The closest longboat pulled along side the canoes and the Rangers disarmed the Frenchmen of whom there were nine in one canoe and five in the other. They transferred the prisoners, two to a boat. They tied off the two canoes to the stern of the two longboats that would bring up the end of the columns when moving in their normal order.

The Ranger that Fogg saw go down in his boat was dead and the man who was showered with splinters could no longer row. The Ranger in the other boat had been creased in the head but was otherwise able to perform his duty. Rather than decrease his detachment by sending back a boat with the dead Ranger and the wounded, Fogg elected to bury the dead Ranger on the small island that lay just west of the Long Island. While Fogg and his section landed, the other eight boats stood off and kept watch. The island was sandy loam and it did not take long to dig a shallow grave. They did not mark the grave so that it would pass unnoticed by any of the enemy.

They were underway within three quarters of an hour, once more moving down lake toward the North Arm as some called it. Fogg elected to remain mid-lake, steering for the island the Rangers said was Dome Island that was about four and one- half miles from where they had buried the Ranger. There was little wind on the lake this morning and they made good time. Being in mid-lake, it was not necessary to creep along and watch the shores for an ambush. In this part of the lake the distance across was, in most places well over a mile, giving plenty of notice of any approaching enemy boats. Fogg's encounter with the four canoes assured him that he probably was much larger than any French force afloat on the lake at this time. On shore he would need to be careful as the French were known to put out large patrols, two or three hundred not being unusual. Major Rogers had made that mistake when he mistook an advance party for the main party last winter. There were estimated to be four to six hundred in that French scout. So far, Fogg had been fortunate with his casualties but he knew that his luck would not hold forever.

They approached the Dome Island with caution, the column splitting and going around the two sides to observe it. When they reached the north end, they could see the entrance to the North Arm or Northwest Bay plus the entrance to what was termed the First Narrows. The island was about eighteen hundred feet long and a little over a half mile to the next closest island on the west. He decided to tie up his boats to the east shore. It was a mile or so to the east shore of the lake and he posted a watch on the crest of the island to watch the other three directions, each with a spy glass. He would rotate them every half hour as he planned to stay here no more than two hours to let the men rest after the fight in the morning. They had been there for an hour and a half when the watch on the north end whistled the alarm. Fogg, Gris and the Sergeant Major went running to the north end. The Corporal in charge pointed down lake to a small flashing speck just starting to appear in the narrows. Fogg raised his glass and focused on the spot. Sure enough, he could make out a line of boats approaching from the north. The sun reflected off the wet oars causing the flashing. Fogg could make out three boats, but could not tell what kind they were. He sent Gris and the Sergeant Major back down to the boats to make ready to get underway, as he preferred to meet an enemy out on the lake where he had the advantage in firepower that the swivels gave him.

When they had first spotted the boats, they were just visible through the islands in the Narrows, which put them about three to four miles away. As Fogg observed them, they steadily came on south up the lake. As they cleared the Narrows and the headland on the east side he could make out that they were longboats and therefore probably English. The elevation of the island gave Fogg an advantage of being able to see the boats easily. From down on the water level, the boats could not yet make out Fogg's boats lying tied up to the east shore of the island. They were pulling directly for the island that Fogg and his men were on.

As the boats pulled even with the two islands just northwest of the domed island one of the Rangers said, "Them's Stockbridge Indians in that lead boat!" Fogg once more brought his glass up and he could make out the figure standing at the tiller of the lead boat. No mistaking, it was Putnam. The boats came steadily on until they were just a little over a half mile away. Fogg saw Putnam hold up his hand and the boats lost headway as all hands stopped rowing. Fogg saw Putnam hand the tiller over to the man next to him and draw out his spy glass. He was looking at the boats that were now visible from his position. Fogg sent one of the Rangers down to tell Captain Gris to have a Ranger go out and stand in the boats so that Putnam could see him. The fellow ran off down to the main party and soon Fogg saw Putnam give the signal to proceed forward. Fogg gave the rest a "job well done" and went down to greet Putnam.

In a short time, Putnam's flotilla pulled up along side Fogg's and nested with them.

Putnam was his usual self, "Brother Fogg and Brother Gris, what the hell are you fellows doing out here on this lovely day?" giving both of them a friendly grip.

"One of our jobs is to go up into that great bay there and look for signs of Monsieur Marin and his boats. The other mission was to look for signs of Israel Putnam upon the lake as His Lordship was ever so slightly concerned that you had not yet returned. By the way, where is your other boat, as you left with four of His Majesty's longboats?" Fogg added the last sentence just to twist Putnam's queue.

"The side got stove in. We had sails up and running before the wind. One of the boats hit a submerged rock or ridge on the east side of the lake just opposite the Major's rock. The boat was one that had wintered under the ice and most likely had a bad spot. Some of them boats weren't put into deep enough water last year. The ice on this lake freezes down two to three feet in the shallow places. I stepped into a bad spot this last winter and ended up standing on the bottom in the sand dry as a bone, if you please. What have you got for a hungry man," adding with a big grin "I managed to save my three Connecticut boats."

"Just cold rations but your welcome to them," replied Gris, handing Putnam his haversack. "Help yourself."

"What did you see on the lake and how far did you go?" asked Fogg.

"We went a little further than we was supposed to," replied Putnam, rummaging through Gris' ration bag. My orders was to scout just past the First Narrows, there, a couple of miles or so. I went for the or so."

"How many 'or so' miles was that?" questioned Fogg.

"All the way down past the middle set of narrows," mumbled Putnam, with a mouth full of one of Gris' last pieces of cornbread.

"That's about four more miles than you were supposed to go," said Gris, "and that's the last of my cornbread."

"Actually about seven, as I went all the way to the bluff point on the east side and I'm probably doin you a favor as this is mighty stale-tasting cornbread," was Putnam's reply. "Got anything stronger than lake water to drink?" Fogg just shook his head, incredulously.

## Chapter 39

It was decided that they would join forces and proceed first up the North Arm and then together back up lake to the English camp. Fogg gave Putnam the two canoes to redistribute his men as all four crews were sailing in three boats. It was also decided that they did not need their French prisoners if going hunting for Marin. Putnam pointed out a set of two islands directly west of the domed one. He suggested putting them on the small one. It was separated from the larger one by what looked to be four or five hundred feet and the larger one was separated from the main land by about half that. His reasoning was that, by the time they got to the mainland, it would be too late for them to interfere in any way. If they all could not swim then it would take longer for them to get back into the war but they would no longer be Fogg's problem.

They shoved off, pulling for the island that Putnam had pointed out. It took less than twenty minutes to cross over and disembark the Frenchmen among a great deal of protesting. Fogg left them two-day's supplies. It would be more than enough for them to make it to one of the French lookout camps or to the English camp at the head of the lake; their choice.

From the island to the mouth of the North Arm it was only two miles and their flotilla covered the distance in very little time. The plan had been set previously and the two columns were to split. Gris' plus Putnam's boats would take the west shore of the bay and Fogg would take the eastern or outer shore. The columns split and they each went their separate route.

Fogg worked his boats slowly along the shoreline, two doing the searching and the remaining boats standing off to cover a retreat in case of an attack. The agreed upon plan was that if attacked the other column was to cross over and help provide cover as the bay was on average about three quarters of a mile wide in most spots. There were several places that could have been used but there were no marks to indicated that anyone had landed. There was no signal from Gris or Putnam that they were having any better luck.

At the mouth of the bay, there was a stream that ran into it that was capable of floating a boat. Fogg reached this part of the bay before the other column. He waited for the others to join him before taking his boat up the stream. They tied one of the long lines to his sternpost, letting it trail behind him as he cautiously proceeded up the creek. The other end was being held by the hands in two of the other boats. The plan was to extract Fogg's boat by hand over hand if it was attacked. This would be much quicker than his crew attempting to row back out. When they reached the end of the first line, one of the Rangers bent a second line on to it and they let it pay out. When Fogg was about one hundred feet up the creek, the Stockbridge in the bow signaled for them to stop. He pointed to the west bank. Fogg moved the boat closer and, when it struck bottom, the two Stockbridge jumped out and waded ashore. Within a few minutes they were back in the boat.

It seemed that the French, or at least a big party, had already decided to depart this part of the lake. The Stockbridge told Fogg that there had been many boats in here, enough to carry at least two hundred Frenchmen. They had probably passed by Putnam somewhere in the narrows unaware that his scout was even there. That many boats would surely have attacked his three boats. They extracted Fogg's boat from the stream and all three met out in the middle of the bay. Their best plan was to proceed to mid-lake and if the wind were right, run in front of it up lake. They decided to suggest to Lord Howe that the Rangers put a good size scouting force out on the lake to deny the French the use of the lake for spying purposes. This would force them to use the overland routes which would slow down their communications.

The wind was with them and the Rangers got an appreciated free ride home. Fogg passed the word over the other column "that the smoking lamp was lit." The only disruption in the return trip was when the lead boat spotted several other boats out on the lake. It turned out to be a small Ranger scout that was making a run down lake as far as the first big bay on the west side, the dark one, just below Diamond Island. They calculated to be back in before sundown.

The rest of the journey was so uneventful that those not on watch slept.

# Chapter 40

Since Fogg and his detachment departed on June 19th a great deal of activity had been happening in the English camp. Due to the intelligence of the French observation parties being so close, questions were raised regarding the security of the camp. It was decided that parties of two or three hundred men would be stationed at night on the hill which over looked the road. In conjunction with this, a smaller party was set each night to guard the teams. Included in this round of orders were explicit instructions for approaching the camp at night. This included that the approaching party stop and wait until challenged by the guard and then proceeding only when told to.

Daily large detachments were designated to escort the wagons and teams that were hauling supplies up from the Half Way Brook and then to escort the empty wagons and trucks back down to the same area. These detachments would number three to four hundred men. At the same time, work parties of the same size were sent out to maintain the road. There was a constant stream of wagons going up and down the road in an effort to transport the five hundred and thirty-six thousand pounds of supplies needed to support the army for just one week. By the time they took Crown Point the supply line would stretch over an estimated one hundred twenty miles long from Albany.

There were also work parties sent out on wood details, to lend additional hands to the bateaux-men at the boat yard and the never ending fatigue duties of just maintaining a camp of this size. It was a must to move the "necessaries" every few days and fill in the old ones. The provost was kept busy at night just patrolling the camp to make sure that it did not become "fouled" due to soldiers being too lazy to walk to the "necessary".

There were the usual rounds of courts-martial to be held. The typical courts-martial required the presence of at least fourteen officers, depending upon the offense, two of them being field grade and the rest line grade. All of this put a strain on the officer corps of the army but was a necessary function of maintaining discipline.

General Abercromby issued an order that released all of the officers and soldiers who were included in the capitulation of Fort William Henry from their parole. This was due to the behavior of the

180

Indians who were with Montcalm and the failure of Montcalm and his officers to stop the action. This order was mainly to cover officers as private soldiers were expected just to do as they were told.

Each regiment had been issued a small number of rifled firelocks. On a couple of occasions, the men issued these were sent out to fire at marks in specially designated areas. There were also parties sent out from camp to these same areas, who were unable to draw their charges from their firelocks. It was necessary for them to discharge their muskets to clear them. They were also instructed to retrieve as many of the spent balls as possible. Firing was always done in a visible designated area at a specific time to eliminate the possibility of alarming the camp. On certain days it was required to review the arms and ammunition of the entire army and the shortages made up.

Another activity that was being carried out was the instruction of the troops in the making of gabions, those round wicker frames, that when filled with dirt, were used for siege work. It was planned to lay siege to both St. Frederick and its outpost at Carillon. Others were instructed in the construction of fascines, used with the gabions. A call was also issued for any NCOs or Privates who had served during any siege work.

A major problem that had arisen was that supplies were being left out in the open. The General had ordered that the additional tents be turned over to the bateaux-men and that the any water-proofed cloths and flys be used to secure the supplies stored on shore and already loaded in the boats. It was made an offense to use any of these covers for any personal purpose. Considering that the supply line extended from New York Town to Lake George via Albany it was a prudent order. Lord Howe had just spent the last month and a half getting the necessary supplies to support an army of this size to the lake head. One rainstorm lasting only a few minutes could wipe out all that effort.

The main body of the regulars were now in the camp and a very large proportion of the provincials were encamped. There were still some stragglers in the process of moving up from Albany and as yet Sir William Johnson and his Mohawks were not gracing the camp with their presence. It would be difficult for the ordinary citizen to realize that this encampment rivaled the population of the majority of the metropolitan places in North America. On a daily basis it fluctuated between seventeen thousand to nineteen thousand, depending on how many men were out in the various detachments. Some of the Rangers who had been on perimeter patrol claimed, "It were near like ten mile…" around the outside of the camp.

It was at this bustling encampment that Fogg and his now expanded flotilla put in just as the sun was starting to set. He sent a messenger to Lord Howe to inform him that they were back and Putnam was with them and they awaited his pleasure.

## Chapter 41

Fogg and Gris did not meet with Howe until the next day as Howe had gone down to Halfway Brook to see about correcting some flaws in the supply line. When they arrived at the headquarters, Putnam was already there and had just finished his report. Howe motioned for them to come in and have a seat at the table that he was using for a desk.

"Gentlemen, good morning. Major Putnam has just finished his report including the part that he shared with your detachment. Good manuver to form one flotilla. I would dare say that your assumption that you were the largest force on the lake was probably true. Enlighten me to the events that took place prior to your meeting Putnam. Help yourselves to tea and there is also some coffee." Both declined the offer. They took turns recounting their scout. When they got to the part about running down the four canoes, Howe stopped them.

"You are saying that the swivel with grape at less than fifty yards disintegrated the canoe?"

"Yes," replied Fogg, "but it was probably due to the angle and the grape holding together longer than usual. It may also only have seemed that way. It probably took away enough of the stern so that it sank immediately and of course the occupants were lined up in a row from that angle."

"What is your opinion?" Howe asked of Captain Gris.

"Your Lordship, I would not have believed it myself if I had not seen it," replied Gris.

"Extraordinary, simply extraordinary! Please continue Major." Fogg continued with the remainder of the report, being careful to include all parts. When he finished, Howe sat there for a minute. He suddenly seemed to return from wherever he was.

"Well then, Major Putnam, Moneypenny has yours and Major Rogers' orders for you. I shan't keep you any longer. Thank you for your report." Putnam stood and saluted, said goodbye to Fogg and Gris and departed. They sat there another moment while Howe seemed to gather his thoughts for the next move. Finally he spoke, telling them that it was his plan to have Rogers put out several scouts. These scouts were to observe South Bay, Lake George and

Ticonderoga, all by land. He had also ordered parties out on the lake as far as five miles past the First Narrows. They were to make no effort to hide as they were intended to take the attention away from the land scouts.

"Major Fogg and Captain Gris, I want you to make another sortie down the lake. Last June 7th Major Rogers did a reconnaissance of the north end of the lake. There is a small bay or a cove there that is suitable for our purposes to land the army. I want to determine if Major Rogers' report is still good. You will have to spy it out from a distance as an approach too close might tip the French off as to our plans for the landing. I am told that there is a point on the east side across the lake from this cove where you can see it with a glass. The point is slightly south and about halfway between it and the place the Rangers refer to as Major Rogers' Rock. Your Sergeant Major will know where it stands. It is important that you determine if we can get the majority or all of our boats into this cove. Rogers says that there is a sandy beach if not too deep, it will be suitable." With that he stopped. "Any questions?" Both indicated that it seemed clear enough and they wondered when the Ranger scouting parties would head out onto the lake. Howe said that the Rangers' orders stated that they should depart some time either late morning or very early afternoon. Fogg then begged his leave, as they needed to get their men started and coordinate the first part of their passage with the Rangers.

"Good hunting, Gentlemen. I expect to hear from you in no more than five days. When you return, I will give you the full details of the plan to take Crown Point and Carillon from the French." They saluted and walked out of the headquarters, bidding adieu to Alexander, who simply said good luck and to please write out a report as soon as they returned. He had records of almost everything that the army had accomplished up to this point, but nothing in writing of their missions so far.

On the way back to their camp, they went to the Ranger camp to find out who was going to make the scout on the lake. They were directed to the officer in charge, one of Rogers' regulars who had been learning the business of ranging in the Cadet Company. He indicated that he would be going out just after noon and that they would rendezvous just off of the mouth of the creek where Fogg's boats were nested. This gave them a little under four hours to get their men packed and ready. Fogg sent Gris back to camp to start the process and he went down to the boat works. At the boat works, using his order from Lord Howe that he should be supplied with whatever he needed, he drew one of the new twenty foot cedar whale boats that had been constructed for scouting. It had five oarlocks and a tiller oar and carried only six men. They were fast and could outrun any other type of boat on the lake including the two-man birch canoes. The cedar whaler was so light that two men could carry it if necessary. Using the tiller oar he sculled it up the creek to where his other boats were tied up. He instructed the bateaux-men to tie it up to the stern post of his boat. They informed him that they had numbered the boats as they all would be issued soon and they would need some identification. His was boat number one of Fogg's Flotilla. They had painted FF1 on the bow. They laughed when he told them to put FF ½ on the new cedar whaler.

By the time that Fogg arrived back up at the camp Gris and the Sergeant Major had the men almost ready. They only needed to check the ammunition and draw whatever shortages they had and they would be ready to shove off whenever the Rangers were. Fogg went to check his own gear and took one more look at his map before putting it away. He never carried the map out into the field with him, unless absolutely necessary. The loss of it to the French would be disastrous. As maps of this part of the world went, it was a very detailed map of the area especially with Fogg's notes and marking upon it. Fogg checked to make sure that he had enough ammunition for his fusil and pistols. He had not fired his fusil at all during the last sojourn upon the lake. He checked each round to make sure that there was no moisture damage, the biggest threat to ammunition when on the lake. When he got over to where Gris and the Sergeant Major were standing, they handed him a packet wrapped in linen. It contained the major part of his rations for the trip. They were not bringing any bread with them. Instead kegs of Navy biscuits that would be stored in the boats. It was fresh from the bakery, if Navy biscuits could ever be considered fresh. Both were holding a cup and they handed one to Fogg. It was the last of the morning pot of coffee that the Sergeant Major had brewed. Since meeting them he had become a very good coffee brewer. They also had a large slice of bread with a big slab of butter on it.

"Best eat up Sir. This will be the last fresh-baked bread that we'll be having for a while," offered the Sergeant Major.

"Tell me, Sergeant Major. How do we have fresh bread on a Thursday morning when we aren't due to draw a bread ration until Saturday?"

"It's a miracle Sir! It just appeared in camp when it found out we were fixing to go down lake. A miracle," replied the Sergeant Major.

"It seems that a lot of miracles happen in your presence, Sergeant Major," said Gris with a slight grin.

"Why Sir! It is just my sainted mother looking out for her poor boy," said with as much piety as possible. At which statement they all had a good laugh and when they had finished their brief repast Fogg gave the orders to get the detachment moving to the boats.

# Chapter 42

The Sergeant Major had the men fall-in and marched them down to the creek where the boats were tied up. The bateaux-men assigned to each boat had refitted the boats with all the necessary provisions. When they arrived at the boat area, the Sergeant Major assigned the men to their newly numbered boats. They all marveled at the new "scout-type" whaler, but also got a chuckle out of its hull designation, FF ½. Although the Sergeant Major had explained that the FF stood for Fogg's Flotilla, there was a great speculation among the Rangers, being the rough lot they were as for what it could also stand. The boats were tied up in the creek in a nest, that is to say with five tied to shore and then another tied to the stern. The one tied to the stern was off-set so that its bow went a little past the stern to facilitate going from one boat to the other. They were tied this way as the entire creek was full of boats as far up as possible. Fogg's boat, FF1, was tied up on the outside, downstream side of the nest. This put it in a position to lead off. The rest of the boats were tied up in order of position in line astern.

By the time they made the last minute checks and got everyone in the boats, the main Ranger scouting party was just pulling out from their docking position a little downstream from Fogg's. He waited until the Rangers were almost finished and were moving out of the creek before he gave the order to "cast off". The "bow hook" used his pole to push off from the boats next to them and swung the bow downstream. One oarsman in the bow and one in the stern used their oars to pole away from the others. All oars, except the previous mentioned two, were in "up oars" position. When clear, the command to "down oars" was given and then "all hands haul away". The boats moved downstream, the coxswains maintaining the boats' positions both in line and center stream. By the time Fogg's flotilla had cleared the creek they were only fifty yards astern of the last boat in the Ranger line.

The lead Ranger boat gave the signal to halt and Fogg pulled his boat ahead, even with it. He and the officer in charge held a brief conference. Fogg outlined his plan, which was to appear to be part of the Rangers' scout group. He would bring up the end of the line and remain there until dark. He also suggested that they split up when entering the islands in the First Narrows in order to confuse anyone observing them. After dark, he and his flotilla would draw ahead and proceed down lake until just before daylight. They would then pull ashore and conceal the boats, wait until dark and then commence on down the lake to their appointed observation post.

When asked by the Ranger officer where that would be, Fogg replied, "If you do not know then you cannot tell if captured." Even the strongest man who had his intestines tacked to a tree and was forced to run around it would tell anything just to have it finished with a swift blow from the tomahawk.

Fogg let the line move ahead and fell in behind the last Ranger boat. It was a quiet trip as the boats moved down mid-lake. Fortunately, it was a calm day with just a little wind blowing in from the northwest. All the rest of the afternoon they moved at the slow steady pace to arrive at the entrance to the narrows while it was still light.

This progress did not pass unnoticed by the French observation posts situated on the side of the mountains on both sides of the lake. To the French, it appeared that the English had launched a scout in force upon the lake. From the number of boats they estimated that there could be at least 450 to 500 men in this scout. The French officer in charge of the post on the west side made the decision to send a small party of two, swift, three-man canoes to shadow them and report to the officer in charge of the last observation post before the landing just above the first falls in La Chute. He would take care of it from there. He cautioned them to be careful, as it was important that the message get through. They were to follow them through the narrows and then pass them in the dark. He made them repeat the order just to be certain. After they left, he also sent three of the Indians to go on foot to deliver the same message. He knew that they would arrive at the same destination not much more than a couple of hours behind the canoes, if not before. These people could maintain the same trotting pace all day long on no more than an occasional mouthful of pemmican and a swig of water from any brook or stream. He had lived among them most of his life and try as he might he could never keep up that pace. He could run most Europeans into the ground but not any Indians. He greatly admired their ability to do this. Some of their other traits he did not admire so much, yet he did admire their women. He forgot about the English boats as his mind drifted off to recollect as to just how much he had admired a couple of those women, although not simultaneously.

The post on the east side was in the process of sending runners to cut over to Wood Creek and go to Carillon and report the movement of a sizable English force on the lake when one of the lookouts spotted the two canoes leave the shore on the opposite side and start down the lake. They canceled the runners and went back to their normal routine.

There was still plenty of light left when they arrived at the First Narrows and, according to their plan, the line of boats broke up into what appeared to be smaller sections. These sections then spread out to inspect the islands that filled the Narrows. The boats would approach an island, stand off while they inspected it with a glass, and then move in close to shore to get into the shadows caused by the sun setting lower in the west. Part would move to the next island repeat the same process while the other part would move off around the island and then head for the opposite side, where their other section was waiting there. It was hoped that the movement, splitting up and rejoining of forces, would make it difficult for the French observation posts to keep track of all of the boats.

There was a very large, long island just north of the mouth of the North Arm that was shielded from the view of the known observation post on the west side of the lake, the island hid it from the view of the one that the English knew existed on the east side of the lake. It had a small natural bay on its west side and it was here that Fogg pulled his boats in under the shadows produced by the trees on the island and the small mountain on the east shore of the North Arm. He set a watch and told the men that they should try to get some sleep. He sent two men over to the outward side of the island and two men to the south end as additional alarm posts.

As soon as it was dark enough to call in the sentries they got underway. Fogg had made it a standing order that the oars on the boats were to be wrapped in wool strips at all times. Even during daylight hours, it was advantageous to be quiet. Slowly, they pulled out of the bay and past the island. It was a full moon but the sky was overcast so that the lake was not lit up. Fogg hoped it would stay that way for the entire night as he hoped to be at the southern end of the lake by daylight. The wind had changed and was blowing from the south so the boats were getting an assist from it. It was shortly after one o'clock and they were approaching the vicinity of the mountain on the east side called the Nose when the cloud cover started to break up. Fogg gave the signal to pull into shore to take advantage of the shadows.

No sooner had they moved into the shadows when one of the Stockbridge, in another boat, spotted movement out on the lake. The word spread quickly through the line and the entire flotilla froze in place. Fogg soon spotted the object moving on the lake and took out his glass to see if he could get a better view. It appeared to be two canoes moving down the lake, most likely headed for the first French outpost at the foot of the lake. They were sparing no effort and therefore might have been messengers sent to warn of the large English party spotted at the Narrows. They most likely did not know that Fogg's group was on this part of the lake or they would have been more cautious. As there was no way that he could stop them without making a great deal of noise, he decided to let them go. In another one and a half to two hours he would be at his objective and off the lake. He waited twenty minutes and then gave the order to get underway, as by now the two canoes would be at least a mile or so ahead of him.

They had covered about fifteen miles since leaving the island and the Sergeant Major estimated they had about another three or four more miles to go due to having to follow the shoreline. They moved along the shore as far out as they could without losing the advantage of the shadows. They would be visible to anyone on the shore but not to anyone out on the lake or on the other side. After they had rounded the Nose, they made for a spot identifiable by the large flat rock that ran down to the water. On its north end was a small cove where they could pull up the boats and conceal them in the woods along the shore. The main party would stay here under Gris, Fogg would take the cedar whaler and go to the point to observe the proposed landing place that Howe had indicated. The cedar whaler was made to hold five rowers, one coxswain and a bow hook. Fogg took with him four Rangers and two Stockbridge. He placed one Stockbridge in the bow and the other in the last rowing seat. They did not like to row but were capable of doing an excellent job if and when they wanted to. The plan was that if either party got into difficulty the other was to make for the firing with all haste. Fogg and his small party set off for the point, which was about two miles away. Gris immediately put out his sentries and got his men settled in for a long day.

The cedar whaler was extremely fast and handled well. It responded to the tiller like a racehorse. They had been underway for about five minutes when the Stockbridge, who was rowing, touched Fogg's knee and pointed toward the west side of the lake. He had spotted a fire on the mountain that the Rangers called the Major's Rock Fogg guessed it was the French outpost that the Sergeant Major had told him about. By land it was only about three miles from the French advance camp at the foot of the lake. For the Indians that was just a short trot. Fogg had been told that the Indians played inter-village lacrosse with each village as the goal and sometimes this was ten or so miles.

The last few yards they coasted into the shore.  It was a sandy beach and the majority of the point was cut off from the main land by a marshy area that was full of cattails.  They picked the boat up and carried it inland a ways and covered it over with brush.  One of the Stockbridge swept out their tracks on the beach.  Fogg set one Stockbridge and two Rangers to watch the approach from the mainland and left one Ranger with the boat.  He took the one remaining Ranger and Stockbridge with him to the north side of the point.  They approached the shore carefully but there were no signs of any French activity on this point.  Now they waited for daylight.

As it turned light, the Stockbridge pointed to the small island that was just north of them and made a noise like a sheep.  Fogg took out his glass and sure enough he could see some sheep on the island.  He then turned his attention to observing the other shore of the lake.

The place that Howe had indicated would be the main landing place was a little over a half mile away and the cove faced south.  From his position, Fogg could see the sand that lined the shore and it presented a gentle slope up a few feet.  From there to the French advance outpost it was, in Fogg's estimation a little over another half mile.  The closest sentry to Howe's proposed landing was half way between the camp and the cove, probably a quarter mile.  Fogg could just barely see him because of the height of the grass, almost up to the sentry's waist.  He could see the French soldiers at their camp going through their morning routine.  They had just started to stir.  Fogg watched them on and off for a couple of hours.  They changed guards, they sent out patrols, they did the usual camp stuff.  He saw what appeared to be patrols of Canadians with Indians come in from the south west, most likely from the lookout post.  The Ranger with him told Fogg that the French had regular patrol trails that covered that side of the lake and the valley just beyond.  It was one of these patrol trails in that valley that they were on when they had the Snowshoe Fight.  Supposedly, the French had a plank bridge that spanned the La Chute a little further down, but Fogg could not see it or the works that were reported to be on both sides.  He was looking at what the Rangers called the French Narrows.

They had one breath-holding moment when a canoe appeared from behind the Sheep Island and headed on an angle into the bay that lay to their right.  It came on steadily, headed for the center of the bay.  When it reached a point about twenty feet from the shore it turned and headed back north along the shoreline.  One of the paddlers jumped out and was standing in water up to his knees.  As he moved along ,the canoe kept up with him and he would reach down into the water and throw something into the canoe.  Fogg put his glass on the canoe and finally made out that he appeared to be throwing clams into the canoe. The canoe and the clammer continued along the bay moving steadily away from Fogg's post.

The Ranger whispered to Fogg, "The Indians eat them freshwater clams in a soup. It's a little strong but nourishing. They's probably Canadian courier de bois or la malice. Some of them's lived with the Indians so long there ain't much difference 'cept their French is better. They's the French Rangers. French regulars is just like our English regulars, begging your pardon Sir, afraid of real woods 'cause there ain't no real woods left in Europe and England or so they say."

Fogg nodded his head in understanding and went back to observing the landing place. There was still no activity in that vicinity, which probably meant that they did not patrol it at all. They held their position all morning. The sky was clouding over and off to the west it looked like rain. They had intended to wait until dark to withdraw but if it rained Fogg decided to do it then. They would hug the shore line back to the flat rock area where they left Gris and the rest of the command. About one o'clock it started to sprinkle and then the sky opened up. The lake got a little choppy but that was good for their retreat. Fogg gave the order to pull in the sentries and get the boat into the water. They launched and pulled along the shore line, the cedar whaler making good headway even with the slight chop. It took a little more time to get back to Gris' position then it had to make the original trip. When they reached the spot where the boats were, two Rangers grabbed the bow and everyone jumped out into the shallow water. It took less than half a minute for them to conceal the boat and disappear into the bush. Gris and the Sergeant Major had come over to where they landed. Gris indicated that he was set up closer to the open area of the flat rocks where he could see the lake better, so they moved up to there.

"The landing is almost like Lord Howe described. I think it is a little narrower than Rogers thought, but I could be wrong. The French do not patrol the cove itself. What about the observation post across the lake?" asked Fogg.

"There has been some activity off and on. They do not take too much care to conceal themselves. They probably figure they own this end of the lake. They have a couple of boats tied up between the land and that island just south of the big rock face. Can't see them now because of the rain. Maybe three at the most," Gris pointed out.

"Good. We'll sit here until it gets dark and then move on up lake. I would like to take the time to stave in the bottom of their boats, but it is better if we just slip away and leave them with their notion of owning this end of the lake."

"Agreed, Major. No sense putting them more on guard," replied the Sergeant Major, Gris nodded in agreement.

"Right. Tell the men to rest as best they can in this weather. We'll be busy all night to get up lake far enough so as not to make anyone suspicious of where we have been," was Fogg's order.

# Chapter 43

It continued to rain and by seven o'clock that evening the lake was dark enough to conceal their movements. Fogg gave the order to man the boats and all the crews quickly responded. Anything to get this part of the mission over. Rowing would be a great deal more warming than sitting huddled in a wet blanket under a dripping pine tree. It had been two days since they had been able to warm themselves around a fire. The flotilla formed up in its two columns and moved up lake along the eastern shore until clearing the promontory the Rangers called the Nose. When they cleared the Nose, Fogg signaled to move out into mid lake. Around nine o'clock the rain stopped and the clouds began to disappear. Along with this change in the weather a breeze started to blow in from the northwest. Fogg signaled to step the masts and the breeze carried them up lake. This time they were thankful that the full moon was only two days old and lit up the lake.

*If this wind holds,* Fogg was thinking, *we will be south of the First Narrows by daylight and at the camp by mid morning. Let us hope there are no French on the lake between us and this end of the Narrows.*

The wind held true and by false dawn they were two thirds of the way through the Narrows when the Stockbridge in Gris' boat pointed toward the western shore. Gris signaled Fogg who turned his glass in that direction, making a sweep to find the object of the alarm. There it was, just lake-ward of the large island they had hid behind on their outward voyage, a line of boats or canoes making for the opposite side of the lake or the big island that lay in the center. Fogg signaled for the coxswain to move the boat closer to Gris' column and the two lines swung toward each other.

Fogg said to Gris, now only a few yards away, "We'll maintain our course straight down the middle. Set your line to fill the intervals so that if they maintain their present course we'll cross the 'T' and both columns can fire as they bear. One round from every swivel should give them pause to think about following us."

As the two lines drew closer to converging, Fogg maintained an eye on them with his glass. The rain had let up a little but the wind still held. The other line of boats were not under sail but were rowing

194

and, at their present course, Fogg's flotilla would either cut across in front of them or perhaps even cut through the first quarter of their line. Fogg could make out that the other boats did not have swivels or that the swivels were not mounted. All that he could see were a few men in each boat with muskets. He still could not make out if they were French as no uniforms showed. He had one of the Rangers who was not rowing break out the quarter-size ensign and run it up the mast. This brought a rather loud "Huzzah" from the line of boats running perpendicular to Fogg's. The lead boat went to "up oars" and started to loose headway, followed by the remainder. The man in the bow of the lead boat held his firelock up horizontal over his head, signaling they meant no harm. Fogg signaled for his flotilla to down sails and drift. The majority of Fogg's boats were within range of the other line. He signaled for the lead boat to approach. The man in charge of that boat gave the command to "down oars" and they began to pull toward Fogg's boat.

"Mr. Gris, if this goes wrong, do not hesitate to fire. Understood?"

"Understood Major, understood," was Gris' short reply. The man in the other boat spoke, still holding his musket over his head.

"Major Fogg? Lieutenant Caleb Brown, Connecticut Rangers. We were told we might find you out here. How was your journey? Might we join in and follow you to the camp? Your numbers look mighty impressive when seen from a distance."

"Well Lieutenant Brown, Connecticut Rangers, how did you know it was my detachment?" asked Fogg.

"When we left for our scout, Major Putnam told me to keep an eye for you how many boats you had, including the new cedar whaler. Ain't another one of them out on the lake as yet, Sir."

"Very well, Lieutenant. Bring your boats in behind ours and break them up to even out the lines. Can you rig to sail?"

"Aye Sir. We just need to step the masts."

"Very well. Signal when you are ready. We'll pull ahead so that you only need to fall in behind as we pass." Brown's line fell in behind Fogg and. within five minutes, they had their masts stepped and were ready to sail. Fogg gave the signal to hoist the sails and within a minute all of the boats were underway. Fogg's little flotilla had grown to sixteen boats with the addition of Brown's five. As Fogg looked back, it was easy to see that some of Brown's men, being from Connecticut, were no strangers to a longboat. Fogg now hoped that they might catch some French boats in the southern end of the lake.

Fogg calculated that from where they were now it was twelve to fourteen miles up lake to the landing at the English camp. He called over to Gris whose line was, about fifty yards off to his starboard.

"Captain Gris! We'll work our way up lake tacking back and forth to scour the large islands. I propose that when we come to an island that if it is on my side of the lake I'll take the landward side and you the lake side. Agreed?"

"Agreed, Sir!"

The first large island lay just south of their present position about a mile away. They ran up to it and dropped the sails as they approached. The passage between the mainland and the island was only a couple of hundred feet wide and the water not more than a couple of fathoms deep. The island was thickly covered with trees as was the mainland. There were no signs of where any boats or canoes had been pulled up on shore. It appeared as if no one had ever landed there. When they cleared the south end and Fogg could see Gris' line he signaled to raise sails and they move on out across the lake to the large island on the opposite shore. This island lay just opposite the mouth of the North Arm and just above the island where they had put the Frenchmen ashore on their first sortie on the lake.

Gris did the landward passage this time. Most of the channel was wide, five-hundred feet or so, but one spot was only about half that distance and the water not more than a fathom. The island itself was over three quarters of a mile long and at least a quarter mile at its widest point. It was covered in the center part by a thick stand of evergreens and the outer section was chocked with brush. On the outer side, there were no signs of any boat activity but Gris discovered two places where there was plenty of signs. As he moved to the south end, the Stockbridge in his boat tugged at his arm and pointed to a spot just ahead of them. Gris gave the signal to up oars and took out his glass. There at the spot where the Stockbridge pointed was, just barley visible, the tip of a canoe pulled upon the shore. He gave the signal to move forward and passed the word back to the Connecticut Rangers that when they came even with the end of the island to hold station and keep a sharp watch on the water between the island and the shore. He signaled for the line to hold position and he pulled his boat over to Fogg's.

"Major, there is a canoe pulled up on shore and concealed. Do you want to take the time to put a party ashore to sweep the island?"

Fogg thought for a minute and replied, "Yes. We'll send Brown's men back to cover the north end. Put four sections ashore

196

on this end and have them form a double skirmish line and sweep north. Station two boats in the channel at about half way to watch both north and south. The other four will stand off as a reserve, two on each side. Any firing and they are to move toward the sound, but only land if requested or ordered. Put the Sergeant Major in charge of the shore party."

The orders were relayed and the various parties took their stations. The bateaux-men stood ready with the boats at the landing points in case of a needed withdrawal. As the Rangers moved north on the island, the ones who came to the point where the canoe had been sighted discovered a second one. They uncovered both and pushed them into the water to be retrieved by one of the guarding boat crews. The Sergeant Major had stationed himself in the center of the lines and moved cautiously up the island. He had just enough men so that they were able to see each other and his two lines were staggered to fill in the intervals. His men would move and stop, listening for any movement on the part of anyone hiding. Twice he thought he heard movement but it remained quiet.

The skirmish line was three quarters of the way up the island and had cleared the stand of trees. There was only the brush left for cover. One of the Rangers in Gris' boats saw a movement in the brush along the water's edge. Gris directed his boat toward the movement and as he approached, there was a splash as a man slipped on the wet rocks on the shore and a leg and foot appeared in the space between the brush and the water. Just as Gris was about to call to the man in French to surrender, two Rangers appeared out of the brush with their muskets pointed down at where the man was hiding. Gris saw them motion with their muskets toward the water and slowly the man appeared out of the brush, standing in water just above his knees, his hands held over his head. He had no musket or any arms at all and was wearing only his breeches and a brown-dyed linen workman's smock. Gris called for him to move toward the boat but he indicated that he could not swim. Gris told him to walk out as far as he could, which he did. One of the Rangers threw him a line and he grabbed hold of it and they pulled him in. All this time the other boats kept their muskets trained on the shore.

Soon the Rangers on shore started to appear in the brush and Fogg thought that they had only garnered one prisoner. When the Sergeant Major appeared he had in tow four more, all gagged and bound together in a line with a rope around their necks as was the Indian fashion for moving prisoners. Fogg gave the order to get them into the boats and called up the boats that belonged to the shore party.

Soon, all were turned around and heading back up lake toward the English camp.

Fogg and Gris held a council and decided that they had enough intelligence and prisoners for their efforts out on the lake. The flotilla set sail directly for the English camp, five prisoners and two canoes richer than they had been at the beginning of the day. Upon landing, they sent the prisoners to headquarters and made sure that their men were on their way back to their camp under the command of the Sergeant Major. Fogg and Gris then went to headquarters themselves to report on their scout.

Having received the prisoners, Lord Howe was most anxious to hear their report. Fogg reported that the landing appeared to him to be slightly smaller than he understood it to be from Rogers' report. However he had noticed that there was plenty of room from the landing spot down to the French camp and all of the shore was sloping. There would be more than enough room for the army once the French were driven off. He reported he could not see the bridge or any of the works because of the angle and the waist high grass. He also reported that there was a great deal of movement on the patrol trails, which he concluded were the changing of the observation parties. Howe thanked them and ordered them to get some rest and dry clothes. He told them that he planned to put out more Ranger patrols on both the lake and the land starting tomorrow. He inquired if they were up to another sortie the day after tomorrow. Fogg looked to Gris who nodded his head in the affirmative.

"Good, gentlemen, good. Be back here tomorrow evening and we'll discuss your next sortie. That will be all, gentlemen. Goodnight." When they got back to their camp it was very quiet. They found the Sergeant Major sitting in front of his tent finishing his supper. They sat down with him and one of the Rangers brought them over two plates with food. The best that could be said about it was that it was hot.

"First thing tomorrow, get after the men to repair their kit. Also, set a work detail to go down to the boats to lend a hand to the bateaux-men. We are going out again day after tomorrow. If we have any men who are sick or hurt, get replacements for them. We will want a full compliment whenever we go out from now on. I am going to request from Lord Howe if we can get another two sections to bring our boats up to a dozen. I would not be surprised to see the French increase the number of boats they have on the lake. They must know we are getting ready to move. Well, that's it for now as I'm off to bed. I think these moccasins have attached themselves to my feet."

198

Gris stood up also. "Me also. I'm too tired to take off my moccasins so I think I'll just use my tomahawk and hack off my feet."

With which the Sergeant Major replied, "Try not to ruin your stockings Sir. I'd like them as you will have no further use of them."

# Chapter 44

The men spent the day getting ready to go back out on the scout. There was plenty of work to be done on the boats. Two men from each section were assigned to assist the bateaux-men at the boats. Any boat that looked like it might be in need of some re-caulking was hauled up and the outside inspected and, if needed, new oakum was inserted. All of the muffling on the oars and badly worn oar pegs were replaced. The wool muffling on the oars acted like an abrasive on the pegs. All of the oars were inspected and any with the slightest cracks were returned to the yard and new ones drawn. Each boat also carried two extra oars.

Two men from each section were assigned to inspect the cartridges. They collected every other man's cartridge box and extra cartridges. When these were all inspected and replaced, if necessary, they would then return them, collect the remainder, and repeat the process. Next, they would open the extra cartridge kegs, inspect the cartridges and then replace the seals. Any defective kegs were returned to the coopers and a new one drawn.

Four men from each section were sent to the stores to draw rations for the rest of their group for two weeks, as they had to be back at the head of the lake by July 8th. The remainder of the men worked on the various normal fatigues that went with maintaining a camp. There were tents and other unit equipment to repair plus individual equipment. Several men had to go to the artificers to have muskets repaired. The Rangers and Light Infantry had a priority at the artificers. Their firelocks were repaired ahead of the battalion soldiers. This was because they were constantly out on scouts or patrols and required that their firelocks be in prime condition.

The day went by with every member of Fogg's Flotilla making preparation to once more go out on the lake. The Sergeant Major spent the day going from fatigue detail to fatigue detail making sure that all of the jobs were being completed to his satisfaction. It had also been necessary to replace a dozen men who were not fit for duty due to various ailments. The most prevalent ailment among the men was dysentery. No matter how much it was preached that clean water and clean eating utensils were a necessity on campaign, there was always that percentage of soldiers who did not pay heed. He had always found that a jigger of rum in the canteen would help purify the water. Major Fogg had told him how Roman Legionnaires put vinegar or sour wine in their water to accomplish the same thing plus to better quench their thirst. He had tried it but found the rum more to his liking. The Major knew many things like that.

That evening Fogg and Gris went over to the headquarters to meet with Lord Howe. When they arrived, they found Major Rogers there. Lord Howe introduced them, as they were unacquainted except by reputation. Rogers inquired as to how his Rangers were doing. Fogg replied that they were perhaps some of the finest irregulars that he had ever had the privilege to serve alongside. This helped sooth Rogers' well-known, over-blown ego.

"So, you have served with other irregulars? Here in North America?" asked Rogers.

"Not here in North America, but in various other places," replied Fogg, not offering any more than that. Rogers started to speak but Lord Howe put an end to the conversation.

"Gentlemen, as I have told you earlier, I want to put patrols out on both the lake and the land. I want land patrols to harass the observation posts that are situated on this end of the lake and some to penetrate as far as Carillon. It will be impossible for our entire army to progress down the lake without being observed, but the less time that they have to warn the main French force the better. Major Rogers, you will put out your normal-size patrols in order to cover the most area as possible." Lord Howe paused for a moment to allow them to digest what he had said.

He continued, "Major Fogg, your little Armada will work as a back up force on the lake. I have given you the two extra boats with their sections that you requested. You will proceed down lake past the First Narrows, say here," pointing to a spot on the map, "just past the islands where the lake opens up again, in the area of this large point, here on the east. Here you can act as a rally or fall-back point for the Ranger patrols. The size of your flotilla, along with any of Major Rogers' boats that fall back to it, is more than a match, I believe, for anything the French can or will put on the lake. Questions?"

Fogg spoke up, "Yes Sir. A question for Major Rogers, if I may. Is there any recognition signal that your men use out on the lake? When we met the Connecticut Rangers out there we had difficulty recognizing each other until I ran up an ensign."

"We do not have that type of signal," replied Major Rogers. "Perhaps we should establish one."

"Might I suggest a couple of pennants? One red to be flown on top and one green under it for your boats and a blue one under the red for my boats. They can be flown from the mast if it is up or even tied to an oar. Best not to have them flying all the time only when approaching another body of boats," suggested Fogg.

"Agreed," was Rogers' only answer.

"Splendid, gentlemen, splendid! Then I shall expect you to take to the lake at first light or sooner if you like. Major Rogers, I want all of your scouts back here by, say July 2nd, one week. Major Fogg, you have your orders, you are to act as the deterrent after the Ranger scouts have been withdrawn. Alright gentlemen, good hunting."

As they left the headquarters tent, Rogers remarked, "I don't know how you manage to come off so well Mr. Fogg. No one has ever heard of you before and you show up, a Major, and are given an independent command answering only to Lord Howe. On top of that, you are given my Rangers and boats my Rangers could be using. Can you answer me that?" Fogg could sense the hostility in Rogers' voice. Gris had told him that Rogers had an ego larger than the legends about him told by the Rangers and probably propagated by Rogers himself. He was determined to not have a conflict with Rogers, as it would not be in the best interests of Lord Howe or his original employer.

"I am not sure, Major Rogers, what exactly you are implying. I did not set out to draft your Rangers. As a matter of fact, we had a mixed unit when we first left Albany with half of our force from the 80th Foot. Lord Howe changed the composition of the force. As you stated, we are under the direct command of His Lordship and I would assume that when this campaign is over our little unit will be disbanded. I doubt that when this war is over anyone will even remember that we existed. However, I do believe that people will remember Major Robert Rogers of the Rangers. I should hope that answers your question, Major Rogers. Good night Sir." Fogg and Gris turned off to where their camp was, leaving Rogers standing in the roadway. It was dark out but Gris would have sworn that Fogg was grinning.

When they got to their camp, all was quiet. The majority of the men had turned in. They knew it would be an early reveille as the Sergeant Major had warned them that they might be out on the lake way before daylight. He was waiting for them, sitting by the cooking fire, smoking his pipe.

"Any last minute changes, Sir?"

"None, Sergeant Major. Tell the NCO in charge of the sentries to wake us at the end of the Dog Watch. Good night."

"Good night, Sir. There will be coffee when you wake. Good night, Captain Gris."

"Good night Sergeant Major and I took off my moccasins last night so you're out of luck with my stockings."

It seemed to Fogg that he had just pulled his blankets around himself when the Sergeant Major was shaking his feet. Reluctantly he pulled on clean stockings, his moccasins and his Indian leggings. He had changed all of the rest of his clothing last night before turning in. True to his word, the Sergeant Major had coffee ready. He was just taking his first sip when Gris crawled out of his tent.

"Good morning, Fogg." Gris skipped the military protocol as they were standing alone.

"Good morning, Gris. Looks like it will be a nice day for an outing on the lake. I think that we will alter our operation this sortie. We will have twelve longboats plus the cedar whaler. I would like to use three lines. I'll take the center, you on the left and the Sergeant Major on the right. What do you think?"

"That should work well. If we have an action that requires line ahead, how do you want us to maneuver?" asked Gris.

"How about forming on the center with the Sergeant Major's line moving into place first and then yours. Agreed?"

"Agreed."

Within forty-five minutes, all of the men were up and ready. Fogg gave the command for the Sergeant Major to fall them in and led off to the boats. It only took a five-minute march to the boats and just one hour and fifteen minutes from their reveille, Fogg's flotilla was under way down the creek to their rendezvous point on the lake. The lake was just becoming visible in the gray of false dawn. The boats formed up and Fogg signaled to hold position while they waited for the various Ranger patrols to come out on the lake.

They did not have to wait long before the Ranger boats started to appear from the mouth of the creek and their various beaching points. They all passed by Fogg's boats and the Rangers exchanged comments between the boats in hushed voices. Some comments related to good luck, others related to the marital status of parents and so forth. When the last patrol passed them and were a ways down the lake, Fogg gave the command to get under way. He watched the patrols fan out to their various destinations and he held a course in mid-lake directly for the point where Diamond Island lay. With his glass, he could see some of the lead Ranger patrols off to the east moving up toward the long island that lay just north of the bay called South Arm. The patrol that was headed toward the North Arm had disappeared along the shoreline north of the islands that lay there. The flotilla held its course and speed toward the Diamond Island. Fogg was hoping for a south wind to come up so that he could rig the sails and make tacks back and forth to hold his position. All of the patrols had orders to fall back on his flotilla if attacked, but Fogg wanted to be sure that he could support the Rangers if necessary. The entire day passed in this manner. At the mouth of the First Narrows Fogg held his position. All of the boats had orders to rendezvous at the large island, mid lake just south of the entrance to the Narrows. When Fogg arrived at the island, there were two of the patrols already there. The two boats that were scouting the North Arm had not yet arrived nor had the patrol that was supposed to scout the entrance to the Narrows. Fogg nested his boats on the south end of the island and had the Sergeant Major get the men encamped in a defensive placement. He and Gris then went to find the men in command of each patrol. He took their reports, Gris recording them in his journal. As they were just finishing the reports, the other patrols came in. The patrol from the North Arm had discovered some traces of boats on the western shore but they were at least two days old and a search on shore uncovered no hidden boats. They surmised that it might have been a re-supply for the observation post on the mountain that, by tomorrow, would be driven off by a land patrol. The patrol from the entrance of the Narrows reported that they had spotted some French boats far off heading down lake, perhaps a half dozen. The reflections off the water made it difficult to determine exactly how many. Fogg thanked them all for their reports and suggested that they encamp on the island tonight and get underway tomorrow morning at false dawn. This would allow them to be seen approaching the islands at the Narrows. This should drive any French hiding there down the lake. The purpose of their mission was to free the southern end of the lake from French observation posts and patrols.

## Chapter 45

The Rangers were up and ready to move as soon as there was enough light on the lake for them to be seen. The patrols spread out in front of Fogg's boats, which held mid lake. It was just under two miles to the entrance of the Narrows. Fogg had given the Rangers a ten minute lead as they had to fan out to cover the islands on both sides of the lake. There were a half dozen or so islands that were sizable enough to hide an ambush party. The remainder could perhaps hide one or two men, but not their boat or canoe very well. The Ranger patrols consisted of at least two boats so they were able to pass on both sides of the smaller islands and see the whole island. If you were hiding from one side you would be seen from the other. The larger islands required a closer scrutiny and would take longer to scout. Fogg's Flotilla in mid-lake also made it more difficult to depart the islands without being seen. Not impossible but more difficult.

As one of the patrols approached the large island that Fogg had used to hide his boats on his last trip a canoe emerged from the north end of the island. It was one of the middle-size canoes that the French used that had six paddlers. Fogg was tempted to send the cedar whaler after it but decided against it. He could not afford to lose the cedar and this just might be bait to lure one of his boats off by itself. He signaled to the Rangers not to pursue it. Within minutes it had disappeared behind one of the other islands and did not appear again until later, way down lake from them. It took the patrols all morning to completely inspect all of the islands. Fogg sent Gris' section down lake to just opposite the large bay distinguished by a large red rock and hold station there. From that point he could see down lake at least five miles to where the last set of islands were situated. He could observe these and the ones that lay on the east shore about halfway in-between. It was shortly before noon when Fogg and the patrols came up to Gris' position. Fogg pulled his boat alongside Gris.

"Well, Captain Gris, did you see any movement?"

"None, Sir. If there were any French at the set of islands they may have moved along the inshore side and if they held to the shore line the shadows would have helped conceal them."

"That is probably a good assumption. I think we can let the patrols go on ahead and we'll hold mid lake. I'll have one of the two boat patrols check those two small islands on the west shore and then cut across to join the others. We will all meet at those last two islands there. I would like to station one section there to watch down lake. Do you want the assignment or would you like to give your men a break and let the Sergeant Major's section do it? He might be getting tired of following me around."

"If he wants to take the point, it is good with me," was Gris' reply.

Fogg signaled him up and he drew his line alongside Fogg's. Fogg told him of the plan and he said his lads were itching to be out in the forefront. With that, Fogg gave him the go ahead and his boats fairly leaped out ahead. Fogg relayed the orders to the Ranger patrols and they dispersed to their assigned targets. Fogg and Gris slowly moved their boats down lake in a two-line formation, just far enough apart to be able to row. This made it very difficult to count them from the shore unless you were situated up on one of the mountains. As they moved down lake they spotted a couple of flashes from either a looking glass or a signal mirror from the top of the big mountain on the west shore. He had instructed Gris and the Sergeant Major to keep a sharp eye on the mountain on the east shore just above the point with the bluff. This is where he planned on spending the night as they should be able to defend themselves due to the shape of the point. The rest of the day passed without incident. All of the patrols scouted the islands only discovering where some boats or canoes had been beached in the last few days but nothing new. What Fogg thought were two islands turned out to be three. The patrol that checked the larger one found evidence of a campfire on the island, but it too was at least two-days old. Fogg ordered all of the boats to the point with the bluff for the night. When they had landed he set up a defensive perimeter to the land side and three observation posts to the lake side. He put these up in the trees where they had the advantage of height to increase the distance they could see out onto the lake. When it got dark, one of the lookouts called down that he had spotted lights. One on the big mountain across the lake and the other slightly to the north of it but down closer to the water. Fogg warned all of the lookouts to look alive. Fifteen minutes later, the lookout on the north side of the bluff passed along the word that he had spotted a flickering light up on the mountain to the north of them on the east side. It would be only a mile or so away.

Fogg sent the word along that he wanted all patrol leaders to meet him at his central position. When they were all there he held a small council of war. He surmised from what the lookouts had reported that the French on the far side had seen them land and signaled to the other two parties. The one down close to the lake might be heading for their boats and the ones above them to the north might be considering attempting to take prisoners for intelligence purposes. The area on which Fogg had landed was a rounded point that stuck out into the lake about a quarter mile and was just about as wide. His men were stretched too thin to adequately defend the neck of the point and guard against an attack from the lakeside at the same time. He decided to pull his men off from the point and assume a defensive posture out on the lake. He gave the order for everyone to fall back to their boats and prepare to get underway.

When he had all of the boats out a couple of hundred yards on the lake, he formed his flotilla into two lines ahead with the Ranger boats forming on his two columns. When everyone was in position Fogg had each boat pass its bow line to the boat ahead of it. The lead and aft boats in each column then passed a line to the boat opposite it. The boats were spaced out about six feet apart fore and aft and double that between the two lines. The lines connecting the boats held Fogg's little flotilla in formation with out a great deal of effort on the part of the occupants. In each boat a quarter of the men went on watch and the rest settled in to sleep as best they could.

It was a little after two hours of sitting on the lake that they heard voices coming from the eastern shore. French voices! Fogg listened carefully to what they were saying. It seemed that they were confused as to why the lookout on the other side had told them that there was an English party camped on the point. There was no sign of any party having been there, at least not in the dark. Pretty soon he heard another sound, that funny hollow sound a paddle makes when it strikes the side of the canoe, followed by a whispered "Merde!" and then a "Sshhhhhh!" both of these were followed by a "Qui vive?" from the point. A long silence and then a cautious voice from the lake proclaiming that they were French. The voice from the shore told them to come in closer, slowly. The voices on the lake were coming from aft or south of Fogg's Flotilla but in closer to the shore. Fogg passed the word along for the two forward boats to man their oars and start to pull on his signal. It took a few minutes but eventually the two lines started to make some headway and slowly inched away from the point and the French. Fogg was not sure how many French were present and did not intend to engage them in the dark. After a half hour of rowing he gave the command to stand down. They lay like this the rest of the night.

When the sky started to gather a little light he had the bow hook pull his boat in close to Gris'.

"Captain, we will untie the boats and come about in line. I'll adjust the distance between my line to accommodate your boats sailing at the intervals. Once we get around, we'll pull for the point and hope we catch the French canoes still on the shore. If they are there, we'll rake them with the swivels and then have every boat pour musket fire into the French as they pass. I plan to come within fifty yards of the shore so we might expect some casualties."

"Very good Sir. I'll pass the word along to my boats. Wish us luck," replied Gris.

" I am hoping that if we bloody them they will start to pull back to Carillon." Fogg made his parting remark as he pushed his boat away from Gris'. They gave each other a salute and went about getting ready. The men accomplished the separating of the boats with remarkable quiet and within ten minutes the flotilla was underway and coming about to run up lake opposite the point. The bateaux-men had the swivels uncovered, primed and gave the signal that they were ready for action. The bateaux-man in command of Fogg's boat angled it in so to bring the line within fifty yards of the shore. Fogg took out his glass and scanned the shoreline looking for signs of the French. Sure enough, he could make out their canoes pulled partially up on the shore. There were six canoes and two bateaux. That many boats could mean a part of at least forty from the other shore and heaven only knows how many from the mountain. At least only the ones with boats could chase him if necessary. Fogg kept an eye on the French as his boats pulled closer to the point. He could see the sentries walking their posts and he could also make out figures on the ground rolled in either their great coats or blankets. His boats maintained their approach.

*Can't they see the boats? There is not enough mist to hide us. Is this a trap?* All of this went through Fogg's mind as his boats maintained their approach. Then it became obvious to him. *We are coming from the north end of the lake. They think we are French!* They were within seventy-five yards from the shore when he saw the closest sentry move forward toward the water-s edge, still holding his firelock on his shoulder. The sentry brought his right hand up to his mouth and Fogg heard him call, "Qui vive?" Immediately Fogg called back, "Francais!" The sentry half turned his back and waved them on in toward the shore. Fogg turned to look at Gris who was just off his starboard stern quarter. Gris gave him the thumbs up sign that he was ready for action.

Fogg's boat was now at the fifty-yard distance mark and had pulled parallel to the shore. The first third of his boats were just pulling even with the beached watercraft when the sentry turned back around toward them. In the ensuing minutes the light had improved and he could now see that the person standing in the stern of the lead boat was wearing a red jacket and the men rowing did not look like French voyageurs. As the sentry started to bring his musket up to fire, Fogg gave the command.

"Swivels, fire as you bear on the boats. Muskets pick your targets on the ground!" No more had he finished then there was a crash as the first six boats fired almost simultaneously, their grape shot raking the canoes and the men sleeping on the ground behind them. Some had been startled awake by the voice in English giving the command to fire, but others were still asleep. Fogg regretted firing upon them while they slept but it was either them or his men. The ones who woke up, jumped up and ran away from the shore to escape the slaughter that was going on there as boat after boat passed and fired. The ones toward the end of the line turned their swivels upon the troops who were just south of the beached boats. As the last of Fogg's boats passed the center of the point, the French managed to rally and get off a volley at the departing boats. Soon, Fogg's men were out of range and he gave the command to come back around south. As he passed each boat, he called for a casualties report. Only the last two boats had been hit with fire; so quickly had they gone in and withdrew. They had a half dozen casualties plus two killed. Four of the casualties were minor and two were serious enough to be debilitating. He gave the orders to redistribute the people in the boats so that no boat was carrying any more than one wounded man. He asked the Sergeant Major what the practice was for men killed out on the lake. The Sergeant Major recommended to weight them down and bury them "at sea" so the Indians would not be able to dig them up. Fogg agreed but wanted to get further out from the shore before doing so. They pulled for mid-lake to bury the dead, tend to the wounded and to check their gear. He had the Sergeant Major get the names of the dead and wounded as he would have to report them to Major Rogers. The last two boats were from Rogers' patrols.

They spent about an hour and a half taking care of all of the tasks. Then the Ranger boats went about their assigned patrols. Two boats were assigned to advance down the lake as far as the French Narrows to reconnoiter the French camp and bridge located there. They had been warned to maintain a good distance and use their spyglass. Fogg re-cautioned them about approaching the camp too closely. That part of the lake was a cul-de-sac, easily cut off due to the point were Fogg and his party had spied on the French. It was only a third of a mile across the lake at the point.

Fogg and his boats maintained a position in mid-lake. He had scanned the shoreline where the French had been ambushed and could see that the boats and canoes were probably beyond repair. They would be having a long walk back to Wood Creek and Carillon. The rest of the day was quiet as their pace only required half of the crew to row. By mid-morning they had advanced down lake as far as the Nose and were holding station mid-lake there, in plain sight of the French lookout on Mount Pelee, called by the English Bald Rock. Fogg guessed that the patrol stationed there had heard the firing from earlier that morning. He hoped that the presence of his flotilla would keep the French more interested than the two boats that were working their way along the east shore, clinging to the shadows from the trees. Fogg intended to make any of the lookouts more interested in what he was doing. From his place on the lake, he could see across to the foot of Mount Pelee where it met a little bay. He could see that the shoreline was clear and offered a fairly good landing place. He decided to make a feint for that beach.

From the top of the mountain, the French lookouts spotted the three lines of English boats pulling toward the bay at the foot of their mountain. They reported it to the officer in charge, a regular officer from troupe de terre. Although he had been in this part of the world for a while, he hesitated. Finally, one of the senior Canadian officers suggested that they send out a party to ambush them when they landed. The French numbered a little over two hundred and if they occupied the ledges at the bottom of the mountain they could deliver a great deal of damage to the English. Soon, all of the patrol, except for two dozen who remained on top, was moving down the side of the mountain. Fogg could see the movement from his position on the lake by using his glass. He decided to keep on for the bay but at the last minute change direction for another one just south of it. His boats kept on course toward the original bay and the French kept on moving down to their intended positions. At two hundred yards, Fogg could see that they, the French, were in position on the ledges and in a good position to shoot down on his boats if he were to land. His boats would not be in range of the French until they actually landed so he took them in to within fifty yards from shore. He was tempted to fire a volley from the swivels but thought better of it, as he could not see all of the French. He gave the signal to turn to port and the boats sheared off along the shoreline and away from the French ambush.

The French commander cursed the damned English now, not sure if he should hold tight or pursue them. He decided to send three Canadians down to follow along the shore and see what and to where they were off. The last of the English boats was just rounding the little point at the entrance to the next bay when the Canadians reached the bottom of the cliff. They trotted along the deer path that ran parallel to the water's edge. Cautiously, they approached the point. There, they climbed up on to a large rock that sat at the water's edge. To their surprise the English had pulled into the large bay and had landed their lead boats. One of the Canadians dropped off the rock and headed back toward the main party. There was still time to ambush the English Rangers.

Fogg immediately put out a screen and then sent a half-section scout toward the original bay. This included two of the Stockbridge Rangers. The two Canadians on the rock saw the approach of the Rangers and decided that they would be better off if they rejoined their comrades. There was a small brook that trickled into the lake at the base of the large rock where the Canadians had been watching. Now, while the Canadians were quite woods-wise, they were in a hurry and had jumped down where the brook ran next to the rock. It was a very muddy area and, consequently, they left very neat tracks. When the Stockbridge came to that point, they immediately saw the tracks and advised the young officer in charge of the Rangers that they should return and tell Fogg. It was indeed fortunate as, by the time they reached the flotilla at the landing, a party of at least one-hundred seventy-five French was on its way toward them. Fogg gave the command to withdraw to the boats and pull out of range of the French muskets. By the time the French reached the landing place, Fogg's boat was just pulling away from the shore. The French commenced firing at him as they came out of the bushes, but by then he was fifty yards away and moving at an angle to them. The closest anyone came was a ball that skipped off the water and hit the side of the boat, spent. It had just enough energy left to lodge in the port gunwale next to where Fogg was standing. The Ranger sitting nearby reached out and plucked it out of the wood with just his fingers. He tossed it to Fogg.

"Here you go, Major, this one had your name on it. Hang on to it and you'll be safe 'cause they can't use it if it's in your pocket!"

Fogg smiled and said "Thank you." *I guess one more won't hurt, I'll put you with the rest of them.*

## Chapter 46

Fogg pulled his boats out into the Lake a quarter of a mile and then moved parallel to the shore. The French on the shore followed him until they came to the base of the Bald Rock. At this point, they could not go along the shore so were compelled to go back up the mountain to their outpost. The French in the outpost could see Fogg's boats as they moved along past the rock. Before reaching the next point, Fogg gave the signal to pull for mid-lake and once there he adjusted his position to remain hidden from view of the French camp at the second or French Narrows behind the point from where he had observed the proposed landing place from. Holding station at that point, he and Gris scanned the shoreline of the lake for a glimpse of the Ranger patrol that had gone to observe the French camp. From here they could see most of the west side of the lake. They waited the rest of the afternoon, watching the shore for any activity.

When darkness came Fogg decided to take the cedar whaler and make a quick scout of the bay just the other side of the point. He was confident that it could out run any boat the French had on the Lake. He took three men from his boat and the one just aft of his plus one Stockbridge. They approached the shoreline off the point until they could make it out in the dark. Cautiously, they moved around the point and into the bay. In the dark he could make out the silhouette of Isle aux Mouton and they heard an occasional sheep. About half way around the bay, they heard more than saw an object up against the rocks, as the waves striking against it made a hollow sound. They approached with caution not sure if it was a hollow log or a boat. When they reached it they saw that it was indeed a longboat up against the shore upside down. There was a large hole in the bottom where it had been smashed out from the inside. Fogg figured that the occupants must have scuttled it to keep the French from using it but it had been driven into the bay by the wind and had beached itself. The number on the hull was indeed one of the Ranger boats that had been sent to scout the camp and landing.

Fogg ordered a line tied to the longboat and then they rolled it upright and pulled for a spot between the island and the point. As they moved forward, the boat filled with water and soon was dragging on the bottom. They backed down the cedar whaler until they were over the sunken boat. One of the Rangers reached down as far as he could in the water and cut the line. When they controlled this end of the lake after this campaign, they would come back and salvage it. It was probably in just enough water so that a boat had to be directly over it before seeing it. He would need to make a note in his journal that at least one of the two boats was lost. He would have to check with one of the Ranger NCOs as to how many men might have been in them. He thought that it might have been at least twelve to a boat but was not sure.

After cutting loose the damaged longboat, he gave the order to pull toward the French campsite. When they cleared the island, Fogg could see the glow from at least three fires in the direction of the camp. He could not see if there were any lights on the east shore because the large point in the end of the lake blocked his view. Using his glass, he could make out shadowy figures in the French camp moving back and forth on a regular basis. He guessed that these might be the sentries. Although he had fought the French twice before, he did not totally understand how or why they did some things. Here he was dealing also with La Marine who were, for the most part, Canadians and did some things completely different than the regular French troops. From what Gris and the Sergeant Major had told him, and from his own brief observations, the Canadians were a formidable antagonist when opposed in the bush. They were equal to and, in some cases, superior to their native allies. This was especially true in the winter when the natives disliked venturing too far from home. The Canadians would don their snowshoes and attack a post or settlement one-hundred miles away. These Canadians were the reason the English employed so many Rangers.

Fogg crept as far down into the tail of the lake as he felt safe doing. He did not want a French group of canoes or boats returning to the camp to cut him off from the lake. This is what he feared had happened to the Rangers. He gave the order to turn about and head back toward the flotilla. He kept to the west shoreline until he was even with the point on the west side, just south of the island. He then crossed the lake and made for the position where his boats should be waiting. The moon being in its last quarter he almost missed them in the dark. Gris had tied all the boats up in the nest formation that they had found so useful before. He, Gris and the Sergeant Major met in Fogg's boat, which was in the center line. Fogg explained what they had found and they both concurred that perhaps both boats were lost. One of the Sergeant Major's Rangers had mentioned earlier that he thought that he had heard firing from down lake when they were pulling out from the bay where the French had fired on them. He had dismissed it as perhaps an echo from that firing, thinking that his ears were playing tricks on him. Fogg made the decision that they would return up lake to the rendezvous point in the morning, wait, and see how many of the Ranger boats made it.

When the sky started to lighten, Fogg gave the order to get underway. The rendezvous point was about two miles up lake where it became much broader. From mid-lake, it was possible to see a mile both east and west. The view up and down lake was at least a mile and a half to the north and five miles to the south. This made it very difficult for anyone to surprise you during the day. By the time Fogg reached the rendezvous the Ranger boats were already there except for the two that had been assigned to scout the camp and landing. Fogg nested all the boats and waited for another hour. There was no sign of the two boats as far as Fogg could see down lake.

The advantage of nesting the boats was that it facilitated having officer and NCO calls. The men simply stepped from one boat to another until they arrive at the middle. The disadvantage lay in that it took a little longer to separate the nest and get under way. By eight o'clock, Fogg had decided to send all of the Ranger boats back up lake so that Lord Howe would have intelligence up to at least yesterday for the north end of the lake and whatever they gleaned on the way back south. To insure their safe arrival, he dispatched the Sergeant Major to escort them up lake as far as the south end of the First Narrows. He was to remain there and the rest of the flotilla would join him by late afternoon. Fogg and Gris decided to move up lake as far as the area called the Nose and then search both sides of the lake going north. They would stay one hundred yards off shore and set a man to watch the other column of boats. All others were to watch the shoreline for any signs of the missing boat. They had been searching for about an hour and a half when the lookout in Fogg's boat sang out.

"There's a signal from Captain Gris' boat, Sir. He's waving us to come on over to his side." Fogg gave the command and his column turned and moved toward the point on the west side of the lake, across from the point that he had spied on the proposed landing place. Cutting straight across the lake made him visible from the French camp if they had sentries out as far as the meadow just north of the landing place. Gris' position was already too close to the French patrol trails on the west side of the lake. Gris had moved toward the middle of the bay on his side, which not only increased his distance from the shore but put him in a better position to observe toward where any French boats might come from.

As Fogg approached Gris' column, he could see that they had a man in the boat all wrapped up in a blanket and one of the Rangers was holding a bottle of rum for him to drink. Fogg pulled his boat along side Gris'.

"Keep a sharp lookout." he cautioned. "Who is this, Captain?"

"Ranger Berra. He was in Sergeant Jarvis' boat. Tell the Major what you told me," replied Gris.

"Aye, Sir. Well, Major we was pulled up close on the south side of that point there. That one that looks so black cause of the pines," pointing toward the point across the lake. "The Sergeant was just putting a couple of the boys ashore to spy when a bunch of Frenchies jumped us. They come out of nowhere, must have been hiding along the shore toward the north of that little bay. Was five or six boats of 'um, we didn't have time to use the swivels, barely time to fire a few rounds from the muskets. Some of 'um came off of the point itself. Well, Sir, they killed six or eight, best I can tell."

"How did you manage to make it out alive?" questioned Fogg.

"I think I was lucky, Sir. A ball or something hit me here in the head," indicating a large lump on the side of his skull. "Being thick skulled, like me mother always said, it only put me out. When I came around I was a laying face down on the beach with the water just barley touching me nose. Had blood all crusted down on this side of me head. I think the Frenchies took me for dead or thought I was a going to die. There was five other boys laying there on the shore also but I was the one the farther up. Anyways, I stuck it out until it got dark and then I pulled a log that was there into the water and clung to it and headed for the flat rock where we sometime rendezvous. The wind was blowing too hard from the southeast and I couldn't make it so I ended up over here. I figured it was better than staying on the same side less they come back."

"Good report Ranger. Anything else you remember?"

"Well, Sir, Major. I don't talk the French lingo but I heard a couple of them Frenchies say Sur Langy a couple of times and a man answered them who I took to be this Langy. I heard of him but ain't never seed him and I dasn't open my eyes no way."

Fogg thought for a moment. "All right, Captain Gris. Transfer this Ranger to one of the middle boats and we'll get under way. We'll pull toward the flat rock site and see if anyone else made it. There is a good chance that Sieur Langis has taken fifteen or more prisoners who may or may not know of the proposed landing place. We need to meet the Sergeant Major lest the French come back out on the lake with a larger force if they learn we are still around." Looking up toward Bald Rock, *They already know that we are but may be mistaken as to our exact number and intent. Maybe, just maybe they might come out after us.* "You take your boats and head straight for the rendezvous. I'll check the rock area and follow you on down. Splitting up may delude them even further into thinking we are an easy prey."

Gris nodded his head and gave the command for his boats to head south to the rendezvous point. Fogg and his boats pulled toward the flat rock area on the east side in search of any other survivors. Fogg's men searched the flat rock area for any sign of survivors but found none. The Stockbridge found some signs that the French had been there also, maybe two, three days ago and had camped. It looked like they had come in from the mountains on the east, perhaps over from Wood Creek. It was only four or five miles between the two bodies of water, depending upon where you crossed.

Fogg gave the order to return to the boats and they headed for the rendezvous point. All the way back up the lake he kept one Stockbridge in the after boat with his spy glass watching toward the north end of the lake. He, Gris and the Sergeant Major had spoken about this Langis and Fogg understood him to be a "plus bien partizan". Langis had been fighting the Bostonaise all of his life. *That's all right, Monsieur Langis, I have been fighting les Francais for a great deal of my life and that is a hell of a lot longer than you could ever imagine!* With that Fogg settled down to catch a nap as they headed south. His body did not require much physical rest to renew itself for he could go for days without sleep. However, he did need mental rest on a more regular basis. Cat naps fulfilled that need for him.

# Chapter 47

The rendezvous point was a medium-sized island just southeast of the entrance to the North Arm, about a quarter mile off the point that formed the southeastern end of the Arm. The sun was just starting to go down when they made the rendezvous with the Sergeant Major's boats. They tied up the boats on the west side of the island in three, small nests, one for each column when underway. The Sergeant Major had new orders for Fogg from Lord Howe. As usual, they were verbal so that no written record would remain to give away any of their dealings.

"The message from His Lordship is as follows, 'Party is on for Julius' fifth anniversary. I will meet you there. Bring presents.' That was all Sir," reported the Sergeant Major.

"Thank you Sergeant Major. Did you get any replacements?"

"Yes Sir. I draught enough men out of the other boats to give us a full compliment. I couldn't take any from the dispatch boat 'cause it was one of the new cedar whalers, like ours."

"Very good. Captain, Sergeant Major, let's get the men bedded down. Quarter watches with two Stockbridge to every watch. In the morning, we're going hunting for a present for Lord Howe." Fogg rolled up in his maud. *The army sails on the fifth of July and Howe wants us to meet him there? He cannot mean at the landing place as that would give the whole thing away. I guess the best thing to do is to wait at the northern end of the First Narrows. It should not be too difficult to spot a thousand boats coming down the Lake. Howe had mentioned a false landing once during a conversation, but the place does not mean anything to me. It was a strange name, something akin to Sunday something. Perhaps Gris or the Sergeant Major would know.*

The Sergeant Major woke Fogg just before daylight.

"Sir, the men are asking permission to build small cooking fires. They want to boil up something hot to drink and the like."

Fogg thought it over for a minute and decided that as his was probably the largest force on the lake it would be alright. It might even draw in some French as Howe wanted "presents".

"Alright Sergeant Major. Tell them to make as big fires as they like and if this mist clears off the lake to let them smoke a little. Perhaps it will act like honey to flies."

Within no time, they had several good-size fires going. There was a few hundred years of dead and driftwood on this island. Fogg, Gris and the Sergeant Major worked out a plan of action for the day over a cup of hot coffee with a touch of rum. The naval biscuit wasn't bad if you soaked it a little.

Fogg intended to spend today, June 27th, on the island. Not only would it give his men a much-needed rest but also the opportunity for the French to perhaps attempt to attack them. His boats were fairly well obscured by the overhanging trees on the shore line and they were on the west side of the island. His men took the day to mend equipment, inspect the boats and, in general, take it easy. Some of them used their bean boilers to cook up whatever dried beans or peas they had. One section even took some hominy and jerky and made up a kind of stew. They would not tell anyone how it tasted, but it smelled good. The Sergeant Major told Fogg that these Rangers were not above boiling their moccasins if hungry enough. Everyone slept well that night.

Fogg awoke to the smell of, what passed for, the Sergeant Major's fresh coffee. The plan was to proceed down lake. It was approximately six and half or seven miles to clear the First Narrows. It was another ten or so to the area some referred to as the Nose as it matched a point on the Hudson by the same name. Once in that area they, would split up the Flotilla into the three columns. Gris would proceed down lake on the west side, the Sergeant Major on the east side and Fogg would hold center lake in support of either column. When they were a little north of the Nose, he would send the cedar whaler out ahead of his column. Only its six-man crew with the coxswain, acting as the lookout, would man it. It would be the bait dangling a mile out from the main column.

They got underway about two hours after daylight when the mist had cleared and visibility on the lake was good. It was necessary for them to be able to see well. The French needed be able to see the bait. The men rowed in good spirits, knowing that the Major usually had a good plan and that maybe, just maybe, "Fogg's Luck" as they called it now, would hold for yet another fight with the French. By mid-morning they were just south of the Nose and Fogg gave the signal to split up. He took the crew for FF ½ from the first two boats in his column with a bateaux-man as the coxswain and in command of the cedar. He watched as the cedar pulled away from them. The crew was just pulling at a normal rate and the cedar was doing almost

218

double the speed of a longboat. The cedar carried no extra weight, even the muskets and accoutrements of the men were left back in their regular boats. Speed was the weapon of FF ½.

When the cedar reached its lead distance, the coxswain signaled to Fogg who was watching through his glass. It was a subtle signal as the French were, most likely ,watching. He simply took off his cap, scratched his head and put the cap back on. Fogg swept both shores looking for the other two columns that were on station. He kept a careful watch on the cedar as it moved down lake making a short, zig-zag course as it moved. Fogg and the other two columns were just a little north of the Bald Rock and the cedar had just cleared the point south of Isle aux Mouton when Fogg saw the cedar suddenly come to port and head on a southwest course. It was still moving at an easy pace. Fogg saw the smoke from the lead French boat as several muskets fired at the cedar. The cedar was out of their range and the rounds fell short. Fogg counted the boats as they came out from behind the point. There were six bateaux and they were overloaded. Fogg watched as a canoe pulled out ahead of the bateaux. The canoe was fast and it was barely closing the distance to the cedar. It looked like there were a couple of men in the canoe who were only riding so that meant they were the firepower. The bateaux were now past the point and had still not discovered that Fogg was coming down the middle of the lake. He could see the Sergeant Major's boats with the men straining at the oars, now pulling straight across the bay to Fogg's starboard.

When the canoe looked like it would pull into range of the cedar the coxswain would increase the stroke just enough to keep out of range. Fogg could see the canoe respond as the paddlers bent to their task. He turned his glass to where Gris' boats were and could see that they were on a course to meet the cedar. The French bateaux had altered course slightly to the southwest when it became apparent that they had spotted Fogg's column of four boats. They turned to attack him, leaving the cedar to what they thought would be an eventual rundown by the canoe as, after all, no whaler could outrun a canoe. The French commander undoubtedly thought that his six boats were a match for Fogg's four. He had scanned Fogg with the glass and saw no swivels mounted on the fore posts.

Fogg headed his boats directly into a collision course with the French and gave the command to form a line abreast from the center. The French had been proceeding in a staggered or offset line ahead. They still hesitated as Fogg's boats came into formation. Fogg gave the command to mount the swivels, which were already loaded. It was at this point that the French boats spotted the Sergeant Major's column, now coming in on their port side. The odds now changed from six to four to eight to six in favor of the English with the added element of the swivels. Fogg could see the French commander in the lead boat quickly swinging his glass back and forth from one column to the other. He made a quick turn to the canoe that was unaware of what was going on behind it. Fogg saw him turn to the coxswain of his boat and the boats started to come around to the west, away from the Sergeant Major's column. Now, the French boats were pulling with all their might toward the French camp at the foot of the lake. They had been about four hundred yards apart when the French had made their turn. By the time Fogg made the point, the Sergeant Major's boats were even with his. The Sergeant Major shouted across to Fogg one word, LANGY, pointing toward the French boats. Fogg signaled for them to form to his starboard and give chase. Now, all eight boats were pulling for all they were worth to come up to a range where they could fire. *Come now Monsieur Langis, terror of the North American woods, stand and fight. Let's even the odds.* He signaled to the Sergeant Major to halt and establish a fallback station and help cut off the canoe.

As the Sergeant Major's boats turned to take up a station that cut off the canoe from the north end of the lake and the camp, Fogg turned his attention back toward the French boats. He could see the man that the Sergeant Major had pointed out looking back at the four remaining English boats. *Yes, there are only four boats chasing you now. You out number us, in your end of the lake.* Fogg's boats were cutting down the distance between them and the French boats. It was now about three hundred yards and closing. Fogg could see the French camp, there were two more boats pulled up on the shore and a small cannon at the south end of the camp. He decided to follow the Frenchman in as far as he could without putting his boat in too much jeopardy from the gun. *You are foxy, Monsieur Langis. You want to hide under the cover of your gun. Perhaps today is not the day for us to meet but I will work at it.* When they had closed to two hundred yards, Fogg decided it was too close to the gun and gave the order to come about. His boats assumed a line ahead and pulled for the rally point with the Sergeant Major. When he reached it he could see up lake to Gris' boats. He could make out the canoe being pulled along behind the last boat in the column. He gave the signal to proceed up lake and within a few minutes all three columns were headed toward the Narrows. Fogg called over to Gris, inquiring as to how many "presents" he had acquired. Gris held up his hands indicating six and then dropping two. Fogg nodded his head indicating that he understood. Gris then held up one finger and then took two and drew them along his cheek. Fogg did not understand what he meant. The lead NCO in his boat told him that it meant one was an Indian. Fogg signaled for the boats to move closer.

When he drew along side Gris' boat he asked. "Where is the Indian?"

"There in the center of the second boat." Fogg let his boat drop back until it was even with the second boat. There sat an Indian who was obviously very different than the Stockbridge Rangers. He was almost completely naked except for a wool breechclout and was wearing a pair of burgundy hose with the feet cut off. He was barefoot. He was bound hand and foot. His arms were behind him and were tied crossed and then tied to his feet. Around his neck was a leather thong with one end in the hands of a Stockbridge Ranger. The Stockbridge Ranger looked at Fogg and then inclined his head toward the other native.

"Abenaki!" was all that he said. Fogg had heard some of the stories of the French-Abenaki raids into New England. Some as far south as the Stockbridge villages. There was no love lost between the two. Although he thought that the way the prisoner was tied was a little excessive he decided to let it be. These people had been fighting their war for hundreds of years. The Stockbridge would have fared no better and perhaps worse in the hands of the Abenaki and the French. He inquired as to the other French prisoners and the Rangers indicated they were in the third and forth boats. Fogg dropped back to see them. Two of them looked to be Canadian civilians, perhaps la malice. The third was wearing a blue justacorp and it was difficult to tell to what regiment he belonged.

In French, Fogg asked. "What regiment?" The Frenchman sat silently, a dour look on his face. He was perhaps in his early to mid-thirties.

Fogg asked again, "What regiment?" and again nothing.

Again in French, "Give them to the Stockbridge. They are of no use to me." The Rangers just looked at him but the Frenchmen all responded at once. "La Rousillion Royale".

Fogg smiled and said, "Merci. How many men at Carillion?"

One of the Canadians replied, "Seven thousand and more coming every day." A Ranger sitting next to them reached down into his coat and pulled out a French gorget, tapping it and nodding toward the Canadian.

"That is more regulars then there are in all of New France," replied Fogg. "Gentlemen are not supposed to lie. Ensign, is it?" Fogg used the lowest rank to see if he could get the response he wanted.

"Someone has given you false numbers about the regulars. It is Lieutenant Renard."

With that Fogg started to laugh. The Frenchman looked at him like he was mad. One of the Rangers asked what the Frenchman said that was so funny. When Fogg explained that "renard" in French meant fox, all of the Rangers in both boats started to laugh as well.

"Well, Monsieur Renard, it would seem that you have been outfoxed today and my men thank you for a good laugh!" said Fogg, speaking in French. With that, he gave the signal to move back into position and his column drew back into the center and up even with the other two. Fogg took one more look back in the direction of the French camp. There was no sign of any French boats on the lake. Fogg had decided to occupy the large island in the middle of the lake at the north end of the First Narrows. It had enough area and was a half mile from the west side and a little under that on the east. It afforded a good view in both directions up and down lake. From there he could control the Narrows and make contact with any other Ranger patrols on the lake. His presence there would cause the French to send messengers only at night or by land. He planned on putting out screens at night to block especially the west passage. There would be no fires for the next couple of nights.

*     *     *

For the next two days they lay on the island, watching the lake, putting out four-boat patrols to sweep the Narrows from their island south to the entrance of The Narrows. Both nights they put two boats out on the lake between the island and mainland on both sides. The patrol from the second night thought that they heard a boat, but could not see it. It seemed to be moving to the south and they had spotted no Ranger patrols going north. Fogg put out eight boats on the third night, Friday, June 30th, with Gris in command. This put the boats just at about one hundred yards apart. It was an overcast night with little light. The Rangers would need to rely upon their hearing and instincts to catch a French fish this night. They moved into position about an hour after dark, using the number of strokes to determine distance. Any boat coming from north or south was to be stopped. Fogg hoped that Howe had suspended all patrols north of the entrance to The Narrows, which would make their task easier.

Sometime around 11:00 PM or so they could hear a commotion out on the lake. It sounded like some muffled cursing, some thuds and then silence. Fogg waited patiently to see if any thing else arose. Ten minutes, fifteen minutes, going on twenty and then the boats started to appear. They had all been moored on the east side of the island so Fogg moved over to that side. When Gris' boat came in, he grabbed the bow line as Gris jumped ashore.

"What went on?" he inquired of Gris.

"A French boat attempted to go down lake. It ran smack into the boat on my east side. The lookout standing in the bow of the French boat fell into the longboat on top of the coxswain. That was the cursing you might have heard. The coxswain is not a small man and the Frenchman was, so he picks the Frenchman up and throws him back into the French boat. The Frenchman hits the first rower and knocks him into the man in front of him. All the fighting you heard was the Frenchmen reacting to being attacked from inside their boat. The only one who knew that they had hit an English boat was the bow lookout who is now unconscious in the bottom of the boat. The lads in our boat grabbed the French boat and pulled it along side. It took the French a few minutes to realize that they were staring into English muskets and by that time the next boat over had come along on their other side."

"Any casualties?" asked Fogg.

"Just the Frenchmen who beat each other up," replied Gris who was having a hard time not to laugh. "We have ten new 'presents' for His Lordship."

"Good. Let's get them secured and the lads bedded down. Quarter watches. Men out on the lake get to sleep first. I'll take the first watch, Sergeant Major the second and you the third." Gris nodded an affirmative reply and went off to turn in. Fogg passed the word to the rest of the boat crews. *This bunch was headed north and that means that an intelligence report will not be getting through. Maybe we can get something worthwhile from them. I may send three boats up lake tomorrow to get these Frenchies to Lord Howe. I can control this part of the Lake with nine boats for a half-day if I get them off before daylight.* Fogg then settled down for the two hour watch reminding himself to tell the Sergeant Major to get them moving on his watch. He was to take one boat from each column and the whole under the command of a senior NCO.

## Chapter 48

When Fogg awoke, the boats with the prisoners were already on their way to the head of the lake. Two of the Stockbridge Rangers had gone with the boats. Fogg asked why two were needed. The Stockbridge told Fogg that they wanted to make sure that the Abenaki reached his destination safely.

"You mean you are afraid he will not reach the English Camp safely?" asked Fogg.

With out blinking an eye, one said, "Him only go as far as Diamond Island. There we set him ashore."

"Diamond Island? Why Diamond Island and why would you set him free?" was all that Fogg could muster.

The Sergeant Major spoke up, "Begging your pardon Sir. You being a stranger to the Lake ain't aware that setting him on Diamond weren't no act of mercy or compassion. Diamond Island is one big rattlesnake den. They didn't say he was free." Fogg decided to let the whole matter pass. These people had their own justice and, while he didn't agree with it, he had not lived through a couple of centuries of their constant inter-tribal warfare. He had learned early on that when it came to the affairs and goings on of the natives, you did not interfere. He had heard that even Sir William Johnson did not interfere in some matters and the Iroquois, at least the Mohawks, looked upon him as one of them. Indeed, it was even rumored that he was repopulating the Mohawk nation at a rapid rate all by himself.

As he sat with Gris and the Sergeant Major having their usual coffee and biscuits, he decided to ask if they knew about the place where Howe said he would make a false landing.

"Do either of you know of a place on the lake that is Sunday something? It may be a cove or a bay."

"Sunday, Sir?" replied the Sergeant Major. "Would you be meaning Sabbath Day Point?"

"Yes! That was it, Sabbath Day Point. Do you know its location?"

"Aye, Sir, that I do. It's about ten or twelve miles down lake from here. Almost two miles north of where we ambushed the French and their boats near the bluff point but on the west side. Late July last, over three hundred of the Jersey Blues was killed, captured or drowned there in an ambush."

"We are to meet Lord Howe there. He says he will depart on the fifth. We shall lay just south of it until the flotilla comes up."

"I believe there is an island just southeast of the point about a mile that we can sit behind until they come up. It is on the other side of the lake and would help confuse the outposts on Pelee," added Gris.

"Splendid idea, Captain Gris. This should not go further than the three of us. If captured, the men can't tell what they do not know."

"Aye, Sir but they are all such liars that the Frenchies wouldn't believe them anyway," chimed in the Sergeant Major. "I would also add that if we leave on the dark of the fourth, we could be in place before daylight. That island could well hide our boats on the east side."

"Done then, we leave on the night of the fourth. What shall we do to keep ourselves busy for the next couple of days?"

"Might I suggest, Major, that we could 'spread our net' so to speak every night? It is a quarter mile from here to the shore. If we put out eight boats they would be spaced at about fifty yards. That is a very tight net. The probability is that any French dispatch boats or canoes will be traveling close off shore. It is a long way out around us to get to mid lake. Chances are they would think they can sneak past, that is if they even know we are here. We may not be visible to an outpost. The land patrols could have driven it north. I am sure that they have deposed the one on the east side closest to the camp and, perhaps, even most of them on the east side. It is a short run down the mountain and a quick canoe trip up Wood Creek to Carillon."

"Agreed. Tell the men to get some rest as they may be up all night. Have the bateaux-men check the muffling." Gris and the Sergeant Major went about setting the men to the various tasks. Fogg took time to update his journal and work on his map. The map was piecemeal in his journal but when he returned to London he would have it redrawn into one map by a cartographer. He wished that he had carried his navigational equipment from his baggage, left at Albany. He could have taken sightings that would have accurately marked the places on his map. Perhaps next time.

The day was relatively quiet. There was only one alarm when they spotted a boat making its way south along close to the shore on their side of the lake. Through his glass, Fogg could make out that there were two boats and that they were French. They had missed the second boat as it must have been hidden by the lead boat. He gave the order for the Sergeant Major's column to man their boats and move around close to the south end of the island and wait for his command. The bateaux-men pulled all of the remaining boats tighter into their nest so that most, if not all, were hidden in the shadow of the trees along the shore line.

The French boats were moving very slowly. From his concealment in the brush, Fogg could see that what appeared to be the man in charge was sweeping the shore and islands with his glass. He watched as they disappeared in behind the large island to his north. He gave the order for Gris to man two of his boats and hold in the nest until the French disappeared past their island, then they were to move out to cut off their retreat from the Sergeant Major.

By the time that the French reappeared from behind the large island both of his ambush parties were in place. The French boats came on, still moving cautiously. Now Fogg could see that the boats had only the necessary crews to handle them. They were carrying supplies. Their final destination was probably the trailhead in the bay of the North Arm. The man with the glass was still keeping up his surveillance of the shores. All of Fogg's men were hugging the ground, concealed behind bushes or on the east slope of the island. When the two boats were even with the island, he gave the signal to attack. The Sergeant Major's boats were headed on an angle toward the point of the Arm and were pulling hard. In a short time, they would be arrayed across the path of the French boats. Immediately, the men in the French boat stopped rowing and their boat slowly lost headway. The officer shouted a command to come about. As he did, Gris' boats shot out from their end of the island. Fogg was watching the French boats closely through his glass. Suddenly, the traps covering the "supplies" flew aside to reveal more men with muskets. As yet, no one was within musket range. The French had sprung their trap too early. Fogg immediately gave the order for the remainder of Gris' column to man their boats. It only took a couple of minutes for them to be underway and a few more to join the other boats of that column.

Now the French boats were closed in at both ends with the possibility of more English being on the island. The officer in charge hesitated too long. The English boats had moved into range for their swivels with both groups moving in line abreast. He gave the command to head for shore. As the oarsmen started to pull, Gris' boat was closest to the French and opened fire with its swivel. They had fired deliberately short. The water about ten yards from the French erupted into a patch of spray, with some of the shot skipping off the water and hitting the side of the boat and a couple of the rowers. One of them slumped over into the man behind him, disrupting his stroke, which, in turn, interfered with the next rower. Consequently, the boat had more power on the one side than the other and started to turn toward Gris' column instead of away. The other boat was making more headway and as the lead boat floundered about he ran into the oars on its starboard side, shearing the last two and entangling his own port rowers into the stern of the lead boat. The impact tumbled the fusiliers, who were standing in the centers of both boats, into a heap. By now both sets of English boats were close enough to cause a great deal of damage with their swivels and muskets.

The French officer held up his hands and called for his men not to fire. In one hand he held a red handkerchief, the French signal of surrender. Gris called, in French, for them to put their arms into bottom of their boat and make, slowly, for the island. Fogg signaled for the closest section to get up and watch them from the shore, at the same time cautioning the remainder to stay down and remain quiet. *It's not that I don't trust the French, it's just that they are so French. This was a neat trick. If they had waited just a little longer, they could have caught our boats completely off guard. I wonder why they did not have any swivels or at least a wall gun on those boats.*

When the French saw the additional men on the island, they gave up all hope of anything. Fogg ordered them all to take off their shoes, hose and accoutrements before they got out of the boats. When they got on shore, he then had them remove all of their justacorps, breeches, etc. They were all now standing there in their shirts. This eliminated, for the most part, any place to hide a weapon. He then had them advance, one at a time. One of the Rangers patted them down in search of any weapons. Sure enough, one of the Canadians had a knife hung round his neck, Indian fashion. Fogg gave the order for them to remove the shirts. The one who appeared to be in charge protested.

Fogg replied, in French, "Very well. Sergeant, shoot the man who had the knife and every one you find with a similar weapon."

The French officer said, "No. No. Do not do that!" and stripped off his shirt commanding his men to do the same.

They recovered eight other knives from among the Canadians. He ordered the prisoners bound and had the Sergeant gather up all the shirts and tie them in a bundle. All of the rest of the clothing they piled off to one side. A crew of Rangers had been emptying out the two French boats of all the arms, accoutrements and supplies. He asked the French officer where they had come from and of course, he refused to answer. He next asked under whose command they were and received the same response. He looked around and picked the youngest Frenchman he could find. He told the Stockbridge to take him over to the other end of the island and castrate him, like they had done after the raid on the mountain. Then he repeated it in French, adding that they would proceed in this manner until someone told him what he wanted to know. Three Stockbridge dragged away the struggling, screaming young man. They could hear his screams for mercy all the way to the far end of the island. Then the screaming stopped briefly and there was one, long, horrifying scream and nothing. Two of the Stockbridge came back. Fogg asked again and got no response. He motioned to the Stockbridge to take another. They picked one of the Canadians who had been wearing a knife. One of the Stockbridge reached into the pile and pulled out the one that the Canadian had been wearing and gave a large grin, making a motion like he was grabbing a set of testicles and making a slicing motion, indicating that he was going to castrate him with his own knife. The man started to kick and struggle hard, but two more Stockbridge grabbed him and they carried him away, like a lamb to the slaughter. He was screaming constantly until he made one last scream and stopped. They could hear the Stockbridge laughing from the other end of the island. Fogg again asked the same questions. This time when the Stockbridge came back one of them had blood all over his hands. They looked at Fogg and he indicated that they should pick another. This time they picked the French officer. The Stockbridge with the blood all over his hands marked the Frenchman by wiping his hands on his face. This proved to be too much for the officer who started to loose his balance. Two of the Stockbridge grabbed him and he shouted to Fogg to stop. This was certain death to a man in the wilderness, all bound up. He would tell him what he wanted to know. To die in battle was one thing, this was something else all together.

The officer explained that they were from the camp at the tail of the lake. Le Sieur Langis had arrived at the idea of the trap. His outpost was on Mount Pelee but he himself was at Carillon at the moment. Le Sieur Trepezec was on the mountain with the lookouts. General Montcalm was at Carillon with eight-thousand regular troops and two-thousand more at St. Frederic. Fogg knew the last part to be an exaggeration as there were probably just over seven thousand regulars or troupe de terre in all of New France.

First in English and then in French, Fogg instructed the Sergeant Major to have the prisoners transported to the small island just west by northwest of this one. It sat in the middle of the lake and

228

was a least a quarter-mile swim from the closest shore. He instructed him to give them back their shirts and one blanket for every other man plus a half cask of biscuits. Fogg calculated that this would last them until the main army arrived. He nodded to the Stockbridge to return the ones they had taken away. The French officer was visibly furious when he saw them approach not covered with blood and obviously with all of their parts in place. The Rangers, once more, got a good laugh at the expense of the French.

"Your ploy seems to work very well, Major," commented Gris.

"Aye Sir. It seems to make the Frenchies quite the song birds, if I may say so," added the Sergeant Major.

"It is a very old Celtic device used against the Romans in England. The largest difference being that the Celts did the cutting for real and, of course, they didn't take the poor Legionnaires out of sight to do it. They just tied him up and let the women hold the poor bastard down while one of the women did the honors with the Legionnaire's own short sword. It does seem to work well," replied Fogg.

The French officer was now protesting that they would die on the island without food or water. Fogg reminded them that they had a whole lake full of water and enough supplies to last a week if they were careful. Perhaps one of their patrols would come along or maybe Sir William Johnson's Mohawks.

"Get them in the boats, Sergeant Major," commanded Fogg, and to Gris, "Do all the French regular officers whine like that or is it just my imagination?"

In ten minutes, they were on their way; all of the French in their own boats with an escort of four longboats. Tonight they would set another trap. This time in the vicinity of the island where they had set the French. Fogg was sure that the French lookouts would have heard and seen the activity today. He called Gris and the Sergeant Major over to where he was standing.

"We are moving the camp tonight, just in case we attracted too much attention today. When it gets dark, we will move to the island that sits at the far end of The Narrows. It is almost exactly in the middle of the lake. There is a large island just south by about a quarter mile but the view north is clear for a couple of miles. Any French south of us will avoid us because we are a much larger force, however to the north may be another matter. Yet I still wonder that they only sent two boats and no swivels. Thoughts?" asked Fogg.

Gris spoke up, "Perhaps they have a shortage of boats on their Lac du St. Sacrement due to the need for supplies and ferrying troops on Lac du Champlain.  We had the same problem until recently.  The Rangers operated with very few boats until the orders for new ones were issued.  After this campaign, we will have a problem with storing them over the winter. Sergeant Major?"

"Captain Gris is probably right, Sir.  If you recall, we did not spot too many boats at the camp at the foot of the lake.  Now, they could have been a little north, 'round the bend where we couldn't see them but like as not, they don't have that many on the lake.  They can walk to Pelee and they use an approach from Wood Creek to get to the sites on the east side of the lake.  They have always kept more boats at the main base at Crown Point, with only a few dispatch and supply boats at Carillon.  In my humble opinion, Sir," answered the Sergeant Major.

"Good.  That's it then.  We move tonight. Inform the men."

## Chapter 49

As soon as it was dark enough they embarked and headed for the new island in their three-column formation. With the oars muffled, they moved silently down the lake. Very little light came from the new moon, the stars providing some additional. There was a light over on the island where they had deposited the French prisoners. Some resourceful soul had managed to start a fire, somehow. Fogg only hoped that it did not cast enough light out onto the lake to make his boats visible to the west-side lookouts. The light was intermittent, as if they were blocking it with a blanket and then removing the blanket. A flashing light would attract more attention. Fogg decided to keep all of his boats concealed on the new island and just observe the lake tomorrow. Perhaps he could surprise yet another French convoy before the arrival of the entire English campaign fleet. When he arrived at the island, he had the men pull all the boats up on shore as far as possible. As it became light enough, he would have them carefully cut branches to cover them. They picked up the cedar whaler and took it to the middle of the island where it could be launched from any direction. Within an hour of their landing, three quarters of the men were turned in, the quarter-watch rotation set.

\*    \*    \*

The men were up before first light and had the boats concealed in a very short time. They had been careful to cut the branches very close to the ground from a ways back on shore. Then they had rubbed dirt on the new cuts, both on the branch and the stump. Some of the men thought it was being too cautious but Fogg had impressed upon the NCOs how important it was not to miss a single detail when it came to concealment. He had purposely made them recall times when an ambush might have been averted if those involved had been more conscious of details. It never paid to jump into an ambush, patience being the watchword.

They then spent the rest of the day, July 2$^{nd}$, watching the lake. Each NCO who was in charge of a section or boat had been issued a spy glass. Each officer had their own glass. This meant there were a possible dozen and a half glasses trained on the lake. They observed no movement on the lake what so ever. One of the Stockbridge thought that he detected a slight movement on the west side of the lake very close under the protection of the shore. When they scanned that area with a few glasses, they spotted nothing. When questioned he said he thought he had seen the flash of a paddle and possibly the light color of a birch canoe, but only for an instant. Fogg thanked him for his diligence.

It was a very long day as it was a cold camp. This meant that it would be at least another day without some sort of warm food or drink. The men complained, as soldiers of all ages have complained, but it did not hinder anyone of them from doing his duty. They considered it gave them bragging rights when in camp with the regulars. Of course, the stories always got a couple of extra days added to them. Elite corps always became slightly more elite in their own minds. It was how you got these men to do the nearly impossible things that they did.

That afternoon, a canoe appeared on the west side of the lake making its way north. They first saw it when it was a little under, by most estimations, a mile away. They lay a plan to attempt to capture it or at least stop it from reaching the French camp. They would wait until it was not quite even with their island and then send out two boats from the south end. Hopefully the French would make a break for the north end. At the same time, they would send two boats out toward the north, keeping the island between them and the canoe. That was a tricky task but a possible one. Fogg also ordered the cedar whaler to be manned and ready with one of the best shots seated in the center seat with two loaded muskets. He also wanted the four strongest rowers at the oars. If the canoe attempted to land or otherwise eluded the other boats, they were to attempt to run the canoe down and dispatch the occupants.

As the canoe drew closer and more even with the island, they could see that it was manned by five natives and a white man, perhaps a Canadian. The only difference between him and the natives was his light, almost blonde, hair. Fogg could tell when the canoe saw the first boats, as they visibly increased their paddling. From his spot, Fogg could see the second set of boats as they started to angle off toward the shore. He hoped it was still too far for the canoe to see them. He decided to launch the cedar whaler and gave the signal. The canoe had come out a little further into the lake to cut across the bay that lay to its left side. When the cedar whaler came into view the occupants of the canoe bent more to their paddles than before and the canoe seemed to leap forward a little more. They also angled it a little more toward the shore. The lead paddler chanced to look up and spotted the two boats that were off to the north of them. Fogg could see him look back over his shoulder and shout something.  The canoe increased its angle toward the shore.

Now the chase was on in earnest.  The canoe was headed for the shore and the relative safety of the forest.  All five of the English boats converged on the canoe.  The cedar whaler was the closest and was rapidly closing the distance.  Fogg's men were fresh to the chase, whereas the canoe occupants had been putting forth a maximum effort for almost twenty minutes.  Just when it seemed that FF ½ was going to overtake the canoe, the canoe seemed to pick up a little more speed.  The men watching from the island had to admire the stamina of the men in the canoe.  The cedar whaler managed to get into musket range just as the canoe reached the shore.  The occupants leaped out of the canoe with their gear and started for the woods.  The marksman in the whaler fired a shot and missed, dropped the musket and grabbed the second.  This time he took aim that was more careful and the white man went down like his legs were swept out from under him.  The two closest natives grabbed him and all disappeared into the woods.  The whaler came about and moved a little off shore, out of musket range.  The other four longboats came up to their side.

Fogg could see that they were having some sort of discussion that he supposed had to do with getting the canoe.  All four longboats then moved in toward shore with their swivels uncovered.  The cedar whaler was in the center of them.  The marksman was in the bow with what appeared to be a small grapple hook.  When they reached within twenty-five feet or so, he tossed the line and caught the canoe, which was bobbing there next to shore.  If the Canadian and the natives were close enough to fire upon the English, they thought better of it because of the four swivels.  Fogg watched as the boats returned.  They came around the island and put in on the east side.  The canoe still had some gear left in it, plus two French muskets.  They were the light fusil de chasse type and perhaps had belonged to the Canadian.  They were too undecorated to have been Indian guns.  There were a couple of packs or pouches that most likely belonged to the Indians and what appeared to be a military dispatch case.  Fogg and Gris took it and attempted to read the contents.  The handwriting was very sloppy but the spelling and grammar were quite impeccable.  It had to have been written by a very well-educated French officer.  It told how the English army was finished loading all of their supplies into the boats.  It gave some figures as to estimated boats, number of men, artillery and how it was being shipped.  It said that the English would be ready to depart in a minimum of two to three days.  They assumed it was written either yesterday or early today.

Fogg congratulated the men who had gone out in the boats. They had indeed brought back a "good catch" for a one-hour fishing trip. He then warned them that they must be even more diligent as he thought that the French would not leave such important information as this solely to one messenger. Gris suggested that they put out small patrols, perhaps as little as two boats to a patrol. In this manner, they could have at least four patrols out on the lake, leaving four and the cedar on the island. Fogg agreed but on the stipulation that none of the boats got any closer than just out of musket range from shore. He had lost very few men to date and did not want to start this close to the beginning of the campaign. He also wanted them all to be back to the island no later than sundown. His column would remain on the island. Any unit in trouble was to head toward the next closest unit and all were to head toward the sound of any firing. Each boat should have still had a three-quarter full magazine of rounds for their swivels and consolidating their firepower was where their strength lay.

The eight boats departed for their various patrol areas. Fogg had stressed the necessity of keeping together to support each other. The two boats were to travel in a line ahead with at least three boat lengths in between. This made them harder to spot from head on as the lead boat would mask the trailing boat. They had practiced this maneuver several times while still in the south end of the lake. It took only three to four strokes to bring the second boat up to form a line abreast and therefore bringing both swivels to bear.

It was difficult for the men who stayed back on the island. Sitting and waiting always seemed to take longer. When they heard some firing from way south of their island, they were extremely puzzled. None of the patrols should have been that far south. The lookouts on the south end of the island kept their glasses trained on that end of the lake, straining for some glimpse of movement. As the day started to terminate and the sky grew darker, the patrols slowly returned. First one, then another and then a third came in. The fourth patrol had everyone a little anxious as it was starting to get dark enough to cut down on the visibility. At last, they appeared out of the dark. They had chased a French boat that was heading south toward the North Arm. They had gotten almost within range and the French put ashore, abandoning the boat. It was a bateaux and had supplies in it with a minimum crew. The French had escaped with their arms but little else. They unloaded the supplies and the Sergeant Major took an inventory of what was there. The best thing that they found was bread packed in casks. It probably had been made at Carillon or Crown Point only a couple of days before. As far as the Rangers were concerned, it was fresh bread and there was a firkin of butter to go with it. There was also some smoked ham that went very well with the bread and butter. If they ever could build fires there was also dried peas, beans and flour. Included in the larder was some salted fish. There were a half dozen bottles of brandy, most likely for the officers, which Fogg had stored away for when the army came up. That would be a time to celebrate their good fortune to that point. All in all, it was a fortunate day. Fogg's Flotilla had put a damper on not one but two French missions. In doing so, they had extended English control of the lake to the complete southern half. The French were still free to move up and down the trails that ran along the ridges above the shore but it was a longer communication route. If the Ranger patrols were successful in pushing the French outposts off of the mountains on the southern end of the lake, that control would be even more complete. To do so meant having to gain control of the mountains where the outposts were located and then occupy them or patrol them on a regular basis.

*    *    *

July 3rd started out to be just another patrol day. Fogg put out several short patrols but all returned within their allotted time without any contact or sight of the enemy. About midmorning one of the lookouts spotted, what appeared to be, three bateaux coming from the southern end of the lake. Through the glass the occupants were all wearing civilian cloths and their nationality was difficult to determine. They did not appear to be heading directly toward the flotillas' little island. Instead, they appeared to be searching as if unsure where they were headed. Fogg decided to launch one column. Gris volunteered and his prepared to get under way. As they cleared the island, they raised the spare oar with the pennants attached. As per the agreement, there was a red one on the top and a blue one underneath. The bateaux seemed to hesitate and then there was a flurry of activity on the lead boat. At last an oar appeared with a red pennant on the top and a green underneath. Rangers! Gris signaled them to follow him on into the island. When he reached shore Fogg was waiting there. The three bateaux pulled up and a young man stepped out of the lead boat.

"Lieutenant Witherbee, Connecticut Rangers. Major Putnam's compliments. We have some supplies for you and dispatches from the General."

"Very good, Lieutenant. Sergeant Major, have the men get these supplies unloaded and take a look at what you need. We took a French supply boat yesterday and therefore may be exchanging some items or sending some back. I would also like you to take back the bateaux itself," replied Fogg. "Now, where are the dispatches?" Witherbee pulled out a dispatch wallet and handed it to Fogg.

"Here they are, Sir. Do you have any casualties? We could take them back with us."

"I'll have the Sergeant Major see if any of the men are not fit for duty. I do not think so but it's best to check." Fogg opened the dispatch case and pulled out two documents. One was in plain English and complimented him on his splendid work to date on the lake. It also thanked him for the presents he had sent along and that they had complimented the authors' collection. It also said that if he had found any more to please send them along with the bearer. It was signed simply, George. The second document was a plain, curvy line with nothing else on it. He stared at it for several moments and then held it up to the light. Gris came over and inquired as to what it was.

"It is a map, my friend, a map."

"A map? Of what, if I may?"

"I would suppose a place on the lake. This line probably represents the shoreline at a given point. And this small pin hole, see the light coming through, is where we are supposed to perhaps rendezvous. Sergeant Major, a moment, if you please."

"Sir?" replied the Sergeant Major.

"Take a look at this and tell me if it resembles any particular place to you" asked Fogg.

The Sergeant Major took the paper and looked at it very carefully, turning it around to get a different perspective of it. He held it up to the light as Fogg had, so the light came through the pinhole.

"I don't know who drew this Sir, but I thinks they are a little turned about I should say."

"Why would that be, Sergeant Major?" was Fogg's reply.

"It looks like they drew part of the west shore line, but it's not exactly right. It's backward." stated the Sergeant Major. "See, here Sir. If we turn the paper around and look at it with the light behind the paper, it is the shore line near the Sabbath Day Point and the pin hole is exactly at the Point. Here, here! What's this? At the bottom right corner. Take a look , Sir." Fogg took the paper and looked where the Sergeant Major had indicated. Sure enough, in the very bottom right corner were five more pin holes. Fogg smiled. *His Lordship is a tricky devil. He has read about some of the methods used in espionage in the Low Country. This information is not available to the common soldier.*

"Well, gentlemen, it appears that we are still on schedule for the same rendezvous. Time and place. Sergeant Major, are you finished with the re-supply?"

"Aye, Sir, that we are. We have filled up our swivel magazines and have an extra two rounds per boat stored in three casks to put in each lead boat. The men are complimented out to sixty rounds per man and we still have the one cask of one hundred rounds per boat, all in good shape. We have good English rations to take us through until after the rendezvous. I am sending back all the captured peas, beans and flour. We have received more parched corn and jerky that we can use better, what with having no fires."

"Damn good job, Sergeant Major. All right Lieutenant Witherbee, you can shove off. Winds in your favor so you can probably sail half-way home. Tell His Lordship, we will await his pleasure at the appointed time and place. God speed." The Lieutenant thanked Major Fogg and ordered his men back into their boats. As soon as they cleared the island, they stepped the masts and were on their way up the lake. The bateaux, being for the most part empty, fairly skipped up the lake, as best a bateaux was capable of skipping. The only man in each who was working was the helmsman.

Fogg's men dined on the new supply of parched corn and jerky, plus an extra shot of rum "all 'round". They all rolled up in dry blankets with full bellies. Life was good, at least for the moment.

## Chapter 50

Fogg had been out in the field for so long that he had to work out what day of the week and month it was by going backwards through the various events recorded in his journal. He finally deduced that today must be Tuesday, July the 4th, 1758. He made a note in the journal as to the date and resolved to enter it each day from now on. He called all the officers and senior NCOs together for a brief Officers' Call. They would patrol the lake, same as yesterday, but he wanted two patrols to proceed down lake about three miles to a point where they could see past the dog leg in the lake. From there, they should be able to observe the entire lake all the way north to the Nose. If necessary, they were to either go ashore and climb a tree to improve the distance or step the mast and put a lookout up there. They had observed no lights from the island on which they had set the French prisoners on the previous night, so he also had one of the patrols check that island on its sweep.

Having set all of his men into action, Fogg sat down and worked on his map. It was coming along nicely, although a bit piecemeal. He drew each segment on a page in his journal. The page next to it with filled with notes on islands, bays, shallows and the like. It was a practice of many years that when in a strange place he would make maps and notes. His cartographer friends in London were always very happy to see him return from one of his journeys.

Today was a long day what with all the patrols out. The men who remained on the island set about all sorts of tasks to keep busy. There was a tall evergreen on the island and the men had cleaned out a path up it to a point just below the top. By leaving the branches on most of the tree, a man could climb up there and not be silhouetted against the sky. They had cut some of the branches and made a small seat there. Fogg took a turn up in the "squirrel's nest" as the men called it. Looking down the lake with his glass, he could see all the way to the point with the bluff where they had had one of their fights. He could also see the top of the mountain just north of it where one of the French parties had came from that night. He caught the flash of the sun off metal just below the summit. Steadying his glass, he was just able to make out a white dot on the top of a bare spot on the mountain. Every now and then he would get a flash from the metal on what he assumed was the man's spyglass. On that side of the mountain, it would not have been from the lens as the sun was off to the rear and south of the man. Fogg wished that he had one of the longer naval glasses, but it was too unwieldy to use in the forest. He guessed that the man was watching one of his patrols, probably the one on the west side. *It is most probably a regular French officer. A woods-wise Canadian would have his glass wrapped or the bright work painted or let tarnish. More and more I find these Canadians to be formidable irregulars. They are on a par with the Panadors or Croats and for the most part have good company level leadership.*

When Fogg came down from the perch, one of the patrols was coming in. They had covered the shortest leg and had come up with nothing. There was not a glimpse of a French boat, canoe or even a floating Frenchman in their area. They had found one place that appeared to have had a boat pulled up, but no tracks as it was rocky. Two boats of Fogg's column requested to go out on the second leg of the patrol. The men who had just returned had no objection. Sitting on a hard boat seat, and pulling on an oar for a couple of hours at a time was not the ordinary soldier's idea of fun. It did, however, beat digging a new necessary. Traveling the lake on skates in the winter, now that was fun.

About mid-afternoon, the last of the patrols came back in. They all reported the same thing. There was no sign of any French activity on the lake. There were plenty of signs where they had been along the shore in the usual places but all at least two days old. It appeared as if the French were pulling themselves in. It must be obvious at the southern end of the lake that the English army was getting ready to move.

Fogg had sat by his pack earlier formulating in his mind a plan to get to the rendezvous point. *Around five o'clock I will have the men start two cooking fires on the middle of the island. We all would appreciate some hot food. We will keep the fires up until it is dark and let the fires start to die down. This should also keep any French lookouts interested in this island for most of the night. When the fires are down enough, we will load all the boats and head for the rendezvous point. Sergeant Major says it is about four miles to this Sabbath Day spot. Land the boats get them covered and wait for the main army to come up. I can't imagine they will arrive at that point until mid or late afternoon.* When Gris and the Sergeant Major returned, he told them of his plan. They both agreed that it was a workable plan. It would put them in a good concealed position to observe the lake. Sergeant Major suggested that they stay to the north side of the point, as they would have a better view of the French end of the lake.  He did not believe that they would have any trouble spotting the English fleet coming down the lake.  A fleet of a thousand boats was a hard thing to hide.  With that, he went off to set the men to gathering firewood.  As the lake flowed north, the south shore was littered with plenty of driftwood that had been sitting there for a hundred years.  The men had also formed a couple of breast works out of the dead trees that were on the island so they chopped up some of that.  After tonight, they would have no use for it as in a couple of days they would sweep the French from this part of North America.

At five o'clock, the men started the fires that they had laid earlier.  Two good-sized ones right in the middle of the island.  In a half hour or so, they had burned down enough to cook on and they kept them at that size until they had cooked up all the rations they needed.  When the cooking was finished, they stoked the fires back up and kept them at that point until Fogg gave the order to start letting them die down.  It took almost another three quarters of an hour for the fires to diminish to the point where they did not illuminate the entire center of the island.  As the light faded, Fogg ordered the men who were farthest away from the light to man their boats.  In all, it consumed almost an hour before they had everyone off the island and were on their way to the rendezvous point.

They moved in their usual three-column formation with the Sergeant Major's column in the center and leading the way.  He led them directly to the spot on the point where they had planned on landing.  Quietly, the men disembarked and pulled the boats up on the shore as far as possible.  They spread the dark-brown sails over the end that stuck out and piled some boughs on them.  Unless you were within twenty-five, or so, feet of the boats and looking for them, they were invisible.  The men then settled in for the remainder of the night.  They were formed in two lines back to back, one facing the lakeside and the other facing the landside.  They used the quarter-section watch system to provide security.  Fogg, Gris and the Sergeant Major were located in the center of the lines.  The night passed slowly, especially with the two alarms that they had.  The first was slightly amusing.  The wind was blowing from the south and therefore from the landside as to where they were sitting.  A deer on the way to get a drink walked across the legs of the last Ranger on that end of the line and actually bumped into him.  The next day, it was a subject of discussion as to who was the most frightened, the deer or the Ranger.  Some ventured to question if the deer had wet itself also.

The second alarm was more serious.  On the ends of the line closest to the point, they had heard a boat or canoe pass close to shore. It then rounded the point and followed the bay to the north. They could hear the men in the craft speaking low in French. They came within a few feet of the ends of the boats that were still in the water. Everyone held their breath until they were past. This was probably the French patrol for which they had been looking for the last couple of days. Neither Fogg nor Gris could make out what had been said. Needless to say, everyone was relieved when the sky started to lighten.

*      *      *

The Sergeant Major took his section and moved to the south side of the point to set up a watch. The army would be approaching from this direction. He also put some of the Stockbridge Rangers out as a screen to the west on the landside of the point. Fogg had wanted to be sure that this site was clear for at least a half mile or so back from the lake. When the main part of the army arrived, they could push the perimeter back more. The Sergeant Major also put a Stockbridge up one of the large trees that hung out over the lake. From a perch almost thirty feet above the lake, the lookout could see anything on the lake to the south for about four miles. Looking north, he could see all the way to the Nose. Fogg estimated that they would see the lead Ranger's boats twenty minutes to a half hour before they would see the vanguard. They had speculated at what over one-thousand boats would look like upon the lake. It would be a spectacle that no one in this army had ever seen before. They also wondered if any more troops from the provinces had come in since they had departed on this patrol. Of course, no one expected the twenty-three thousand troops that the various provincial legislators had boasted they would raise. Half that would be more than anyone would expect, even with the promise of arms, equipment and tents. It was the opinion of most of the Rangers that men who resided along the sea coast, far from the ravages of the French and native allies along the frontier settlements were not about to give up their comfortable beds to sleep rolled in a blanket on the shores of Lake George and Lake Champlain. Of course, some of these very same Rangers were, themselves, from seacoast towns but they considered themselves a step above the normal townsmen.

Fogg and his detachment sat and waited. They knew that the main army would have started to embark as soon as it was light. They did not know how long it would take them to clear the boat landing sites at the head of the lake. They could only speculate as to how long the fleet would be once upon the water. Nor did they have any idea as to how wide it would be. The weather was overcast and it looked like it might rain as they sat and waited.

At approximately three-thirty in the afternoon, the lookout signaled that he had spotted boats on the south approach. Fogg motioned him down and went up in his place. Sure enough, just rounding the point way to the south, he could see a line of longboats spread out across the lake like a skirmish line. He called down to Gris to come on up. With his glass Fogg, could make out that there were Rangers in the boats and on the flank he could see what they called the English boat, a large scow-type thing that was manned by the 80th. In fifteen minutes, they started to see the lead elements of the main body. The army appeared to be laid out in what was supposed to be the normal movement order. There were four columns with the two center ones being regulars, flanked by provincials and, the Rangers. The Light Infantry was in the van and Partridge's Massachusetts Light Infantry in the rear.

Fogg could see that the vanguard consisted of the Rangers on the left, Bradstreet's bateaux-men in the center and the Light Infantry on the right. The main body was divided into what appeared to be sub-divisions in order to provide room to row. Slowly the fleet came on, its speed impeded by its size. It appeared to be making about two miles per hour. When the lead boats were within a mile from Fogg's lookout, he ordered the cedar whaler uncovered and brought around to where he was on the point. By the time he cleared the tree, the boat was waiting. He had the pole with the recognition signal attached hoisted and made for the Ranger column of the vanguard. To his satisfaction, he saw the Ranger signal repeated from the lead boat so he knew Rogers was in that boat. The two boats drew close and Fogg called out to Rogers.

"Good to see you Major Rogers. Happy to report that your men are all in good condition and spirits."

"Good to see you also, Major Fogg. I appreciate your taking care of them for me. Any idea when I will get them back?"

"If you will point me to His Lordship, I may have an answer for you. Guide in on that point and you'll find my little flotilla there. I would suppose that you are headed for the flat bay just beyond."

"You will find Lord Howe, just over there with the Light Infantry, I believe. If not there than most likely in the lead right regular column. We're supposed to screen a couple of miles to the north. I would say about as far as the last point." Fogg saluted Rogers thanking him for the information. Rogers returned the salute and bid him luck. *He must have had a good breakfast.* thought Fogg. *He surely was a hell of a lot more congenial than he was the last time I saw him. Must be he has concluded that I do not want to steal his men or his command.* Fogg ordered the coxswain to head for the light infantry division and the cedar whaler leapt around Rogers whaler and cut through the following boats and across the columns. The Rangers rowing the cedar put their backs into the rowing. They had come to enjoy the ability of the cedar to out maneuver a longboat or a bateaux.

Fogg finally found Howe in the center Light Infantry boat. The coxswain went past and then came back around to run parallel to Howe's boat.

"Good day Your Lordship," giving a salute, "my little flotilla is awaiting you on yonder point."

Howe returned his salute, "Good day to you Major Fogg. I see that you have been busy what with all the packages you sent back to us. I assume that this end of the lake is clear of the French?"

"It would appear to be Sir, as far down as the Nose, there. I am sure that our friends still sit up on Mount Pelee, though I have seen no flashes from their glass today. Yet I doubt they would need a glass to see the fleet."

"No, Major, I do not believe they would. We are stretched up lake for about seven miles, best we can figure." Inclining his head over his shoulder, "Alexander worked it out mathematically. We were two thirds of the way to the First Narrows when the last boats left the launching site. I believe that that part of the fleet is about halfway through the Narrows by now." Taking out his watch, "I believe that they will most likely make the camp a little after six o'clock. I would like you to take Fogg's Flotilla and set up on the north spur of the bay. By then I should be ashore, somewhere in the center of the bay, come find me and we will talk further."

"Very good, Sir. Alright men, pull away for the camp." Fogg saluted and the cedar moved quickly away from the columns. When he reached the point, he called to Gris to bring the boats and follow him over to the first point and have the screen move along the shore to that point.

*     *     *

Fogg made sure that his men were settled in. They were allowed to build fires and so had hot food again. This was a luxury when out on patrol on the lake. From their camp on the north shoulder of the bay, they could see the boats coming into the bay and disembarking. From their point and being close to the water, it appeared as if the whole lake was covered with boats with no water in between.

Fogg commented to Gris, "Can you imagine what this must look like to the French outpost on Mount Pelee?"

"It must appear as if the whole English army in North America is on the lake and headed toward them," replied Gris.

"Lets us go find Lord Howe and see if there is any more information available to us. Tell the Sergeant Major that he should not get too settled in as I have a strange feeling that this is just a bit of theatrics. I would not unload anymore from the boats than he wants to repack and keep the men in our area." Gris went off to find the Sergeant Major and Fogg dug out his journal with its notes. By the time Gris returned, they were ready to go. They took the cedar and its crew minus two and went directly across the bay to the center. There was nothing to mark Lord Howe's tent but it was easy enough to find. He was conversing with a group of officers from various regiments, some Fogg recognized and some not. As he had not spent much time in any camp with the army, they all looked upon him as a stranger. Howe introduced him and Gris around and partially explained their various past missions. The regulars showed their usual disdain for irregulars but kept it to themselves, partially due to Lord Howe and partially due to Fogg being commissioned in the most senior Foot Guards Regiment. Most assuming, correctly, that his being here meant he had friends at court. The provincial officers present just simply did not care for most regulars.

Howe again went over his plan of action for this evening and tomorrow. They were to build up fires and allow the men to cook. As it began to get dark, they were to keep the fires going for about an hour and then let them start to die down. Each regiment was to leave behind enough men to keep the fires going at a low stage until past midnight. In the meantime, the rest of the regiments were to re-man their boats, quietly. They were then to move out onto the lake and await the order to be passed to get under way. The men left behind would catch up with them by morning. Howe could not stress enough how important it was to keep as quiet as possible, especially when going down lake toward the landing. The sound could carry clear up to the outposts on Mount Pelee and any other French outposts that might be on the lake. Major Rogers' boats would be in front and make the approach to reconnoiter the landing. Depending upon what he found they would then proceed. If they had to force the landing the Rangers, Light Infantry and Colonel Bradstreet's men would make the initial assault. After asking if there were any questions and answering the few, Howe dismissed the group except for Fogg, Gris and Rogers.

"Major Fogg, I am going to partially dismantle your little flotilla. With the exception of four, long-boat crews and a crew for the cedar whaler, you will return the remainder to Major Rogers.

Captain Gris will remain with you to command one-half of your reduced flotilla. You will take position in the column on the port side of my boat. When we make the landing, I want you with me to cover any last minute contingencies. You are one of the few officers present who has made an amphibious landing and I may require some experience-tempered advice. You know that we have not practiced any of this?" inquired Howe. Fogg was dumb-founded. The army had practiced for the Rochfort landing for weeks. Some of the very regiments that had participated were with Amherst in Nova Scotia. James Wolfe, himself had been part of that expedition and therefore had the experience of an amphibious landing. He hoped that the French decided not to oppose the landing for if they did it surely would mean many casualties.

"Lord Howe, if I may?" asked Fogg.

"Certainly Major, by all means."

"I would suggest that if the French do oppose this landing that the first row of boats going in should have their swivels mounted and loaded. I would sweep the shore with them at about twenty-five yards or so, just prior to landing. The grass at the landing is about waist high and they could conceal a great many men there just waiting to catch us getting out of the boats."

"Good advice, Major. We will pass the word along to the lead wave." The boats pulled on in silence. Around four AM the boats were approaching the proposed landing site. Lord Howe had Fogg and Lieutenant Clerk transfer to his boat and went forward along with Major Rogers' boat. Cautiously they approached the selected landing spot. A canoe came out of the dark toward them and then turned and disappeared again. They were not sure if it had spotted them or not. It did not raise an alarm. They could not see any sentries but could hear them on the shore. From farther down the tail of the lake, they could see the glow of the fires in the French entrenched camp. Howe gave the signal to withdraw and they made their way back to the main body. He pulled his boat close to Rogers and he, Rogers and Fogg agreed that the landing should be clean as the main part of the French were at the bridge head at the narrows. Fogg transferred back to his own boat and had his detachment get ready to make a landing.

## Chapter 51

The boats were already set in order and Lord Howe gave the order to make the assault. The Ranger boats went in first on the left side of the landing with the provincial left wing close on their heels. The brown-coated companies of the 80th landed in the centre and spread out into an "Open Order" skirmish line, each man about an arm's length apart. Howe had gone in with the 80th and Fogg had followed him in. He could see elements of the 80th working their way forward toward the French camp. The waist-high grass blocked most of the view but he could distinguish the 80th by their helmets from which they got their nickname, "The Leather Capps". Fogg could make out the movement of Rogers and his men on the left and an occasional provincial behind them. There were more provincials on the right of the 80th but Fogg was unable to determine who they were.

A runner came back from the 80th saying that Captain Arnot and his company were a few hundred yards out in front and had met no real resistance. There was some occasional firing but it did not seem to be directed at any particular body. The French could be seen withdrawing toward their camp and across the bridge. Fogg took a quick glance at his watch and noted the time was just after six o'clock. There was little or no firing from most of the advance parties. He learned later that Bradstreet's men had gone down La Chute to land at a point closer to the French "Portage camp" and to dislodge those holding it. The report was that the French did not bother holding it, instead withdrawing across the floating bridge and setting fire to it behind them. Howe and Fogg could see the smoke from the landing place.

"Major Fogg, I believe that perhaps the French have cut off the retreat route of their patrol parties and observation parties. I would suggest that you join Major Rogers' party. The provincials over behind Rogers should be Colonel Lyman's wing. On your way to Rogers tell Lyman to take that hill, there," pointing with his fusil, "and keep an eye out for returning French patrols of which there should be many to our south. Clear, Major?"

"Quite clear, General," replied Fogg.

"Splendid. I want you to stay on that wing with Rogers and observe everything you can. When we move out it will be from that wing. Tell Rogers that I will send a runner to confirm his final destination and that he will be about a half hour ahead of the main force. When I get to your position, we will meet and you can tell me all you have observed. I know from your reputation that you have the 'eye' and the experience to assess things correctly. Off with you and God's speed."

*     *     *

Fogg signaled to his men to follow and they were off at a dogtrot to rendezvous with Major Rogers. Fogg had noticed that the landing was starting to fill up with troops. The Grenadier companies had come ashore directly after the 80th and had moved inland a little to make room for more troops. A quick glance out at the lake showed that it would soon be full of boats. At this point, it was not even a quarter of a mile wide. Shortly Fogg and his men caught up with Colonel Lyman's provincials. It took a moment to find Lyman who was still trying to get his men straightened out from the landing. Fogg passed on the message and pointed out the hill that Howe had indicated. Lyman replied that he would put a company up there and Fogg departed to find Rogers. When he got to Rogers he passed on Lord Howe's message. Rogers spent a brief moment assessing the situation and how his men were dispersed. He issued a few quick orders and the line spread out into a close skirmish line, slightly curved. He told them they could build small fires and cook if they wanted, adjust their gear and take a well deserved break. It might be a few more hours before they were to push on.

"What is your opinion of the landing, Major Fogg?" asked Rogers.

"I think that it was fortunate that the French did not oppose us. They could have done so without too much difficulty. It is a risky thing to attempt an amphibious landing without ever having somehow practiced it. I do believe that everyone landed exactly where they should have and did all the correct things once ashore. The rapid spreading out of the screening units most likely unnerved the French as much as the sight of one thousand boats coming out of the mist," replied Fogg.

"I think for the most part you are correct, Major Fogg. I believe that the most confusing part will be getting all of the army ashore and in good order. We will have to keep moving the forward elements ahead as the rest come ashore, else there will be no room for them to form up. Well, might as well make the best of our little respite. Some of the men have fires going already so there should be something warm to drink."

Fogg and his men found the Sergeant Major who had a small fire going and was boiling water for tea. Some of the men, who had been with Fogg's Flotilla, were close by and they had a small reunion, sharing tea and pooling some of their rations. After getting something to eat, Fogg went over to look at the French Portage Camp. It was a set of thrown up works with some picket work and encompassed a fairly large area. The French were wise to give it up as it was meant to keep out small Ranger raiding parties, not a force the size of the one now sitting opposite it. The bridge was a series of pontoons tied into some of the rocks that formed the narrows. Setting it on fire had mostly damaged the rope work holding it together. Most of the planking and beams were still in good shape. The majority of the boards and timbers had caught up against the rocks and were available for repairing the bridge. Some of Bradstreet's bateaux-men were already salvaging the material. The French had abandoned most of their personal equipment and all of their tents and camp gear.

On his way back to where the Rangers were encamped, Fogg took a good look at the army. It had taken just a little over two hours to get them all ashore. The quick advance of the Rangers and the 80th had insured that the army would not be bunched up on the immediate landing site. As the various components had disembarked, they had moved forward to allow the next wave of boats to come in. Fogg could make out the various areas of the regiments without any difficulty. There were provincial parties busy unloading supplies and some of the artillery barges were ashore waiting to be unloaded. Fogg thought that some of the artillery should have been unloaded and set up already but he was also aware that the artillery had been a problem from the very start. Too many artillerymen had been drawn off to go to Louisburg and Captain Ord had struggled to get as much done as was possible. Fogg had heard that he only had forty-something real gunners, the rest being draughts from the regiments.

When Fogg found his men they said that the Major had sent a runner over to tell him that they were moving out in an hour, which was thirty minutes ago. His men were all ready to go, so they proceeded to go to the head of the Ranger camp where Rogers was. Rogers nodded in recognition. He signaled and a group of four Rangers moved out as the advance or point as some of the Rangers called it. Rogers' party split in to four, separate columns and moved out behind the advance guard. In the tall grass they marched about twenty-four feet apart in what is termed "Double Distance." When they had advanced past the French camp at the bridgehead and were headed into the brush, Rogers signaled once more and they closed in to Extended Order at about twelve feet. When they had passed the deserted French camp, they had caught glimpses of some of the French over on the other side of the river, moving off down the portage road.

Rogers turned around to Fogg, "Major, have you noticed any Indians with the French? I have seen nary a one and there should be hundreds of them."

"We saw only a couple out on the lake over the last two weeks. Perhaps Montcalm does not have that many with him. Any idea what it might mean?" queried Fogg.

"It might mean that they couldn't raise any to come south or that the hellions at La Presentation are putting together a party to visit the Mohawk Valley and threaten our back door."

"That is at least a couple of hundred miles from here and would require them to pass through Iroquois country. Would not the Iroquois oppose them?"

"They ought to but I don't trust the Iroquois nor Sir William entirely. He looks out mainly for his own interests. Johnson was supposed to be here already but you don't see him do you? We could use his few hundred Mohawks to weed out any French ambushes. As it is, we'll have to sacrifice good Rangers instead." *I take it that you do not care much for Sir William. According to quite a few people Johnson is not the only one who looks out mainly for himself. Of course then, that is really human nature, isn't it,* thought Fogg to himself.

Rogers called a halt a few hundred yards above the first set of real falls in La Chute. There were smaller rapids and riffles in it from the French bridge down, but these were the first falls and Fogg thought that they actually were more a set of cataracts than falls. They halted on a small rise just above where the Indian trail was located. He pointed off to the northwest a little and told Fogg that it was over in the valley on the other side of that ridge that the snowshoe fight had occurred. Rogers checked his watch and said that the army should be starting to move in about a half hour. Their mission was to proceed down the Indian trail to where the Bernetz stream joined La Chute. There they were to secure a suitable ford. Rogers pointed out that the rain might have raised all of the fords.

Fogg had seen the map that Howe had, which showed the proposed path down the west side of La Chute. He had been made to understand that the Indian path could be made suitable for the artillery. He wanted to drop down to the path and see for himself.

Rogers said he would meet him at the brook. Fogg and his two-dozen Rangers moved on down the slope to where the path ran along the river. Between it and the river was, at the most, forty yards in most places. Howe's right flank column would be barely able to pass through there as the area was full of some sort of alders that Fogg did not recognize. The path itself was exactly that; a path worn into the earth from years of single-file passage. Fogg could just barley make out Rogers column moving along the ridge and in some places they were too far from each other. The river itself was about twelve to twenty feet wide in most places and was running fast as it tumbled down the cataracts and then twisted back and forth until the next set of falls which Fogg could hear ahead of them. The senior NCO pointed out that they were about two hundred yards from where the two streams joined. The whole of La Chute at this point passed through a valley that had been worn over the thousands of years that the two lakes had joined. Across on the east bank, Fogg could see that the land rose rather steeply. He had no idea how far it was to the portage road from where they were. He also had serious doubts about the army marching down through this area. His opinion was that they should reverse their plan and push their way down the portage road. For some unknown reason both General Abercromby and Lord Howe appeared to be in a hurry to press on to the attack. He realized that they were acting upon faulty reconnaissance. Whoever the officer was that said that the path could be used for artillery was sadly in error.

Fogg and his men moved down the path cautiously, slowing even more as they approached the place where Bernetz joined La Chute. They then proceeded west along the Bernetz until they joined Rogers who was about one hundred yards up from the junction. The forest came right down to the brook on both sides. There was more of the alder that he had seen along the river. One of the Rangers had told him that they called it Cripple Brush because after a day of marching through it and getting swatted by it you felt like a cripple. Bernetz Brook was a stream about ten feet wide and, while usually slow and sluggish at this point, today it was running a little fast and higher than usual. One of the Rangers was working his way across the brook and it was up to his waist. He had his moccasins off and hanging around his neck so Fogg assumed it was muddy on the bottom.

When he came up to Rogers, the Major asked, "Care to go for a swim Major?" Fogg sat down and took off his moccasins and stockings. Without hesitating, he went down the short bank and stepped off into the brook. It was July and the water was still ice cold. There was no gradual getting in. The water started out at almost waist height. Once or twice he felt something hit his legs but in the muddy water he could not see what it was. When he got to the other side, the Ranger reached down and offered him a hand.

"What was in the brook that kept hitting me in the legs?" he asked.

"Trout Sir, this stream is full of trout. Sometimes so many you would think you could walk across on them," was the answer he received.

Fogg moved up the bank and sat down to put on his footgear. The sun was out and it was warm so his clothing would be dry in no time. After he finished, he took in his surroundings while waiting. The area was thickly wooded with lots of brush close to the brook. He could make out a path that led away to the east and looking across the brook, he could see where it ran on that side. He looked at the track, if you could call it that, barely wide enough for two men to pass side by side. This was going to string out Howe's columns to twice their length and at the same time double their marching time to reach the lower falls. He began to wonder about the intelligence that had been presented to Lord Howe in regards to this route. He knew that Rogers and at least one regular officer had made the reconnaissance that resulted in the map which led Howe to select this route. Rogers did not seem too concerned about the route they were taking. When Rogers came over, Fogg asked him if he still thought that Howe's army could travel this route. Rogers just shrugged it off and said that it had grown in a little since late this spring and moved off down the track with his lead elements.

Fogg thought about sending two of his men back to inform Howe of the condition of the route he was planning on taking but thought better of it. It was not his command and perhaps Lord Howe had considered this when making his choice. After all, Howe was an experienced, capable officer. With that, Fogg signaled for his men to move off down the trail after Rogers. They crossed a couple of more small brooks and a swale before starting up a ridge. Rogers had signaled for quiet when they reached a large curve in the river. He indicated that the saw mills were just ahead and that there was a large body of soldiers normally stationed there. He made a swing slightly to the north to put more area between his force and the sawmills. Fogg could hear the falls and determined that these were probably the largest of all that they had passed.

It took them another half hour before Rogers signaled for a halt. The Rangers immediately went down into a defensive position. Rogers motioned for Fogg to come forward to where he was. When

Fogg got up to him, Rogers pointed out the falls and the sawmills. The French had a small set of works thrown up there and it looked like they had been there for a while as the grass had grown back over them. Fogg could see French regulars there, but could only guess at their regiments as he was unable to see distinctive button and pocket patterns. He did spot one officer that was most likely a general officer but could not be sure. Where Rogers had stopped his men was somewhere between two to three hundred yards northeast of the sawmills, on a high ridge that ran off to the north. From this point, Rogers said it was possible to scc both lakes. He pointed out where the French fort, Carillon lay. There was some activity on the rise of ground that blocked their view of the fort, but they could not quite make out what was going on. They could hear the sound of axes. Fogg estimated that they were about four or five hundred yards from that spot. It was difficult to tell due to the trees. He could also observe the road that led up from the bridge at the sawmills toward the fort.

Rogers told Fogg he was taking a small party back to meet up with the Provincials who were following him. He did not want them to run afoul of the sawmill and alert the French. Fogg looked at his watch it was just three hours past noon. The day had slipped by rapidly. It was going to be late in the day before Howe and his columns could get in position to attack the French at the sawmills, perhaps too late. Fogg had taken out his glass and was looking toward the heights to the east, trying to determine where the French were on the height when he heard the firing back off in the direction from which they had come. He quickly turned toward the French at the sawmill, thinking that perhaps the Provincials had run into them. He could see that the French were as confused as he was as to the cause. They were looking in the same direction. The firing continued sharply for what Fogg thought was fifteen or twenty minutes and then started to taper off. Soon there was only occasional firing. Whatever it was, it was over. Fogg was the most senior officer present so he held his position. He sent his senior NCO with half of his detachment back to find Major Rogers and find out what had happened. There was still some occasional firing off in that direction that Fogg took for perhaps pockets of resistance. If one side or the other had broken, there would still be units that were more experienced and they would stand and fight. To most British regulars anything was better than running off into the North American wilderness.

An hour later, the NCO returned with news of the action. It appeared that one of the French outposts or patrols had been returning from the direction of Mount Pelee or someplace and had been forced to leave the patrol trail due to the English army being on  part of it. Some were of the opinion that they were lost and some were of the opinion that they had intentionally ambushed the head of the English columns.  At this point the NCO hesitated.

"Go on man, what else?" asked Fogg.

"Lord Howe was killed,"  said the man, flatly, "almost in the very first of the action."

Fogg was stunned, "Are you positive that he was killed?"

"Yes Sir.  Major Rogers himself told me.  The Major requests that you maintain this position until he returns."

"Does anyone know how many French were in the party?" demanded Fogg.

"They say anywhere from four to five hundred.  We seen a great many dead Frenchmen on this side of the Bernetz.  Major Rogers and some of Lyman's provincials shut the backdoor on the French."  Fogg sat pondering the event as he had heard it.  He wondered how the French, especially the Canadians who were so familiar with the area, had become lost or disoriented.  It was true that the English were blocking the ford that Fogg and Rogers had used to cross the Bernetz.  There had to be at least a half dozen more fords as Rogers had indicated as much.  These two Frenchmen who were in charge of the outpost, Langis and Trepezac, they did not seem to be such incompetents.  Fogg suspected that they had intentionally ambushed the head of the English column, to throw it into panic and perhaps gain some additional time and space.  What they probably had not counted on was Rogers and the Provincials being ahead of them already. He warned the men to keep a sharp eye toward the north-west, just in case some of them had rolled past Rogers and Lyman and were circling around.  He had some of the Rangers watching the French at the bridge to see if any parties came in from the south.  Earlier there had been a trickle of men coming down the portage road but that had died off.  He turned his attention toward the area where he could hear the sounds of many axes.

He could see all the way to the vista cut from the fort along the lakeshore.  There was some activity down in that area also, but the distance was too far to tell exactly what.  It looked like they were putting up some works.  He was unable to determine exactly.  The area from the height in front of him also gave evidence that the French might be constructing some works.  Occasionally, he could see and hear a tree fall.  When there was no other noise from below, he could just hear the sounds of many shovels. In his little band, there were two Stockbridge Rangers.  He decided to send them in on a reconnaissance to see if they could get close enough to observe the

French. They stripped down to just their breechcloths and moccasins and carried only their knives and tomahawks. They smeared some of the black loam that was on the ground on themselves and departed. Fogg marveled at how quickly and silently they disappeared into the forest. One minute they were there and the next they were gone. As he waited for further developments, he jotted down all that had transpired into his journal, including a simple map of their route to this location and a diagram of the French works below him at the sawmill.

His mind kept wandering back to the fact that Howe had been killed. *This is going to put a twist in the whole campaign. Abercromby is a damn good logistical officer but not a field officer. The rest of the officers present are not anywhere near the caliber of Howe. Gage comes the closest but does not have the personality to draw the army together like Howe did. Lee and that ilk are back stabbers. This work that is going on over on that height is going to change things also. They will need to come up with a new plan from the one decided upon previously. This is also going to change my status with the army. No one knows exactly why I am here, not even Abercromby as Howe did not choose to inform him, this being a Royal's matter. I am not authorized to disclose it to General Abercromby. Gris knows, but he was sworn to secrecy by Howe. My mission may have just come to a halt. I can show the General my commission papers and Moneypenny will vouch for my status on Lord Howe's staff. I had best just play it out. Save my Royals' paper as a last resort.*

Fogg's thoughts were disturbed by the return of the two Stockbridge Rangers. They had been able to get close enough to see what the French were up to. They were building a set of earthworks that seemed to stretch all the way across the top of the height. They could not say how far it went but could hear men working in both directions. When asked how high they said as tall as a man. This meant to Fogg that there was a ditch in front of it as deep as a man. Fogg asked about the sound of axes. They said it seemed that the French were cutting trees in front of the line to clear a place to shoot Englishmen. Fogg asked what they were doing with the logs and they said that they were pulling them in behind the lines. Fogg guessed that they were going to eventually put a row or two of logs on top of the works. He asked if they had cut down all the trees and the Stockbridge said no. The trees directly in front of the works were still standing. Fogg found this strange, but considered that they were saving them until last as they were closer and would be less work to get in. He thanked the Stockbridge who redressed and wiped off some of the dirt they had used before going out on the mission.

As the day wore on and the sun started to set, Fogg thought that indeed it had been a long day and that it was going to be an even longer night.

## Chapter 52

Fogg and his party sat on the ridge all night. He had dozed off a few times but not slept. He was awakened by one of the Rangers who said that there was some activity off to the northwest, just below them on the ridge. Fogg moved off to see what it was. Just as he arrived at the point, Major Rogers and a large party of Rangers came in.

"Good morning, Major Fogg. Did you sleep well?" whispered Rogers.

"Like a log, on the bare ground," was Fogg's reply. "What is the news of the army?" Rogers sat down and brought Fogg up to date. Lord Howe was dead, killed with a single shot through the breast. The Light Infantry had responded well to the ambush, having been supported by some Provincials from the left column. He, Rogers, along with some of Lyman's men had closed in on the back of the French ambushers and somewhere around a hundred and fifty had been killed and an equal number captured. Most of the army had become disoriented and spent the night in the woods where they halted. The sporadic firing during the night was as best anyone could tell the English firing at nothing or themselves. He had no idea of the casualties from the last night. The General was withdrawing the army back to the landing place to regroup. Bradstreet's boys had rebuilt the bridge and they were going to punch their way down the portage road.

Rogers had brought a relief party with him, he was returning to the landing, and the General wanted Fogg to come back with him. He was to leave his men at the outpost. On their way back to the landing Fogg observed that the path was littered with English equipment. Men had thrown away everything they did not need immediately. There were even a few muskets, which the Rangers picked up along with the many cartridges scattered along the trail. The powder could be dried out and the lead ball was very valuable. When they reached the landing, Fogg was shocked at the sight that greeted him. Yesterday, they had been an army that had the attitude of conquering the world, or at least this part of North America. Today, they were a slightly disoriented tangle of men. The regiments seemed to be somewhat sorted out but there was no semblance of companies. The Rangers and the 80th seemed to be functioning as

256

cohesive units. The light infantry companies of the regiments seemed to be holding it together. The rest were not doing so well, with the exception of Bradstreet's men. They had rebuilt the bridge and Bradstreet had led a force made up of elements of the 44th Foot and 60th Foot, Captain John Stark's Rangers and two of the Massachusetts regiments down the portage road. Bradstreet kept sending back word as to his progress and he was half way down the road and there were no French in view.

Rogers dropped off his men in his area and he and Fogg continued on over to where the General was set up. Abercromby had spent the night in the woods with the 44th Foot and a part of the 55th. He did not know until morning that most of his army had gone back to the landing.

The General greeted him with, "Major Fogg. Major Rogers tells me you spent the night between the sawmills and the French fort. What can you report?"

"Sir, that is correct. The French have a small force at the sawmills, perhaps two battalions. There appeared to be a general officer there but I do not think they will hold that position. The entire area is surrounded by elevated ground and artillery would have the advantage. I believe they will withdraw. They are in the process of fortifying the height of land between the sawmills and the fort. There are two vistas cut, one along the lake the other along La Chute."

"A works? Are you positive?" asked the General.

"I sent in two Stockbridge Rangers who were able to approach the French and observe their labors. They describe the earthwork as high as a man, with the French pulling logs inside to possibly reinforce the top of the works. They were clearing a field of fire in front of the works. I could not see it myself from our position but I should imagine it would be complete. After all Vauban was a Frenchman and the Marquis de Montcalm is an experienced officer." Abercromby thought for a few moments. He then remarked on how Bradstreet had insisted upon pushing on down the portage road. Major Rogers spoke up saying that Bradstreet's idea was probably the most likely to succeed. He also said that it was time to get his army back on their feet and be ready to move up to where Bradstreet was. He asked Rogers if he would excuse them for a moment. When Rogers left, Abercromby told Fogg that he was not sure what Fogg's position was with the army.

"General, I do not understand your question," was Fogg's answer.

"What I mean is, Major Fogg, how did we end up with you? I have yet to see any other Guards officer in North America. Lord

Howe never explained where he inherited you from. You are the only officer present who is not part of a regiment or assigned to my staff. Can you clarify all this for me?"

"General, I am an observer sent directly to Lord Howe, from Horse Guards. I had only verbal orders to meet and report directly to Lord Howe. The written orders I carried, I delivered directly to his Lordship. Lord Howe did not make me privy to them. The only part that he did impart to me was that I was to observe light infantry and ranger tactics with an eye for the future development of them. That is all that I know, Sir." *Well, it's almost true, at least the observing light infantry and rangers.*

The General took a few minutes to digest all that Fogg had said. Fogg had noticed that the General was a little slow on responses, always careful in what he said.

"Very well, Major Fogg. I believe that I shall leave things as they are. See your friend, Captain Gris, is it? Tell him that he is to give you a half dozen men to act as a reconnaissance section. I shall announce it at the next officers meeting, until then anyone questions it tell them to see Brigadier General Gage, who is taking over the second position. You can report to him when you have anything to report. Otherwise yours is an independent command. That will be all." Fogg gave a brief salute and turned away to seek Captain Gris. The brown coats of the 80th were not difficult to find. Gris spotted him coming along the street.

"Fogg, where have you been? You heard about Lord Howe, yes?"

"Yes, Rogers told me about Lord Howe. I just came from the General. I am to carry on with my mission of observing the light infantry and rangers for further tactical development." Gris looked at him with a blank look and then caught the drift of what was going on.

"Splendid, Major Fogg, splendid. Can I be of any assistance?"

"It is strange you should ask. The General says you are to provide me with at least a half dozen men to man my reconnaissance section," replied Fogg with a grin.

"I will do better than that, my friend. How about a dozen, hand picked by myself and all woods-wise?" offered Gris.

"That would be very kind of you." Stepping closer, "Where will you be on the advance, when it happens." Gris indicated that they would be on the right of the line toward LaChute. Fogg allowed as he might take a short walk over that way when the assault started. He planned on grabbing some food and then heading down the portage road to link up with Bradstreet's force. He also warned Gris of the works that the French were building at the same time telling him that it was not common knowledge.

"Tell me Robert, were you nearby when Howe was hit?"

"No, we were about thirty to forty yards from that position. As you know, the brush is very thick along through there and we could not yet see where the French were firing from, as there was a lot of smoke hanging in the air. I spoke to Moneypenny later and he said that he was only five or six feet from Howe when he was hit and that Howe simply fell over backwards. Moneypenny said his hand quivered a little but it was most likely a nerve reaction. The ball struck him in the breast. He said that he didn't think that he suffered. Too quick," was Gris' reply.

"Sad indeed. Well, I'll see you at the saw mill, if not before. Good luck Robert."

"And the same to you Ethyrial," replied Gris. "If the French take you, dazzle them with your Chinese commission and baffle them with your Mandarin." With that Fogg went to find his main pack that was still in his boat. The bateaux-man who supervised Fogg's boat called to him. All of the Ranger boats and his were off on the far right hand of the beach. Fogg retrieved his pack and took out enough rations for two days and put them in his haversack. He also added to his ammunition, storing it in the haversack as well. He now had enough rounds to complete one and a half days. He sat down on a driftwood log near the bow of his boat and ate the jerky and biscuit that he had set aside. By the time he had finished he saw the twelve men from the 80th coming along the line of boats. There was a corporal in charge. When they got up to him, the corporal started to come to the position of most attention and Fogg cautioned him never to do that when in the proximity of the enemy.

"Corporal Elias, 80th Foot reporting as ordered to Major Fogg."

"Very good, Corporal Elias. Sit your men down and I'll explain what we are up to as I finish my rations." Fogg explained to them, between mouthfuls of food, that they were a reconnaissance group and their next mission would take them down the portage road to meet up with Colonel Bradstreet and his bateaux-men. He told the Corporal to organize his men into three, four-man squads with a senior private in charge of each squad. He also explained that unless they were directed to do differently, they were to always march at the ready and, if fired upon, to go immediately to the down position. When he finished eating and had stowed his pack in the boat, they started out for the footbridge and the head of the portage road. Fogg glanced over his shoulder as they approached the bridge. His men were arranged in the four-man squads with the space of a squad between each squad. As they closed on the bridge, the two files simply folded into one and they crossed the bridge with ease. Once on the other side they opened back to the two files. *These Leather Capps are going to do well. I did not have to give an order for that maneuver. Gris did pick them well.*

Fogg marveled at the ease with which his little section moved down the road. There was no talking, or excessive noise. They automatically opened their files up so that they were moving down the two sides of the road. The men on the left file observing the right side of the road and those on the right observing the left side of the road. The last two men in the last squad kept turning around, sweeping the rear of their march.

Fogg noted that as they left the bridgehead, the road rose as they went up a small hill about twenty-five or thirty feet higher than the level of the bridge. Once they had gained the top, it leveled off and continued that way for about a half mile or so before it started to descend gradually. It remained descending all the way down to the sawmills. Rogers had mentioned that the river fell about two hundred or so feet from lake to lake. The portage road was relatively straight but with just enough curve in it to limit visibility because of the forest. The last one third of it was fairly straight and Fogg could see almost to the last falls. He could make out Bradstreet's men and a piece of a set of works, probably at the sawmills. The French had cleared the portage road along the Indian portage trail. As the Indians did not use wheeled vehicles, the pitch of the hill did not mean anything to them. Fogg thought it must be a hell of a ride when moving anything with wheels down this road.

When he reached the sawmill, he found Bradstreet supervising the repair of the works and the sawmill bridge, which the French had set on fire. Bradstreet turned to look at the party coming down the road and waved Fogg over to where he was.

"You are Major Fogg, are you not?"

"Yes Colonel," replied Fogg. "Did you engage the French or had they already withdrawn?"

"Oh they were gone when we got here. I understand you spent the night on a hill nearby. Which one was it?"

Fogg pointed out the hill. "It was that one. You can observe both lakes from there plus the fort or at least its vistas. I would guess in the fall and winter you could also see part of the fort."

"Are you here to join us or are you on a separate mission?" inquired Bradstreet.

"I am to attempt to see if I can ascertain any more information regarding what the French are up to. I observed two battalions here yesterday and now I would guess that they are between me and the height of the land."

"I would believe that you are correct in thinking that. I would suggest that you might go there," pointing to a mountain that rose to the south of where they stood. It is called Montagne de Serpents de Sonnettes by our French friends. You can call it Rattlesnake Mountain," said Bradstreet with a grin.

"Thank you Colonel, I understood the French. I believe that we will take a stroll up that way. From the direction that I heard the axes, we should be able to see where they are working."

"Good luck and by the way, according to Rogers, the rattlers are on the bottom area of the south-east slope, but you know how Rogers exaggerates," said Bradstreet, trying not to laugh.

"I'm beginning to think that Rogers is not the only one who likes to spin a tale," replied Fogg flashing a big smile to Bradstreet. This was too much for Bradstreet, who could no longer contain himself from laughing. He called after Fogg,

"I think this is not your first war, Mr. Fogg! You take it too seriously." As they headed back up the road to gain the spot where the mountain appeared to begin, Fogg thought to himself, *This Bradstreet is one hell of an officer. His men are the roughest, most undisciplined in the whole army yet so far he has accomplished admirably every job that has been foisted upon him in this campaign.*

*    *    *

Fogg and his men reached the point on the portage road just above the second level stretch where the mountain named for the Rattle Snakes seemed to come down to meet the hill. Yes, there it was and Fogg had not noticed it on the way down to the falls. A faint trail coming in from the south that led up along the east edge of the ridge that ran up the mountain. He wished that he had borrowed a Stockbridge from Rogers. One of them would not have missed it. Fogg noticed that these natives seemed to be more so in tune with nature than the Europeans. Some said they could recognize individual trees and rocks and had a natural compass in their heads, like homing birds.

The trail led up at an easy incline and Fogg's detachment made good progress. Within a half hour they were three quarters of the way up the mountain and had reached a point where the trail came out on a ledge. They sat down to take a breather and Fogg took out his glass to survey the area where the French were working. The French work parties had cleared off the majority of the height so that the two lake vistas were joined. He could see where they had also cleared out a field of fire in front of the area where the works might be. He could not see the works as there were still trees standing along what Fogg supposed to be the front of the works. The line of trees zigzagged back and forth across the height forming a slight horseshoe shape. He still did not have an answer as to why the French were leaving those trees standing. The only thought he could arrive at was that they intended to use them for the finishing row on the top of the earthworks.

There was other activity going on in the area . It looked like they were going to put some minor works out on both flanks of the main works. Fogg could make out men cutting down trees. It was difficult to see a lot of what was happening on the northeast end of the line that ran to Wood Creek. The area was clear due to the vista, but the angle was not good as it was partially hidden by the drop caused by the height. He could see where they were building a redoubt on the meadow below the fort itself. Fogg could also plainly see from his perch why Montcalm had elected to meet the English on the heights. The fort itself was not very impressive. The bastions and platform walls were crib construction filled with earth. The buildings on the parade appeared to be constructed of stone and rose too high above the platform walls. Fogg could not get a good estimate of its size but it did not appear to be that large. He also noticed that it was situated too far back from the point. It did not control the waterway, Wood Creek, that was the southern end of Lake Champlain. He could see that they had constructed a horseshoe-shaped battery out on the point that overlooked the lake. It was connected to the fort by a covered way that appeared wide enough for two ammunition carts to pass each other. Fogg had written all of this down in his journal and made some preliminary maps and sketches. He had not seen very many works in North America, but in Europe, this would have been a poor excuse for the designation of fortress. Maybe if the walls were encased with stone it might be more formidable. Had they built it with sloped earth walls covered with pegged sod it would have been more resistant to the effects of guns. In Fogg's opinion, the engineer who had designed and built the place was not much of an engineer. From his understanding of French Canada, the engineer was probably a relative of the Governor General.

Fogg had seen enough and had made notes and sketches. He would suggest that the engineers should come up to this place and take a look for themselves. He looked up at the pinnacle, which was bald except for some brush, thinking that they might even see more from there. It was mid afternoon by the time they made their way down off of the mountain and to the sawmills.

Bradstreet's men had repaired the bridge and a majority of the army had made it to this point. The General was there and Fogg went to make a report as to what he had observed. The General's aid came back to Fogg and told him to report his findings to General Gage who was his immediate superior, having taken Lord Howe's place. Fogg inquired where he might find General Gage and was told that he was back at the landing supervising the unloading of the remainder of the supplies and artillery. He thanked the Captain, who was the General's aide and told his men that they had to go back to the landing in order to find General Gage. A half-hour later, they were at the landing at what passed for headquarters. Fogg was told to wait and the General would see him shortly. An hour and a half later, the clerk came out and said that General Gage would see him directly. Fogg had sent his men to the 80th depot at the landing so that they might get some hot food. One of the men came back with two plates of food and mugs of tea for Fogg and himself. He said the Corporal had told him to remain with the Major in case he needed a runner. Fogg thanked him and told him to find a comfortable place to sit down and he would call him if needed. Fogg went to take a swig of tea but from the aroma was not sure if it was more tea or rum. The food, while hot ,was unrecognizable. It was most likely some sort of boiled salted beef with some potatoes and onions thrown in. There was a chunk of bread to soak up the flour gravy in the mixture. Fogg had to admit that the bread was much better than the French bread they had confiscated. The French variety had grey pea flour mixed into it, due to the ration shortages in Canada.

*     *     *

It was another hour before the clerk came back out and told Fogg that General Gage could not see him this evening. He was to return in the morning and the General would probably be able to see him then.

"Would you go tell the General, that General Abercromby sent me to report directly to General Gage. I have intelligence taken from the top of the mountain regarding the French works on the height in front of the fort."

The clerk returned in a couple of minutes. "General Gage says that your intelligence should be delivered to General Abercromby as he is directing the assault in person. General Gage is directing the logistics." With that, he turned and re-entered the headquarters. Fogg stood there for a moment, dumbfounded. *What in hell is wrong with these two men? I have told both that I observed the*

*French works from the mountain and had information they needed. What do they do?  They send me back and forth between them. One more try with General Abercromby.  Now I know why Howe was sent on this campaign.*

He signaled to the runner to follow and headed for the 80th depot.  They still had enough light to make the falls and perhaps talk to Abercromby.

## Chapter 53

When Fogg and his detachment arrived at the sawmill it was starting to get dark. He left his men and went off to the spot where the General had established his headquarters. Abercromby was busy going over some papers and within a few minutes he called him in.

"My clerk tells me you have urgent news, Major Fogg."

"Yes General, at least it was earlier today," replied Fogg. "I took my reconnaissance party up the Rattlesnake Mountain this morning based on the sounds that I heard yesterday. From the top, we observed that the French are building an extensive set of works across the top of the height and...."

Abercromby held up his hand. "Yes, yes. I know all about this. Captain Abercrombie and Lieutenant Clerk, the engineer, were up there this afternoon. They have reported that the French have some small works scattered across the top of the height, perhaps a simple abatis but that they are far from a complete set of works," remarked, somewhat curtly.

"Sir, begging the General's pardon but that is not a set of scattered works. It stretches from one side of the heights to the other. It is an earthwork as tall as a man with a ditch in front as deep as a man. I also believe it has a log parapet and ...." again Abercromby cut him short.

"Major Fogg! Captain Abercrombie and Lieutenant Clerk are qualified observers. Captain Abercrombie, while not listed as an engineer, is a competent one and Lieutenant Clerk is a very qualified engineer. While you, Major Fogg, seem to appear out of nowhere with no documentation other than Lord Howe's accepting you on some set of unseen orders. Have you ever seen a set of real works, Major Fogg?" demanded Abercromby.

"I believe that the works in the Lowlands would qualify as real works, Sir," replied Fogg. Abercromby looked furious. Here was a Major standing up to him, a General. Abercromby could see from Fogg's eyes that he was not the least intimidated by him. He suspected that this Major of Foot Guards walked with the blessing of those at Court.

"Do you have a written-out report, Major? If so leave it and I shall take a look and discuss it with Lieutenant Clerk, later," was all that Abercromby said and returned to his paper work.

"I shall have it ready for you in less than twenty minutes, General. Thank you for taking away from your valuable time to hear me out." With that, Fogg turned and walked away. *As soon as I finish this report, I need to find Gris and warn him to be extremely careful tomorrow. I have a feeling that these imbeciles are going to get many good men killed tomorrow, unnecessarily.* Fogg sat down at a plank set across two butts of wood and quickly wrote out what he had seen from the top of the mountain. One thought kept nagging at him while writing out the report. *Why are they leaving those trees in front of the lines standing? Could it be to hide the actual view of the lines from the top of the mountain. I could still see the general outline. Why?* He finished the report along with a quick sketchy map and left the whole for the General to look at, perhaps. It seemed to Fogg that the General had already made up his mind that Clerk's estimation, backed by Captain Abercrombie, was more accurate than Fogg's. Fogg went off to find Gris and his men who had come up the original planned route to the saw mills. His men were still trying to dry out their clothes from having to ford the brook that was slightly higher than it had been the day before. Fogg pulled Gris aside and told him of what he had seen from the mountain top. He also warned him that the General was not hearing anything that he said. Gris informed Fogg that at a council of war held earlier this morning, it appeared that they would continue with the original plan as drawn up weeks ago by Lord Howe. He said that perhaps there was going to be another one tomorrow morning, before the attack. Gris suggested that they might just as well turn in as tomorrow was going to be another long day. Fogg agreed and pulled out his maud that was attached to the top of his haversack and wrapped himself up in it.

They were up well before dawn. Corporal Elias brought them over a cup of very strong tea and some sort of bread baked in the campfire. Gris cautioned Fogg not to eat the crust, as it was ash bread and would wear down the enamel on his teeth. You broke it open and just ate the inside. After having finished the tea and bread, Fogg took his men and went back over to where the headquarters was located. He asked the clerk if the General had any orders for him as it appeared that General Gage was not coming down from the landing place. The clerk said he would inquire when the General came out. Fogg had Elias post a man at the headquarters to come and find him if the General summoned him, which he doubted that he would. He took a walk over by the area where Sir William Johnson and his Indians

266

had encamped the day before. Johnson had brought in about four hundred of them. They were a fit looking group of people. It appeared that they were getting ready for the day's activities, although no one knew, as yet, what that would be. Perhaps they had their own agenda. Sir William was easy to discern. His red hair helped to give him away. He was dressed partially as an Indian. Fogg thought about introducing himself but then decided to wait until a more appropriate time. He looked around the camp and the soldiers that he could observe seemed to be quite professional. They were looking to their weapons and equipment. Some were doing camp chores. Some were simply lounging, about but all had the look that suggested today would be different than most. It was something that you could see in their eyes. Fogg had seen it before in many different places, just before a large battle.

Sometime, just before eight o'clock, there was the call for all division-level officers to assemble. Fogg went over to headquarters, not because he had a large division, but out of curiosity and the fact that no one would think of questioning a Guards officers presence. There had been a second reconnaissance this morning, this time toward the lines. A party of men led by Colonel Bradstreet, Lieutenant Rivez, of the 60th and an engineer had gotten up on the top of the hill far enough to see the area where the French had been working for the last two days and all night. Rivez, a Hugenot whose English was hard to understand, made part of the report. He said, supported by Bradstreet, that they could see only a few places fortified with a couple of logs stacked on top of each other. They could not get any closer than a couple of hundred yards at best due to the French pickets. It appeared to be not a very strong set of works, perhaps only a few feet high at the most. The brush, perhaps the simple abatis seen yesterday obscured most of the view. The engineer said that if there were a set of complete works, it was probably down closer to the fort itself. Fogg ventured a question.

"Colonel Bradstreet, what of the trees that were in front of the lines?" Bradstreet started to answer but General Abercromby cut him off saying that the trees were not important. He called for opinions on how the army should assault the lines. It was brought up that they might best attack in columns each supporting the other. Someone suggested that it would take too long to change from the order to attack in line. The attack in lines with each brigade and wing supporting the other was the selected method. There was no mention of any artillery except for a scheme by Lieutenant Clerk to place a battery on the foot of the Rattlesnake Mountain where it could enfilade the French left. With that, the council was dismissed.

Fogg collared Bradstreet and re-asked his question. "What of the standing trees?"

"I saw no standing trees in front of the lines. They must have cut them all down overnight. By the way, the General said that if I saw you I was to tell you to take your men and go with Sir William and his Mohawks. They are going up on top of the mountain. Good luck." Bradstreet turned and went off to find his men. Fogg stood there for a moment, dumbfounded. He was to be an observer, in the strictest sense. He had questioned Abercromby and some of his officers and now was being intentionally kept from the battle. He gathered up his men and went off to find and meet Sir William. Fogg caught up with Johnson just as he and his Mohawks were getting ready to move out.

"Sir William? Allow me to introduce myself, Major Fogg, 1st Guards. I am ordered to go with you to Rattlesnake Mountain and observe the action from there."

Johnson extended his hand giving Fogg a friendly grip, "Welcome, Major Fogg. It seems we are both being sent into exile. Me for not being here a couple of days sooner and you for?"

"I believe for asking the wrong questions and expecting answers," replied Fogg.

"At least we shall have a good seat for the drama." He called in Iroquois to the Mohawk, who seemed to be in charge, to move on out. Turning to Fogg, Johnson added, "It is an easy language, once you get the gist of it." The Mohawks took off at the dogtrot that Fogg had come to expect from most of the Indians. The Stockbridge had usually traveled at the same pace. It was a ground-eating pace that did not seem to tire them. Of course, it seemed to take its toll on Europeans until they got used to it. Within no time, they were at the spot where the trail had cut up the mountain, but instead of stopping they went on past it. It took them about ten minutes to reach the beginning of the level stretch at the set of the first falls. Here, the Mohawks cut off on a side trail that went south. They were moving up a gentler slope than the one that Fogg had climbed on his first trip to the top of the mountain. It seemed that the Mohawks were more familiar with this area than most had thought. Soon, they entered into a place that was bordered by cliff on its east side and the step slope of another mountain on its west. They continued up this little narrow valley for a few hundred feet and suddenly the lead Mohawk turned toward the cliff wall. To Fogg's amazement, the man started to climb up the side of the cliff on a set of natural stairs set in a deep crack in the mountain. It was more like climbing a ladder as one needed to use their hands due to the steps being a little more than man size.

Within a minute, they were on top of the cliff and moving off across the top of the mountain toward the top. In what seemed a very little time they had gained the ridge on the east side of the mountain just below its pinnacle. Fogg could see they were slightly higher than he had been the day before and it had taken them less time to reach it than it had yesterday.

Sir William said, "A spectacular view, Major, a spectacular view. Those over there are the Green Mountains of the Hampshire Grants. North you can almost see to Crown Point on a real clear day when the haze burns off. The Iroquois have taken advantage of this site for years to observe if there was any movement on the lake and I am told that Roger's and his men have used this spot to observe the Carillon outpost many times." Fogg looked around and found a branch that had a fork in it lying on the ground. He broke it off so it was about four feet long. Fogg took out his glass and sat down on a rock to steady it with the forked stick. He trained the glass toward the spot were the French had been working and looked for the line of trees that they had left standing.

When the glass was focused he exclaimed, "Damn it! I should have known what they were leaving them for. It was too sodden obvious!"

Johnson had moved off toward the top of the mountain and the few Mohawks that were still nearby just looked at him. His own men were set up a few yards below him and did not hear him. *I should have guessed that it was to build an abatis. The damn thing must be at least fifty to sixty feet deep and six to ten feet high. The increase in temperature has caused the leaves to wither more than when Bradstreet saw it. No wonder he could not see the works and why young Clerk did not see them yesterday.* Fogg trained his glass toward his left until he could see the English troops. He could just make out what he guessed to be the English skirmish line at the crest of the hill that came up from the river. They were still several hundred yards off from any contact with the French, except on the right flank. He could not determine where the French pickets were located in that area, even though it was closer to his position. *Damn it! If only we had some way of communicating, some sort of signals. Flags or even mirrors to flash messages.*

He turned back to watching the slow advance of the English skirmishers. He could make out the 80th on the right flank. The bateaux-men were supposed to be in the center and Rogers men on the extreme left of the English line. From his perch he could not determine exactly if this was the case. Stark's New Hampshire Rangers, who were supposed to be the lead element, had no uniforms and would have blended in with the bateaux-men. The leaves of the trees still obscured them and the rangers would have been the farthest away. He heard some popping of gunfire and could see some smoke down below him on the English right flank. The 80th had made contact with French pickets who had been closer to the river on that end. The bank on that side was also a little steeper for the first hundred yards. Fogg could tell from the occasional puffs of smoke that the battle was moving up the hill and toward the lines as the French pickets withdrew in good order. By now, the English skirmishers were starting to break out of the woods and into the cleared space in front of the French works. Fogg could make out patches of green uniforms in the center, so he guessed that the order had been changed and the bateaux-men were on the left flank. Fogg had witnessed many battles, but never one from this far with such a good advantage of height. It appeared to be a little over a mile away to the area where the battle was unfolding. Due to the curve in the lines, he could not see much of the action that he was starting to hear on the north end of the works. It was obvious that the English irregulars were pushing the French pickets in and the French were withdrawing in good order. Fogg could not be certain how large an area was cleared, but he figured that a conservative guess was between two-hundred to three-hundred yards if not more. That was the distance from the edge of the woods to the beginning of the abatis. He knew that the men down there had no idea what was in front of them.

There was a crash of gun fire just below him and he quickly looked up, thinking that perhaps they had been attacked by a French patrol. It was Johnson's Mohawks who were firing at the French in the closest end of the works. It was just a show of bravado, to let the French know that they were above them. Even with the elevation of the mountain, there was no way that a ball from a musket could hit the French. Had the French been standing on the bank of La Chute they would have been safe except for an extremely rare stroke of bad luck. Through his glass he could see the French look up at the mountain briefly and then back to more urgent matters when they realized that whoever was doing the firing was too far off. The Mohawks fired a few more shots and then ceased wasting their precious ammunition. He thought that he heard some additional firing from the bottom of the mountain.

The more he looked at what would be the center of the skirmishers' line, the more he was convinced that something had been fouled up. There appeared to be more men in the center than should have been there, yet he had heard firing over on the English left. A line of provincials emerged from the skirt of the woods and halted a few feet into the clearing. *This must be the covering line for the regulars to form behind from the spaced breaks in the line. I do not see the regulars as yet but they must be right behind them.* The French pickets slowly withdrew toward their lines. The English irregulars pushed them in good order, both sets of light troops doing their jobs very well. Fogg could see that as the English irregulars moved forward their process was slowly retarded until they came to a halt short of the abatis. He could see that they were pinned down from the fire from the works. He could just make out some of the 80th, those closest to him, their brown uniforms blending in with the earth as they went to ground. From his advantage point, he could see the French firing from behind their parapet. He was not sure what the English irregulars could see but he guessed that the French were not visible, only the smoke from their muskets.

It seemed like forever but was, in reality, not that long when a column of English regulars appeared in what should have been the left center of the English line. This brigade formed up and Fogg could make out the uniforms of the 60th and therefore it must have been the 1st Brigade who were a little too far left of where they should have been. He could now make out some of Rogers' men who were moving forward in front of this Brigade. Fogg checked his watch and noted it was just a little after one o'clock in the afternoon. He returned to his glass and watched as the 1st Brigade started to advance on its own. The plan had called for all the Brigades to be in position and advance at the same time, thus stressing the French ability to reinforce any given point. The firing off to the left where the NY Provincials were had precipitated various elements of the English to move forward too early. As they drew up to the abatis, the affects of the French fire could be seen from the mountaintop. The tiny figures in the red coats seemed to wither away under the French volleys. It was hard for Fogg to equate that these were real men from that distance. The entire scène was surreal. You would see the smoke and then hear the sound and in most cases, patches of red were already fallen to the ground before the whole sequence registered as gun fire. Fogg looked up from his glass and around his immediate area. He was sitting on top of a mountain on a clear, sunny July day. He could smell burning tobacco and hear the murmur of men talking, while all the time below him, men were dying. He, who had seen so many battles, had a hard time comprehending if the whole thing was really happening. He shook himself back to reality and returned to his observing.

He could see that there was movement on the edge of the woods and the 2nd and 3rd Brigades were coming out onto the edge of the clearing. The 2nd Brigade, whose post was the left flank was slightly ahead of the 3rd who were to take the center. The 2nd Brigade formed quickly into line and commenced to move forward. For some reason, they went too far right and passed in front of the 3rd Brigade disrupting the 3rd Brigades line of march. Perhaps it was the angle of the French works or perhaps they thought that they should move in support of the 1st Brigade. Fogg had no way of knowing. He only knew that now the French were free to reinforce any part of the line they felt necessary to reinforce. This was happening as Fogg could see a body of men behind the French works moving toward the center where the 2nd Brigade should be making contact.

Fogg could see that some of the English columns had made it through the abatis. What looked like the 55th Foot, from Fogg's perch, had cleared the inner point of the abatis and he could see that even while taking extreme losses some of them had attempted to climb the works. He thought that he saw some highlanders in the mix that had made it through but was not sure as it would have put them too far towards the center from their objective.

It was not yet apparent to the men struggling on the battlefield below him but it was to Fogg. The entire attack was completely disrupted. He was having a difficult time keeping track of who should be where and who was actually where. It would be necessary to regroup and launch the attack again, perhaps this time with the artillery.

## Chapter 54

Fogg watched in disbelief and scribbled notes in his pocket journal. He had seen the attempt to establish a battery on the south side of La Chute, just below the mountain he sat on. He was not certain but it appeared that the officer in charge of the little flotilla towing the gun barges did not seem to know exactly where he was supposed to go. It looked like they hesitated and then went down the wrong channel through the rushes. They came under fire from a French battery on the north shore that either hit or hit near two of the longboats. The flotilla then turned around and went back. He was to hear later that Lieutenant Clerk, the engineer had only described the location to the officer in charge of the boats and that the officers had not seen the location previously. It was questionable if the officer who was waiting at the designated landing location had indeed found the correct place as he had not been there either. Apparently Lieutenant Clerk had only seen the site from up on the mountain.

It was about two o'clock  according to Fogg's watch when the flotilla withdrew. At the same time he could see what appeared to be the Royal Americans withdrawing on the English right flank. He also could see that over toward the center there seemed to be some sort of withdrawal by one of the units. He was not sure, but from the facing it might have been the 44th. He was able to make out one of the Provincial units, possibly a Massachusetts regiment drawing up close to them. He thought that the Provincials might be in support of the regular's withdrawal. Much to his surprise, he watched as the Provincials started to move forward to attempt the very thing that had apparently been decimating the regulars. They encountered the same thing as had the regulars. The abatis slowed them down while the French took advantage of it, pouring fire into them unceasingly. From his vantage point, Fogg could see why the French were able to sustain such a rapid rate of fire. He could see figures that appeared to be loading muskets and then passing them on to the people who were doing the firing. He guessed that the French had placed their best marksmen at the loopholes. He also saw why he had not encountered any of the French boats with swivels mounted. The French had apparently withdrawn all of their swivels to be used for defensive purposes. He could make out at least two and in some cases more on each salient of the lines. He could also see that more Provincials were being poured into the attack. It was at this point that Johnson came down to the spot from where Fogg was watching.

"My Mohawks have elected to leave. They came to fight and they see no reason to stay here. They say that the English General will not stay in this place after today. They have no faith in him as a War Chief and would return home to their Valley. I have tried to dissuade them but to no avail. If the army has started to withdraw when you leave here, I would suggest that you go back the way we came. At the spring on the right, just below the steps, you can follow the small stream out and it will bring you to the portage road."

"Thank you, Sir William. Perhaps we shall meet again," replied Fogg.

"Well if you ever get up to my Valley, please be my guest at Fort Johnson. Also, my Mohawks tell me that they do not think that the French have many of their Indians with them at the moment. They think that perhaps some of the Three Rivers villages may appear in a couple of days. Don't ask me how they know these things but they do. It is uncanny. Good luck and safe journey." With that, they shook hands and Johnson departed. Fogg whistled to his men and gave the signal for the NCOs to meet on him. When they came up, he told them Johnson and his Mohawks had departed and that they should take appropriate care to cover their position as they no longer had the Indians as a screen.

Fogg was aware of a great deal of firing over on the extreme left of the English. As with several other facts that he later learned, this was the section that had first been heavily engaged when what should have been the New Yorkers encountered the French picquets. The Yorkers were to be furnishing the screen for the 42nd and the 46th Foot. The Yorkers, in turn, were supposed to be screened by the Rangers. As it had turned out, the Rangers were too far right and the Yorkers had run directly into the picquets. It appeared to Fogg that it was that heavy firing that seemed to launch all of the rest of the ensuing battle. He could not see very clearly form his vantage point due to the curve in the line and the build up of smoke. He had observed some movement on the far right of the French line of what appeared to be la Marine and la malice, but he could not see the action that followed their movement. He did observe that after a few minutes they seemed to be heading for where there were a great many boats. At first, he thought that perhaps they were going to move up lake and then attack from a vantage further north. However, when the guns from the fort fired upon them, he assumed that they were breaking and trying to run. The guns drove them back to their original position in a set of trenches of which Fogg could just make out one end. Fogg could tell that the regiments on the left made several concentrated attacks, even as some of the other regular regiments were withdrawing. This should have been the 42nd and the 46th.

Throughout the entire attack the irregular troops kept up a sustained fire all along most of the front. In their initial attack they had made it to the abatis and some had penetrated into it. It severed a purpose that Monsieur Montcalm had not intended. It became a shelter for the irregulars who, well versed in bush warfare, used the tree trunks and stumps to conceal themselves and snipe at the French. While they could not see any of the French directly in front of them, some could see those who were on a salient on their flank. Due to the dips and rises in the ground there were places where the inside of the French lines could be seen. It was at these points that they were able to inflict casualties on the French. Even where the French had fired back at them the abatis provided cover. One of Fogg's observations was that the brown uniforms of the 80th seemed to disappear among the trees and withering foliage. However, he could still make out the green of the uniformed Rangers. He had noticed earlier that one of the New York Regiments who were wearing grey or drab also seemed to disappear in the poor light in the bush. He had made a note of this for further study.

Fogg scanned his glass along the length of the line that he was able to view. On the right and the center it appeared as if the majority of the regular regiments had pulled back and were drawn up on the edge of the woods. Fogg assumed that they were there to replenish their ammunition and refresh themselves while waiting for the artillery to be brought forwards. Surely the General and his staff had realized that they could not carry these works without the use of the artillery. Fogg knew that there were four, six pounders at the sawmill falls from the aborted attempt to establish a battery at the foot of the mountain. Even these guns, concentrated on one point, would have caused the French considerable damage to their lines. Fogg could see that the French did not have any artillery that was in a position to use counter-battery fire if the guns were brought up.

As the afternoon wore on, it was clear that the English were not going to bring up any guns and that the sporadic firing by the irregulars and provincial troops was intended to keep the French in their lines. Fogg's watch showed four o'clock and he decided that it was time to get off of this mountain. He signaled to his men and they formed up. Fogg led off down the trail that they had used to reach the top of the mountain earlier that day. The path to the steps was clear.

Following Johnson's advice, they went along the little stream that flowed from the spring. It took them straight out to the portage road. He turned right onto the road and within a short time they were back in the vicinity of the sawmill. The breastworks that the English had reworked were full of wounded men. Fogg took half of his little squad and went on up the hill toward the lines. The road leading down toward the falls was choked with the wounded, some walking, some being carried by their mates. They were all mixed in together, regulars, provincials, this regiment in with that regiment. There appeared to be little if any organization to the evacuation of the wounded. Fogg had inquired of a regular officer if he knew the whereabouts of the General. The officer replied that he had seen the General head up toward the battle when the firing broke out, but he did not know exactly were to find him as he himself had been stuck at the sawmill all day just sorting out supplies as they came forward from the landing.

Fogg led his men up the road toward the top of the hill. He guessed it was just over a quarter of a mile to the edge of the clearings. He came up to another breastwork that had been constructed as a forward rally point. It too was full of wounded with a couple of doctors and surgeon's mates sorting out the wounded. Fogg looked at the faces of some of the men sitting there on the ground. Their faces reflected something that he had seen many times before; the vacant look of men who had stared death in the face and lived to walk away from it. He was sure that the battle was as bad as it had appeared from the top of the mountain. He moved forward toward the edge of the clearing. This area was still cluttered with the remaining whole men of the regiments, although they seemed to resemble some sort of order. He saw Major Eyre of the 44th, whom he had met once at Howe's headquarters. Fogg inquired of him the whereabouts of the General. Eyre mumbled something that sounded like "… what General, we have no General here today…" and pointed off to the right of the line saying more clearly, "Over by the Inniskillings, there." Fogg thanked him and moved off in that direction. He found the General, along with some of his aides, situated on a small outcropping of rocks just to the right of the 27th Foot, the Inniskillings. The General saw Fogg approaching and leaned over to one of the aides and said something. The aide met Fogg about twenty feet from where the General was standing.

"General Abercromby says that I am to tell you to write out a detailed report of the engagement as observed from your vantage point. The General also requests that you make contact with the elements of the 80th that are pinned down in the abatis and tell them

276

to make a withdrawal as soon as possible and establish covering fire for the remainder of the army. They are to pass this along to all the irregulars." Fogg asked him to repeat the order again just to make sure that he was not misunderstanding the aide due to the gunfire. Fogg looked at the General and smiled giving him a smart salute, which went unreturned. *So, you old bastard, you think that you can perhaps silence me by sending me into the arms of the French marksmen. I think that it is you who will be surprised.* With that, Fogg led his men off to the right until he came up to the point where the 60th were drawn up.

"Corporal Elias, you will remain here with the men. Under no circumstances are you to come forward. If I do not make it back here before the bulk of the army pulls back, you are to go to the saw mill and find an officer of the 80th and report to him. Understood?"

"Aye Sir, I understand. Good luck Sir."

With that Fogg turned and, at a trot, started toward the abatis. He ran on a zig-zag course toward where he could see some brown uniforms, keeping low. The French had seen this lone figure moving across the clearing and several of their marksmen had started to shoot at him. Fogg could hear the rounds as they passed close by him. Some of the light infantry had seen him coming and that the French were concentrating on him. They started to cheer him on. When he reached the first cluster of brown, he jumped over a log and landed almost in the middle of them. They recognized him as the officer who had led a small flotilla of raiders on Lake George.

"Good afternoon lads! How do you like the French hospitality so far?" was Fogg's first remark to them. They laughed and said that the French were very generous hosts as they had given them as much lead as they could spare.

"Do you know where Captain Gris is?"

One replied, "I believe that he and a couple of the lads are holed up off to the right about fifty to sixty feet or so. He called to all of us a while back to see how our ammunition was doing. You don't have any spare rounds do you Sir?"

"Sorry lads, only to fit my fusil, which is about half the size of your Bess. I would not worry too much as I think you are going to be pulled back any time now." With that, he jumped up and took off toward where they had indicated that Gris might be found. His move was so fast that it caught the French by surprise. He found himself leaping from one log to another and doing all sorts of twisting and turning to avoid the abatis points. When he was about half way there, he was shouting at the top of his lungs.

"Gris! Gris! Where are you? Gris!"

A voice came from just to his right front, "Here, Fogg, you damn fool, here!" A few more leaps and Fogg found himself down behind a huge log that was covering a half-dozen figures, four in brown and two in the uniform of the 60th light companies. They were all hunkering down as Fogg's little sprint had drawn a great deal of fire toward their position.

Gris looked at him, smiling and said, "Glad to see you could join us, Major. For what earthly reason are you here at this charming French tea party?"

"I am here, Captain Gris, risking life and limb to inform you that your General requests that you irregulars withdraw and set up covering fire to facilitate the withdrawal of the regular army." Gris looked at him in disbelief, the French musket balls whizzing around them like hornets.

"He wants me to withdraw? Does he think that we have spent I'm not sure how many hours here because we wanted to? I will not order these men to expose themselves to this fire for no good reason. We will wait until it starts to get dark. I do not think that we need fear having any Indians sneaking out here in the twilight. I haven't heard a single one all day."

"Calm down my friend," soothed Fogg. "Sir William says his Mohawks do not think the French have any Indians with them or at least only a few. The French sure as hell are not going to come out from behind their works, especially knowing that so many of you have managed to gain cover here all day. You should wait until it gets dusk and then withdraw, straight back until you come to the edge of the woods. From there you should be able to find the roads going down to the sawmill. I think it is about over there," gesturing with a nod of his head.

"You sound like you're not going with us," ventured Gris.

"No. I'm going to work my way across the front here and pass on the word as to what we are about. I'll meet you at the sawmill or the landing. I left your Corporal and his men back there," pointing toward where he had left them. "Good men, well trained. Thanks for their loan."

With that, Fogg was up and moving again before the French could react. Once more the fusillade followed him along until he came to the next pocket of irregulars. This continued until he reached the far right end of the English line. Here, he simply turned and headed west until he came even with the point where he thought the clearing ended. It was difficult to determine due to the vista from the fort. A few shots rang out from his left He could see some French, probably malice, in a set of works there. He was way out of their

278

range and the rounds fell short.  He took off his hat and made a very large sweeping stage bow followed by a gesture that even a Frenchman would understand.  Three of them jumped over the works with their tomahawks drawn and started to run up the slope toward him.  It was about one hundred-fifty to two hundred yards from them to Fogg.  Fogg laid down his fusil and calmly waited for them.  When they were within seventy-five yards, he turned and picked up the fusil and shot the middle one in the center of his chest.  The other two hesitated and then came on with renewed fury.  Fogg laid down his fusil once more and advance a few paces from it, standing with his hands on his hips.  They could not see that his left hand rested on the grip of his dirk or that he had drawn his skein dubgh  from the top of his Indian legging and it was held in his right with the blade resting against his wrist.

The first Frenchman reached him a few yards ahead of his partner, his tomahawk raised above his head to strike Fogg.  As he closed with Fogg, Fogg disappeared from his line of sight, dropping down to one knee and sweeping the mans legs from under him with the hand that held the boot knife.  The man screamed as Fogg slashed across his legs just above the foot.  He went down in a heap and never felt the dirk as it sliced into his neck severing his carotid artery and almost his whole neck.  As Fogg spun from cutting the first man, he came around in time to meet the other one who was swinging his tomahawk from the side toward Fogg's head.  Fogg blocked it by holding up his dirk in the path being traveled by the man's arm.  When the man's arm hit the cutting edge of the dirk, the tomahawk flew out of his hand as the dirk severed all the tendons in his forearm.  Fogg's skein dubgh came up in an arc and plunged deep into the diaphragm of the man, piercing his lungs.  Fogg's spinning movement caused the man to roll off of Fogg gently to Fogg's left and he dumped the man on top of the other.  He then walked over to them and wiped off his dirk and boot knife, picked up his fusil and once more bowed to the French in the works.

He called to them in French, "Who else desires to come out and dance?"  None seemed to care to dance with him.  He continued his journey toward the English lines and the road.  When he reached the position where he thought Gris would come out, he waited until the light started to fail.  In a short time, when he could no longer see the French works, he started to see movement in front of him.  Slowly, the irregulars begun to appear a few at a time.  Fogg took command until one of the 80th officers showed and then he stepped aside to let him command.  As Fogg would have expected, Gris was one of the last to appear.  He was helping a 60th light who seemed to be hit in the leg from the way he dragged it. Two of the 60th who had already come out went and relieved Gris of his burden. Fogg went to where Gris was standing.

Holding out his hand he said, "Glad to see you made it out Robert. I am sorry that I could not have been with you and your men on this day."

"Do not mention it Ethyrial. We know that you would have preferred to be there in the abatis as opposed to up on the mountain. The lads appreciate the fact that you risked your life coming to deliver the order to retreat."

"We should go along the entire line here in our section to see if there are any wounded within sight. I should not ask the lads to go too far back into that hell," remarked Fogg. "It will be very dark soon and it would be easy to become lost in that tangle." They searched for another hour and recovered a few wounded. When it became apparent that they might start losing some of the searchers, Fogg ordered everyone to form up and marched off to the saw mill.

It had indeed been a very long day and promised to be the same tomorrow.

## Chapter 55

The road from the battlefield to the saw mill was strewn with dead, those past help and equipment.    Men had thrown away firelocks, cartridge boxes, haversacks, canteens or anything else that would impede their retreat.    Gris told his men to check all the cartridge boxes and remove all that they found.  They picked up some of the haversacks and dumped out the contents.    By the time they reached the sawmill, they had filled a half-dozen haversacks with cartridges.    Fogg would have liked to carry away the firelocks but it would have proved to be too much of a load.  He ordered the men to destroy or disable as many of the abandoned firelocks as possible.  He disliked leaving them for the enemy to pick up.  One of the items that amazed him was the abundance of shoes that they found along the road.    He wondered how so many men had lost their shoes.    He laughed to himself, *I guess that this is just one of the peculiarities of a campaign.  If you wanted to run away in a hurry, why would you throw away your shoes?  Then again perhaps they had just run out of their shoes.*

The breast work at the sawmill was an even worse scene than he had beheld earlier.  It was now mostly full of dead men, those who had died from their wounds or those that could not be moved.  There were no doctors or surgeon mates left    There also were very few senior rank officers here either.    There were a few subalterns who were urging the stragglers on up the road toward the landing.  Fogg approached one of them from the Highland Regiment.

"What are the orders?" he inquired.

"Orders?  There are no orders except return to the landing soldier!  Now get upon the road," came the curt reply.

Fogg realized that he was covered with dirt and blood.  His gorget was still tucked down inside his waistcoat and his uniform bore no lace.  In the dark, he appeared to be just another soldier from one of the royal regiments or a dark-faced regiment.  He reached inside his waistcoat and pulled the gorget out.

"It is Major Fogg.  We, Captain Gris and I, will take command of the works here.  You get the rest of your men and any stragglers back to the landing.  Don't leave any wounded who can walk on the road.  We have seen no Indians today but that doesn't mean that the French do not have a few. Is that understood?" The young subaltern looked even more dazed than he did before. He tried to say something but just stammered. Fogg took him by the shoulders and held him steady.

"Get a hold of yourself, young man. You are an officer in The Highland Regiment and your regiment lived up to its reputation today. Do not let these other ranks see you not knowing what to do. Do you hear me?" Fogg cautioned him. The young officer seemed to grasp the situation and gained control of himself.

"Aye Sir. I understand your instructions and thank you Sir." With that, he turned and started giving instructions to the men who were moving sluggishly toward the road. Soon, his newly acquired attitude started to affect the men and they were moving along at an improved rate.

Fogg turned to Gris, "Captain, we will stay here a little longer to see if any more stragglers come in. I think we can safely remain here until after midnight. We should be able to navigate the portage without any light. I doubt if the French will be probing this way until it gets light. They should assume, the same as I would, that we are regrouping to attack again tomorrow. Johnson's Mohawks were correct when they said that this General would not stay here after today. Damn! What a waist of men."

"What did we accomplish here today, Ethyrial? All I can see is we accomplished giving the French a great victory to brag about for years to come. We outnumbered them at least three to one, perhaps more and they held us. Where in hell was the artillery?" asked Gris, "Where?"

"I don't know, Robert. There were at least four guns with their crews here at the sawmill. They seem to have been removed as they are not there now. At least I do not see them."

"Perhaps they dumped them in La Chute instead of taking them back. To the Royal Artillery their guns are the same as their colors. They would prefer not to let the French take them," observed Gris. They sat down on a couple of bread barrels. Fogg took out his pipe and tobacco, offering some to Gris. Gris reached inside his coat and took out a leather case. He pulled the top off and inside were some rolled tubes of tobacco. He offer one to Fogg.

"Here, try one of these. I prefer them when in the field. The Indians in Virginia smoke their tobacco this way. They roll it up in a tube. They hold it up to their nose, but I find that a little disgusting so I just put it against my lips." Fogg took one of the tubes and held it up looking at it, rolling it in his fingers, giving it a couple of sniffs. Gris held over one of the torches for him to light it and then lit his own. They sat there in silence, smoking their rolled tobacco and reflecting upon the day.

*　　　*　　　*

Fogg did not realize that he had drifted off until Gris gave him a nudge with his foot. He looked at his watch and it was almost two o'clock in the morning.

"How long have I been asleep?" he asked. "How did I fall asleep sitting up?" "I don't know as I just woke up myself. A couple of the men were awake and on guard so one of the NCOs must have been awake. I think we should be gone from this place. One more check to see if there are any wounded who can walk on their own or with little assistance."

They got up off their barrels and made the rounds of the breastworks. There were no wounded left who could move. Fogg disliked leaving them but knew they had a duty to the men who were hale and could fight again another day. They formed their men up in the road and started back up the portage road to the landing.

"Captain Gris, I have just had a strange thought. If the army has departed in the night, do you suppose they would have destroyed the boats that had no occupants? My next question is if this is so, do you know the best way to get back to the camp at the head of the lake?"

"That, Major, is a very good question or should I say two good questions. I doubt if they would have thought to destroy any remaining boats as they appeared to be in too big a hurry to save their own sodden posteriors. However, if they have destroyed the boats we have two choices to get back up the lake. We can either walk down one of two trails or there is a cache of French canoes at the foot of Mount Pelee on the north side in a bay just before it. One of the Rangers told me about them on a scout I went on and I know him to be on the level."

"By God's fish Captain, you are a handy fellow to have around!" With that, they trudged their way up the portage track. It was not difficult to discern where it was as they could look up and see the sky where the track made a path through the canopy of the trees. The Indians and then the French had used this for so many years that it was well defined. As they approached the bridge at the rapids, they were challenged by a sentry post manned by some Yorkers. The point man of their patrol was a Yorker who had joined the 80th and he answered the challenge in a mixture of Palatine German and English that only another Yorker would have completely understood. Fogg grasped part of it, a reference to the marital status of the challengers' mother at the time of his birth. The sentry post got a good chuckle at the expense of the challenger and they passed them on through.

Fogg was relieved to see that the entire army had not yet departed. He did not relish the thought of the long walk back to the Lake George camp. They found the remaining elements of the 80th guarding their boats. Fogg left the group and he and his six remaining men moved on to where they had left their boats. Bradstreet's bateaux-men, who had been assigned to Fogg's boats, were guarding them. They had pulled them a little way off shore, leaving a couple of men on the beach to watch for Fogg. His other six men were also there waiting for him. They had a small fire going and had made some sort of soup. Fogg was glad to have a mug of it as he realized that it had been at least ten to twelve hours since he had eaten anything. It was now close to three o'clock AM and from what he could tell, a great deal of the army had already departed. He told the men to stand fast while he determined what the orders were.

He decided to walk to where headquarters had been located earlier. He found the shelter that they had set up but there was no one there. The General appeared to have departed and in apparent haste. There were supplies and papers scattered around the place. They had even left candles burning. Fogg picked up a few of the papers and glanced at them. They had only to do with logistics for this campaign. He didn't have the time to sort through them all. He kicked them all into a pile and then dropped one of the candles into the pile. Soon the whole shelter was on fire. *That should handle that security problem. I would have thought they could have done the same.* He moved off to where the 80th boats were located. Gris was still there. Fogg's bonfire had lit up the sky and the whole landing area.

"How do you suppose that happened?" inquired Gris with a bit of amusement in his voice.

"Poor headquarters keeping, I should imagine," replied Fogg. "Have you seen anyone of authority around here or have they all set off for the Lake George camp to make sure it is ready for the army?"

"The only person I could find who outranked me was Colonel Bradstreet. He is not departing until all of his bateaux-men are ready to go. You're probably the second highest ranking officer left on the landing."

"Lets us go and find him. We'll see if we can get this mess mucked out." With that, they departed toward where Gris had last seen Bradstreet. They found him sitting on the bow of one of his boats pulled up on the shore. He had a mug of something in one hand

and a sea-biscuit in the other. He greeted them and offered them a seat on a couple of kegs that were next to the boat.

"No thank you, Colonel. We are curious as to what the orders are, as you appear to be the highest ranking officer left," asked Fogg.

"My orders, Major Fogg, were to see to the evacuation of the remainder of this army. And yours?" was Bradstreet's reply.

"I cannot seem to find anyone who wants to give me any meaningful orders since His Lordship was killed. I do have a proposal, if you are interested."

"Let me hear it, Major. I am opened to any reasonable, sane suggestions as I have not heard too many in the last couple of days."

"Colonel, I suggest that we use the remaining 80th and Rangers to sweep the landing area and pull in any remaining troops. You get them loaded into the boats and commence moving up lake. Captain Gris and I will hold the landing place until it becomes obvious that we have extricated as many stragglers as possible. Gris needs, what, six boats? I have my three boats standing off over there. I do not know about the Rangers boats. What do you think?"

"Agreed Major Fogg. I'll leave Captain Gris one extra longboat just in case you get a last minute rush of stragglers. I have not seen any Rangers as I think the General took them to cover the portion of the army that departed with him. If you don't need it, stave in the hull. Do the same with any other boats that seem to not have crews. Don't want the French getting any of our quality-built boats," the last said with a grin.

Fogg and Gris moved out to organize patrols to sweep the landing and pull in the sentry posts on the bridge. They found about two dozen Rangers still at the landing. Rogers had left them behind to do the same thing Gris and Fogg had done, collect stragglers. As it gradually started to get lighter, Fogg could see that more of the army was still on the landing than he had been able to determine in the dark. It took them several hours to completely cover every unit on the site and to get them moving. It was well into daylight when the last bulk of the army pushed off in their boats. One of the last officers they saw was a Lieutenant from the 44th who seemed annoyed that the General had departed so early ahead of his army. Fogg left a party of six men at the north side of the bridge to watch for any stragglers. When there were no more troops to embark one of the sections set about destroying the few unused boats. They not only stove in the bottoms but also set them on fire for good measure. Eventually, he pulled in the sentry posts and they all embarked for the camp at the head of the lake.

As they pulled away from the shore Fogg could still see smoke rising from the place where the headquarters had stood. and the burning boats. *What a forlorn looking place compared to, what was it four or five days ago, when we first landed. We were an army set to conquer all of North America and now we are an army in full retreat. The question is how far will General Abercromby retreat? This will not be a very flattering report that goes to my employer.*

Very quiet crews rowed up lake as even the wind seemed to be against them.

# Chapter 56

When they were about opposite the site of the Jersey Blues' ambush, the wind changed and they were able to step the masts and hoist the sails on their longboats. This was welcomed by the men as they were exhausted from the last five days. Shortly after noon, by Fogg's watch, they were in sight of the camp at the head of the lake. Fogg gave the order to head into their usual birth in the creek but they were unable to do so as the creek was choked with boats. They made for a point slightly off to the east where there were none and beached their boats. The men hoisted their packs and other gear and formed up to march to their camp site. The bateaux-men posted a guard on the boats and the rest went off to find Colonel Bradstreet. They marched along the beach to the point where the creek came into the lake. The boats were so closely packed that they crossed the creek by walking from one boat to the next. All along the way they had been forced to walk around or step over soldiers who were still lying on the beach. They were all mixed in together; regulars and provincials with no distinction between regiments. They found some of the 80th along the way and took those that were able to walk along with them. The ones who could not move with help, Gris assured that he would send a party back for them.

When they finally reached their camp, they found that the situation was only slightly better there. The whole army seemed to be dazed, unable to think rationally. Fogg left Gris and the men of the 80th and went off toward where his camp had been when he departed so many days ago. He found his tent, the only one in the area as all the rest had been struck. The only person in the camp was a ranger who had been wounded early on in one of the skirmishes that had taken place coming up to the lake. Rogers had left him to guard Fogg's tent and possessions.

"The Major's compliments, Sir. I am to remain in your service until you no longer need me. He was a feared that some one of them regulars might pilfer your kit. There's some hot water on for tea or whatever you want. The Major says you can mess with the Ranger officers over yonder at that fly, there."

"Very good, Ranger...?"

"Grubbs, Sir, Ranger Private Samuel Grubbs, Major's Company."

"Well, Ranger Grubbs, you can give my compliments to the Major and tell him I would be honored to mess with the Ranger officers. First, I intend to take a stroll down to the lake and get about two weeks worth of grime and blood off of me. Then I think I'll have some of the tea you were offering. What do you think of that?"

"I'll pass on your compliments to the Major. I don't know about all that bathing. Don't seem like it would be healthy except in the spring and fall what with the vapors and such in summer and winter," replied Ranger Grubbs, shaking his head negatively.

"Perhaps I'll leave my hat on just as assurance against the vapors." Fogg offered, trying to look as serious as possible. Grubbs thought a minute or two and then replied as that might just do the trick though he himself had never heard of it.

Fogg went back down to the place on the beach were they had left the boats, carrying clean small cloths with him, along with his pistol and dirk. He left his cloths in his boat along with the guard and stripped down and plunged into the water. It was July but Lake George could still be cold, especially as compared to the hot July weather. Fogg could feel the water cleansing his body. He stood up in the shallow water and took the chunk of soap he had carried into the lake with him and started to scrub himself from head to toe. A couple of the bateaux-men stood in the boat watching him, shaking their heads. These English officers had some strange ideas and bathing was one of them. It took Fogg almost a half hour to get himself clean and dried off. As he sat on the bow of one of the boats, drying his legs and feet to put his hose and moccasins on, he asked the bateaux-men if they had found Colonel Bradstreet and if so what were Bradstreet's orders. They informed him that the Colonel had put forth his previous plan to attack the French on the western frontier and that the General seemed in favor of it. It meant that they would probably be leaving shortly, taking a great many of the boats with them. Fogg informed them that if they left he would request that Bradstreet leave FF1 here at the lake along with one bateaux-man, a volunteer of course.

Fogg went back up to his camp and put on a clean waistcoat, his light-infantry gaiters, a gift from the 60th, and his spare red coat. He changed his moccasins for a pair of plain tie shoes. He put on his accoutrement belt to hold his dirk and dropped his gorget into his waistcoat. As was the practice of the majority of officers, he put his sash on with his coat over it. He poured himself a cup of the soldiers tea and took a walk around the camp. There were field hospitals set

288

up in each regimental area, the army encamping on the same spots they had occupied before embarking against Carillon. Fogg could see that they were attempting to take care of the wounded. He observed men carrying litters from the direction of the beach toward the regiment sites. As he walked through the camps he could see wounded men in every street. Some were lying in the tents, some sitting in the streets. These were either the slightly wounded or ones who had been taken care of by the surgeons and their mates. There was also a steady stream of litters being carried off to the burying ground, medicine being what it was.

Fogg found the headquarters tent but was told that the General was not available today, and most likely would not be tomorrow also. Fogg thanked the aide and walked on over to the 80th cantonment. He found his friend Gris who was sitting in front of his tent along with another 80th officer that he introduced as Captain Hugh Arnot. Gris refilled Fogg's mug with a mixture of soldiers' tea and rum. Sitting on a small camp table was a large loaf of fresh bread. Fogg realized that he was hungry and tried to recall when he had last eaten.

"Hugh, here, was in one of the lead elements and they got closer to the works than we did. He says that the section in front of him appeared to be well constructed," remarked Gris.

"Well constructed, how?" queried Fogg.

"The timbers appeared to be notched and well laid up with a frieze. This being just short of the abatis. We could not see the works themselves until we were well into the abatis. Our men gave a good account of themselves in spite of the circumstances. We were able to inflict some casualties on the French due to the unevenness of their works. We concentrated our fire on the parts of the salient where we were at their flank. The works dipped down due to the ground, giving us the opportunity," recounted Arnot.

"We did not get a close look at the works," interjected Gris. "We were able to fire into a part of their lines, though. The angle was not too great but we could occasionally see a Frenchman."

"Did you find that the abatis provided your men good cover?" asked Arnot.

"Yes, I think in that instance it worked against the defenders, giving us cover. Without it we could not have spent, what three hours or so, that close to the line. You traveled along a great deal of the line Fogg. What did you observe?" said Gris, turning to Fogg.

"I did not notice that the section I moved along was framed or notched. It seemed to be much rougher. The spaces being filled in with dirt thrown up from the ditch in front and with some pieces of the abatis entwined into it.  My guess is that it depended on which regiment was in that section and if the officers were being true to their duty.  My guess is that if we sat down a hundred men we would get a hundred different impressions of the works and twice as many impressions of the battle," stated Fogg.  "I suspect that this particular campaign will be discussed for a goodly long time as everyone will have an opinion, including those who were not there.  And with that, gentlemen, I shall bid you good night.  It has been a long day, no, a long two weeks and I need a decent night's sleep."  Fogg wound his way back to his camp through the darkening evening.  As he sat on a stump in front of his tent, removing his gaiters and shoes, he reflected on a course of action.  He had decided to leave word at General Abercromby's headquarters that he, as a volunteer was departing for Albany and thence to New York.  He intended to write his full report to his employer on the way down river.  Fogg was aware that the General had already sent one of his aides, Cunningham or something along that line, down river and home to report.  This in an attempt to stem off some of the criticism that was sure to follow.  The largest English army ever assembled in North America had been defeated and forced to retreat by a force one third its size.

When he lay down on his bearskin rolled in his maud, the various events of the past weeks slowly drifted through his mind until they stopped as his body shut down from fatigue.

*     *     *

Fogg sat bolt upright, awake in an instance.  It took him a moment to realize that he was lying in his tent and that the sound of guns and men dying was in his head, a dream.  He sat there for a moment staring out the open flap of his tent.  He could hear men stirring in the other parts of the camp.  He got up, dressed and stepped out of his tent.  Private Grubbs was there with a fire going, a pot simmering on it.

"Good morn', Sir.  I've coffee boilin' here for you.  Sergeant Major says that you're partial to coffee."

"Thank you, Grubbs.  When it is ready, pour me a cup and I'll be back directly," motioning over his shoulder in the direction of the necessaries.  By the time he returned, Grubbs had a mug of coffee sitting on the stump next to his tent along with a couple of the scone-type breads that the Yankees called biscuits.  They were mostly flour and baking soda but served with a slab of butter they went well with coffee.  Fogg looked around while having his coffee.  He could see up to the Ranger-entrenched camp.  There was a lot of activity there.  It appeared as if there were several patrols getting ready to go out.  This made sense as it was going to be necessary to keep an eye on the

French who surely would press their advantage, especially if they had acquired a number of Indians as had been expected. Even if the Indians had not materialized the expected Canadians were a threat being almost as woods-wise or equal to the Indians. Some of the Canadian "bush runners" had lived most of their lives with the Indians. Fogg imagined that Rogers would be putting patrols both out on the lake and also to the east toward the tail of Wood Creek. It would have been advantageous to have Sir William and his Mohawks, as they were very familiar with the area that cut on over through the mountains to the Mohawk. This was their shortcut from the Mohawk Valley to Lake George. Johnson said that a war party could easily traverse this in a day and a half when motivated.

He turned and looked toward the direction of the regular camp. There was activity in that direction also. It appeared as if some of the army might be striking its tents or simply airing them. He could not quite determine which it was. He could make out some wagons just heading out of camp down the Fort Edward road. They appeared to contain both wounded and baggage. In Fogg's estimation, the guard appeared to be light if the enemy was suspected to be in the vicinity. Fogg took out his writing desk and quickly penned a brief note addressed to the General's Staff, stating that he, as a volunteer, was withdrawing his services and moving back to Albany or possibly New York for the remainder of the campaign season. He then penned another to Bradstreet, requesting that the cedar whaler FF½ be left at Lake George under the care of Major Rogers in case Fogg was requested to return to the Lake. Finally, he wrote a message to Gris saying that he would see him, most likely in Albany, and if not, at the level space where he would leave a message for him.

He then packed his things in his knapsack and haversack, changed into his moccasins and mitasses. He put his raw-linen smock over his waistcoat and buckled on his accoutrement belt. Originally, the smock had been made to pull over but Fogg had split it down the front to make it easier to put on and off. He gave Grubbs the messages and instructions to strike his camp and take all of the remaining gear to Captain Gris of the 80th. He also gave Grubbs two shillings saying it was just in case there was something that Grubbs might need. With that, he hove up his packs taking his fusil in his right hand. Grubbs gave him a salute and wished him fair-travel weather. Fogg returned the salute with his left hand and turned toward the Fort Edward road. Within fifteen minutes, he was clear of the camp. Once out of sight of the camp, he left the road and cut east until he was about one hundred and fifty to two hundred yards from the road, moving along the deer track that ran almost parallel. He moved along at the same pace as light troops and rangers moved. He would trot so many paces and then walk so many paces. He had been told that the Indians could travel all day long stopping only briefly for water.

In about an hour, he overtook one of the wagon convoys that he had seen leave just before him. They were moving slowly down the road, the escort troops strung out. Fogg hoped that for their sake there were no enemy patrols out as yet. When he came up to the Halfway Brook depot there were at least a couple of the wagon convoys sitting there. He had originally planned to stop there, but changed his mind. He did not want to be bothered with too many questions and perhaps saddled with a bunch of wagons. Fogg was not sure who was in charge of this post. He thought that it was a provincial officer, a Colonel Nichols who was in command.

Just below the Halfway Brook, he crossed the road and picked up another animal track. This time he did not use the trot but moved silently down the track, his eyes constantly scanning the ground for signs and around him for any movement or anything else tell-tale. He almost missed the moved over piece of broken branch. He stopped and took a step backwards crouching down and examining the branch. It had been pushed aside about the width of two fingers and the leaves had left the dark forest mulch exposed. Fogg could just make out the impression of the edge of a foot wearing a moccasin and it looked like it was moving in the same direction that he was. He moved down the track a little further walking crouched down. Sure enough, there was another slight impression with another partially over it, at least two people. Fogg glanced off to his left The road and the track were coming closer together as they moved south. He left the track moving off toward the west slowly climbing a small ridge that ran south. The woods were mostly hardwoods with a sprinkle of firs. As he moved along, Fogg would go slowly from one clump of firs to the next or to a large tree.

He had kept up this snail's pace for at least an hour and was making one of his periodic stops to listen when he caught just the faint sound of someone or thing moving off to his left front quarter. He immediately went immobile and slowly went all the way to ground. He was just shy of a fir tree whose branches came almost down to the ground. Slowly he inched forward until he was situated under the tree. He remained perfectly still, only his eyes moving very slowly back and forth across the landscape.

There! A slight movement in the hardwoods by a big tree. There were two men sitting close by it, one on each side watching the road. Fogg decided that he was in for a long wait unless he could inch back out and keep the tree between him and them. He decided to wait a while and see what played out. He had been there for what he estimated to be fifteen or twenty minutes when he heard sounds coming down the track. As quietly as he could and with as little movement as possible he turned his head until he could see in the direction that the sound was coming from. The two men had heard it also. There were two more men moving down the track, the one in the front occasionally looking down at the track like he was trying to read it. Fogg heard the chirp of a squirrel from the direction of the two by the tree. The two on the track froze and looked in the direction of the squirrel chirp. One of the ones by the tree raised his hand and motioned to them. They moved off over to the tree and squatted down. Fogg could not hear them but from their gestures they seemed to be indicating something back up the track in the direction they came from. The two by the tree kept indicating the road but the other two shook their heads and pointed back up the track. Finally, all four got up and moved back up the track in the direction of Halfway Brook.

Fogg waited until after they were long gone from sight and slowly made his way out from under the opposite side of the fir tree. He then remained crouched and trotted off to the south. When he had gone about two hundred or so paces he cut south-west for two hundred more and then south for three hundred. At that point, he stopped to catch his breath and listen to the forest. He could hear birds signing off in all directions. When he had rested enough and was sure that there was nothing moving in the forest, he moved off at a walk to the south-east back toward the road. He did not know why but he had the feeling that he was the object of their search. He did not know how they had gotten in front of him, perhaps they had been mounted as far as the Halfway Brook. Perhaps someone did not want him to reach Albany. Fort Edward might not be a good place to stop. He still had supplies to last at the least four days in the field, six if he rationed it. He could be in Albany in three if not two days. Once he reached the lower depots close to Albany he could commandeer a horse and if not there at the depot at the Flatts. He decided that that was his course of action. Avoid the road until he hit the falls at Cohoes. By that time, he would be way below a point where anyone would be looking for him. They were most likely looking for someone who looked like an English officer, not a provincial ranger. A couple of day's growth of beard and he would look like any one of a hundred provincials straggling down the road from the lake.

For the next day and a half he traveled parallel to the road. He slept half way up a large fir tree, sitting on a couple of branches with the upper part of his body in between two other branches. After a few minutes the owl, who occupied the other part of the tree ignored him. He was up and moving before dawn and well down the track by first light. Once he had an alarm when he heard two blue jays behind him warning all the other birds in the forest that there was a "thief" in the forest. The Rangers had told him that this was usually a good sign that there was a human moving about. They said that the Iroquois called the jay a good luck bird as he kept watch on their villages and camps. Fogg remained still until he heard all the other birds take up singing again and then he moved on. Soon, he began to recognize the landscape and knew that he was getting closer to the place where the Mohawk joined the Hudson. Within a short time, he could hear the sound of the falls in both rivers. He kept moving along through the woods until he came to the point where they started to thin out near the Mohawk. He moved along just inside of the edge, heading west toward where he could reach the ford. There were a couple of soldiers on both sides of the ford and it appeared to Fogg that they were not the least bit interested in anyone who was crossing the river. Fogg decided that boldness was the order of the day, as they, whoever they were, would not have been looking for him this far south. The English regular mentality would not have imagined a regular officer not obtaining a mount at Fort Edward or a boat ride. To imagine that he would have traveled this far on foot was unthinkable. He brushed off his clothes, took the neckerchief off of his head and fixed his round hat from its ride in his haversack. He started to reach inside his waistcoat to pull out his gorget but changed his mind. If challenged he would display it.

He back tracked a little through the edge of the wood until he could not see the sentries. He emerged from the woods and was onto the road in less than a minute. He strode down the road toward the ford looking as if he was on parade at Whitehall. One of the soldiers looked up and saw him coming toward them. They had been leaning on a rail fence that somewhat funneled the traffic into the immediate area of the ford. The one who spotted him nudged the other and they both came a little more erect. Fogg was not sure if this was a good sign or a bad one but continued on his way directly toward them. One stepped forward and, holding his firelock at the ready ,challenged him.

"You there, Doodle, where do you think you are going? Deserting are we?"

"I beg your pardon," said Fogg in his best snob officer accent, "are you speaking to me in that tone?" as he reached inside his waistcoat and withdrew the gorget letting it fall outside the hunting smock. The soldier hesitated, not sure what to do next. Fogg walked right up to within a few feet of him and demanded that he come to the position of most attention when speaking to superior officer. Now the solider was completely befuddled as this apparently was a field-grade officer who was used to getting what he demanded.

"Well, speak up Private!" demanded Fogg.

"I, uh, we, er," stammered the soldier. The other one came to his rescue, stepping smartly forward his musket held at present.

"Sir, we have been ordered to challenge all provincials coming this way due to their deserting in large numbers. From your attire we thought that you were a provincial. We had no way of determining that you were an officer, Sir." Fogg looked them both up and down like they were on inspection. He shook his head and walked around them. Finally, he gave them a carry on and went across the ford. When he got to the other side, the two there were already at the position of present and he passed without incident, returning their salute without a comment. He decided to put the gorget back and appear less like an officer and more like a Ranger. He stopped and retied the kerchief back on to his head and put his hat on over it like he had observed some of the Rangers doing. He walked past the regular camp and no one even glanced in his direction. The Rangers moved around large regular camps like the servants in a large household, the regulars ignored them. He walked up to the landing master who did not recognize him until he spoke.

"Good Lord! I did not recognize you. Where have you been?" he asked.

"I have been all the way to the French post at Carillon or Ticonderoga, if you prefer. I have just walked from the Lake George camp to here," replied Fogg.

"Walked? Did you say walked? You could have taken one of our boats down river to here from Fort Edward."

Fogg stepped up close and replied, "I think that there are people who do not want me to return down river to New York with my observations of the campaign."

"Do not fear Brother, we'll get you down river. I have some of your baggage here. Is there more?" was the landing masters reply.

"There is a small trunk over across the river at the headquarters, but it is nothing of great importance."

"We will get you set to go down river as soon as possible. I will get your trunk collected and send it along later. There is a kitchen girl across the river who fancies me. I'll put the trunk in care of Daddy. Agreed?" asked the landing master.

"Very well, it sounds good. Is there someplace I can get some sleep, undisturbed, and then change my clothes?" The landing master motioned for Fogg to follow him as he walked over to a large pile of barrels covered with a tarp. There was a wall of other barrels stacked in front of it. He walked around the stack of barrels and picked up the tarp. There was an opening underneath and he crouched down to pass through. Fogg heard the sound of a flint striker and within a minute the landing master had lit a candle lantern. They were inside a space built out of barrels, planks and canvas tarps that had a camp bed in it along with all of the other necessary items for someone to remain hidden for a couple of days.

"Just like in the old days," said the landing master, "a place for a Brother to stay for a couple of days or a couple of weeks. I'll let you sleep for however long you want. All of the arrangements will be made by the time you wake." With that, he disappeared back out through the flap. Fogg took off his accoutrement belt and smock. He flopped down on the bed, pulled a blanket over himself and fell to sleep immediately.

# Chapter 57

It was daylight when Fogg stepped out of the makeshift quarters. He had donned civilian clothes for traveling. The figure dressed in dark grey was someone you might not notice and would be hard pressed to remember if asked. He had left his fusil and hunting bag along with the rest of his field gear, in the shelter to be sent along later. He had only his dirk and pistols. His skein dubgh had been shifted to the special pocket sewn into the inside, under part of his left sleeve. This was a very old practice among highwaymen and others in a similar line of business. He had his pocket journal and a traveling pen and ink set tucked into a waterproof envelope securely in his inside coat skirt pocket.

The landing master offered him a cup of coffee, some bread, cheese and, some sausage. The boat would be ready in half an hour. It would take him down river all the way to New York. They were carrying the post and therefore had clear sailing all the way to the government landing. They would put Fogg ashore wherever he desired. Fogg wanted to know if they could run Hell's Gate to put him ashore on Long Island?

"You've seen the men running the rapids on the river? Hell's Gate will be a leisurely row for this bunch. The Coxs'n grew up on Long Island and comes from a long line of smugglers. He's run the Hell Gate both ways on many an occasion, in the dark. Why Long Island?" asked the landing master.

"No one will be interested in a traveler coming from Long Island. I can cross at the Peck's Slip ferry and be within a short distance from The Green Tree. I will need a secure place to stay until I get my packet shipped to home." The landing master nodded his head in agreement. They spent the next half hour making final arrangements for the remainder of Fogg's kit to be shipped down river. They also made arrangements for it to be taken care of should the landing operation be changed or moved. Fogg was assured by the landing master that there were plenty who were on the level and would take care of it as if it were there own.

A bateaux-man came over to the landing master's lean-to saying that the boat was ready to shove off. The landing master walked over to the pier and shook hands with Fogg, wishing him a good voyage. The crew pulled the boat out into the river and hoisted the sail. While the tide was working against them the wind was in their favor and they made good headway. When the tide changed sometime after one o'clock in the afternoon the wind was still in their favor and the boat fairly flew down the river. Their voyage was a leisurely one with the wind always at their back or from the northwest. They passed a great many vessels of all types plying the river. There were a couple of navy transports at anchor riding out the tide and unfavorable winds for going north. The smaller boats, like the sloops peculiar to the river, seemed to ignore both the wind and the tide. They would make a tack from east to west and then a long tack from west to north east. Fogg's boat was flying a royal ensign to indicate it was on His Majesty's Service. They received several salutes from various military vessels which they returned. There was a small brick hearth in the center of the boat. It was filled with sand and a brazier sat in the sand. One of the crew brewed up tea, which they laced with rum. The Coxs'n proudly told Fogg that it was very good Barbados rum by way of Long Island. It somehow missed the Customs House in New York. The rest of the crew allowed, with a very loud laugh, that it added to its flavor. Fogg toasted their health and continued prosperity. They stayed on the river all day and just before eleven o'clock PM they pulled over to the east bank.

"We're just above Kingston. We'll pull up here until it gets light. We don't want to take the chance of running into a larger vessel or any of the freebooters who frequent the river at night. Someone might have mistaken our ensign for a sign we are carrying a commodity other than the post or a King's messenger," the Coxs'n informed Fogg. They had extinguished all their lights about an hour before. Up until that time, Fogg had worked in his journal, consolidating notes and refreshing his memory. He would have a complete report for posting on the next available ship by the time he had been in New York for a day.

"Coxs'n, how far have we come?" asked Fogg in a whisper.

"We're down river from Albany about seventy-five or so English miles, maybe more like eighty what with the twists and turns in the river. Hopefully, the wind will hold and we'll make good time tomorrow. We'll have you on Long Island by tomorrow evening, Mr. Fogg, latest," was the Coxs'n's reply. Fogg pulled out his maud and wrapped up in it. The breeze was warm and gentle but damp. The slight rocking of the boat made falling asleep easy. He only awoke once when they changed the watch. Next thing he knew was the Coxs'n nudging him with his foot.

"Tea and the sun are up, Mr. Fogg. We're getting ready to get underway." Fogg opened his eyes and was not sure which sun the Coxs'n was speaking of as it was still dark or at least false dawn. Off to the east there was no hint of the sun because of the mountains. They pulled out to mid-river and hoisted the sail. The wind was not quite as strong as yesterday and a few points more to the west but it still held. It was still dark when they passed Kingston where only a few lights were showing.

In less than three hours they were in the Tappan Zee and an hour later they were off Yonkers. The Coxs'n informed Fogg that they were less than five miles from the entrance to the Bronx River. If they pushed on, they would be at the upper end of Long Island in a couple of hours. There was a tavern there where they could stop and have a meal cooked by a real cook. It was located just past Rycken's Island at the entrance to the Bowery Bay. From there, it would be a short run down to opposite Peck's Slip. Fogg agreed to the plan. On the way through to the west end of Long Island Sound he devised an alternative. His new plan was, if possible, to obtain a mount at the tavern and ride down to the Rapalje landing and cross from there. This way the boat could return either to the Hudson or coast down the east side of Manhattan. There would be no connection to Fogg or the boat having been on the Long Island shore. If asked why they were in the East River, the Coxs'n could say that they had delivered a bateaux-man, wounded at Ticonderoga, to his relatives on the North Shore of Long Island. No one would ever question such a motive or reason.

"That would be a good plan, Mr. Fogg. A cousin runs the tavern and he can get you a good mount. If anybody ever asks, he'll tell them the wounded man story. Been foxing the authorities for years in this part of the world. A good many of us have been here longer than the English, no insult intended Mr. Fogg." Fogg assured him that none was taken as he himself had been involved in some shady business when he was younger, a long time ago. *You would not believe me if I told you what and how long ago. This is not my first trip to America.*

They made landfall at the tavern's dock just before noon. The tavern keeper was boisterously happy over the arrival of his cousin. After a great deal of back slapping and gleeful banter, he bade them sit down. Calling to a black woman, who was in the back of the tavern, they served up tankards of local ale for the boat crew and the woman went off to the summer kitchen to retrieve food. The Coxs'n informed his cousin that the gentleman required a horse in order to ride down to the Breuckelen village. The tavern keeper walked to the back door and called to another unseen person. This one was a black man who was working out back.

"Amos, go to the smithy and get a good horse for this gentleman. Tell the smithy that it will be going to Breuckelen and that I'll get it back to him. Tell him that this needs to be a horse that did not wander from its home, at least a home here on the island. Do you understand all that?" The black man indicated that he did and went off on his quest. Within a half hour, he was back and the horse was tied up in the back of the tavern. Fogg offered to pay for the food and drink and give something for the horse. Neither the Coxs'n nor the tavern keeper would hear of it. Fogg thanked them and then gave them some money to be applied to the relief any widows or orphans of which they might be aware of. This they accepted saying that they knew of some who might use it.

Fogg mounted his new ride and set off down the road indicated by the tavern keeper. The road, actually no more than a wagon track, followed down along the side of the East River. It wandered inland in the places were the salt grass marshes made it too impassible. It was obvious to Fogg that it had been used for a very long time. Perhaps it was like most of the other so-called roads here in North America, an old Indian trail expanded to a road by the European settlers.

It was a leisurely ride, the solitude being broken by an occasional farmstead. The greatest amount of the ride being out in the open meadows with the occasional short trek through a stand of trees. The farmsteads on the northern section of the ride sported for the most part English-type barns, but as Fogg progressed further south the barns changed to the same Dutch style ones that he had observed on the Hudson. The Dutch had spread to southwestern Long Island very early on. The farm at the point where he could ferry over to Manhattan had been started in 1620, the same year that the religious refugees from Plymouth had landed in Massachusetts Bay. New York, then New Amsterdam was already a settled town looking to expand.

Fogg arrived at the ferry landing just before noon. There was a boat halfway across the river headed toward the Breuckelen shore. Fogg sat down, took out his pipe and proceeded to wait for the ferry. As he sat there, a couple of young boys came up to watch the ferry approach. They looked Fogg over in his London tailored suit. One commented to the other, in Dutch, that he must be an Englishman from his funny looking clothes. They got a big laugh out of that comment as did the ferryman who was standing by to receive the ferry. Fogg stood up, stretched and said in Dutch that he thought that

Dutch farm boys should have better manners than to make fun of their elders. With that the two took off, running up the road away from the landing. The ferryman made no comment but busied himself in his work. He did not want to get involved with an English gentleman who spoke Dutch like a Netherlander.

The ferry made shore and a couple of men and a woman got off and went on up the hill toward the farms. They bid good day to the ferryman in Dutch, who responded with a grunt and a tip of his hat. The ferry was a scow-type thing, big enough for a half-dozen people or a couple of men with horses. Fogg told the ferryman that the horse should go to the Rapalje farm and that the owner would pick it up in a day or two. He gave the man a shilling to cover the expense, pointing out to him that arrangements had been made with the owner for the amount. He then gave him six pence for delivering the horse to the farm. Hoisting his saddle bag and haversack, he boarded the ferry. He asked the ferryman on the boat, in Dutch, how much to make the run now. He heard the amount and paid it. As they crossed the river, the ferryman asked if he had been on Long Island on business. Fogg replied that he had indeed been on business and that he had been trying to make arrangements to buy hay and straw. The ferryman allowed as the island was a good place to do that. That was the end of their conversation as the breeze had come up and the ferry was not an easy vessel to maneuver. It took them a little longer than usual to make Peck's Slip. When they landed, Fogg shouldered his kit and set off for the Green Bay Tree Tavern. The walk was a meandering one. First west on Ferry Street to Clift, then south to Beckman's and thence west again to Gold on over to William then south, once more, to Fair. Once on Fair Street, he went straight west until he arrived at the door of the Green Bay Tree, which sat just off the Broadway.

It was now early afternoon and some of the regulars were settled in at their favorite tables. Some of them glanced up at Fogg as he entered, but most ignored him as strangers came in here all the time. Daddy Hopkins was just coming out of the kitchen area when Fogg entered. Daddy looked up and started to say something, but Fogg gave a little shake of his head and Hopkins clammed up. He delivered the two bowls he was carrying and came over to the table where Fogg had seated himself.

"What will it be Mister?" inquired Hopkins.

"I'm a tired traveler, looking for a place to lodge for a couple of days. Can you accommodate me, Mr. ...?"

"Hopkins. Yes I can accommodate you. We have a couple of rooms that we let out on a short term to gentlemen like yourself and we serve the best food in New York Town. Follow me and I'll show you to the rooms," replied Daddy, indicating that Fogg should follow him. They went across the tavern to the back of the common room and Hopkins opened a door that led to a flight of stairs to the second floor. This was a different way than they had gone previously to the Lodge room. When they arrived in a small hall that had only three doors in it, Hopkins opened one and motioned for Fogg to enter. It was a very small room with nothing in it but a bench and one other door.

"This is the changing room for the Lodge," said Hopkins, opening the other door showing Fogg the Lodge room. He then went over to the wall and pushed up the candle scones on the wall. The panel opened and Hopkins stepped inside to another set of stairs.

"Wait here a moment," he said as he disappeared. In a few seconds, there was enough light to illuminate the stairs. Fogg went up into a garret room that was completely finished and furnished. The daylight was coming in through a sky light that had a set of Roman blinds. There was carpeting on the floor and several candle sticks and lanterns.

"Before you strike a light at night, make sure the blind is closed. There is a peep hole in the panel below so you can tell if there is anyone in the changing room or not. No one uses the back stairs except 'guests' and they are all select," instructed Hopkins.

"Thank you, Brother Hopkins. I need a space to finish a report and will need passage to England on the very next vessel out of here. Preferably, a Royal Navy dispatch packet but I will take almost anything. Can you help along that line?"

"I will see what I can arrange, Brother Fogg. What news of Brother Gris? He is well I hope?"

"When last I saw him a few days ago, he was none the worse for romping through the woods and fighting the French," replied Fogg.

"That is good as he is a good man. I will bring you up some food shortly, unless you care to come down."

"I think I'll just settle in and get started on finishing my report," replied Fogg. Hopkins left and Fogg took out all of his notes and writing material, spreading them on the desk that he pulled over to underneath the skylight. By the time Hopkins came back with some food, Fogg had arranged all his notes and maps into a semblance of order and was just getting ready to start writing. Hopkins put the food on the table and asked Fogg if he minded if he, Hopkins, sat a moment. Fogg indicated that it would be his pleasure to have company.

"If it is not asking too much, Brother Fogg, what happened up there on the lakes? We have heard a few rumors here but you were there. There is a messenger of the General Abercromby here in New York who has spread some tales among the upper crust but he does not ring true to me."

Fogg was astounded, "Cunningham, here? He is still in New York? He had at least a one day start on me and the use of the transport system. Are you sure he is still here?" queried Fogg.

"Yes, I am sure. The wind has not been favorable for his departure. There is a frigate standing by to carry him to England but they are stalled by the wind," replied Hopkins.

"Daddy, you have got to get me on a ship for England as soon as possible. Is there a way for a ship to clear this port without going through the usual process?"

"Do you mean a somewhat illegal way?" asked Hopkins.

"Well, we are Brothers to the corsair," was Fogg's answer.

"Then I know just the corsair, a square and upright fellow. You can tell me your adventures some other time as I need to start making arrangements," replied Hopkins as he rose and headed for the door.

"Do you require extra money?" Fogg called after him.

"None, Brother, none! You can put something into the widows and orphans box when you get ready to depart," called Hopkins back and disappeared into the dark space that was the stairwell. Fogg finished his meal and went back to his work. By the time he had finished his report, it had been necessary to pull the skylight cover and light the candles. He sat back and looked at the document. It consisted of several pages and covered his activities from the time he left New York until his recent return. There were details regarding the great efficiency of getting the army up to the initial landing at Ticonderoga. From that point on it became apparent to Fogg that the efficiency started to decline and declined rapidly after the death of Lord Howe. As was usual with his reports to his employer Fogg not only included the facts as he observed them, but also included points that he thought were the key weak points. One of the key points that he stressed in this instance was the lack of accurate information and the consequent ignoring or misinterpretation of it by the General and his staff. He did not skip or gloss over the fact that Lord Howe was also responsible for some actions that led to very bad consequences, mainly his death. By remaining with the carrying out of a preconceived plan, the army had met with disaster. Had these plans been altered to meet the conditions found in the field, the whole affair might have turned out differently. Fogg had just finished bundling up the papers and tying them into a package when a knock came at the door. It was Daddy Hopkins returning with news of the arrangements and more food.

"You will be leaving here later tonight. A guide will take you back across to Long Island where you will be taken aboard a fast schooner that belongs to one of our Brothers. He has letters of marque so the Royal Navy won't be interested in him at all. He will deliver you to any port at home that you like as he intends to cruise off of the southeastern French ports," was Hopkins news.

"Good. I have just finished the report and am preparing it for the trip. Here is a copy of it that I would have you see to its being shipped on the same transport as the General's aide and messenger. It is not quite the same as the one I am carrying. It will be interesting to see whose hands it gets delivered to," handing Hopkins a packet.

"I will see that it gets taken care of. I will call you in a few hours. Eat your supper while it is still warm," replied Hopkins, taking the packet and once more disappearing down the stairs. Fogg sat down to eat and, when finished, he packed his gear in readiness for his departure. When he had it all packed, he stretched out on the bed to rest. He marveled at how quiet this room was. There was no sound from the tavern below or from the street even though the tavern was just off The Broadway. He got up from the bed and walked over to the closest wall and rapped on it. It was just a dull thud. He went back to the bed and stretched out once more. Where had he heard that type of sound before? As he started to drift off to sleep he still pondered the question.

## Chapter 58

Fogg awoke to a distant voice calling him.

"Wake up Brother Fogg, time to depart." Fogg slowly opened his eyes and the answer to his question upon lying down came to him.

"It is built like an icehouse, isn't it Brother Hopkins?" Hopkins stared at him for a moment, not sure what he had heard. Then he realized that Fogg was talking about the tavern.

"Yes it is. The whole upper stories are filled with sawdust. Down below in the tavern it sounds just like any other in the town. Up in the Lodge rooms and here the outside world is shut out by the effect of the sawdust between the walls. It also is warmer in the winter and cooler in the summer. No conversation leaks out of these rooms. Your guide is here, best be moving." Fogg had already commenced to putting on his boots. He slipped on his coat, shouldered his gear and they went down the stairs to the tavern below. It was dark except for the light from a couple of candles burning on one of the tables where a figure was sitting.

"This is a nephew of mine, a good lad. He will guide you over to Breuckelen and to the vessel what is tied up in a shipyard over there. He will introduce you to the Captain who is aware of your coming. Good luck Brother Fogg and God's speed," shaking Fogg's hand.

"I thank you for your hospitality, Brother Hopkins. Perhaps I will travel this way again. Put this in the widows and orphans box for me," handing Hopkins a small leather pouch that contained five sovereigns. Hopkins opened the pouch and spilled the coins into his hand, staring in disbelief. It was a small fortune that would bring relief to many widows and orphans for a while to come. Hopkins started to say something but Fogg had already disappeared out the door. Fogg and his guide made their way back down to the river, avoiding some of the streets by cutting through alleys between buildings. Their intent was to avoid, not only the watch who roamed the streets to guard against fires, but also the press gangs who prowled the streets near the waterfront. There were both Royal Navy and civilian press gangs "recruiting" to man ships. Sometimes these would meet and because the Royal Navy press gangs usually had

305

armed Marines in accompaniment, the civilian press gangs would become the "pressed". The Royal Navy had learned how to elevate the "press gang" to an art. Therefore, Fogg and his guide avoided everyone.

When they reached the quay, his guide indicated that he should hang back until the guide signaled to him. The fellow went forward, crouching low crossing the street that ran along the water. Shortly, a light was flashed from the spot where the guide had disappeared. Fogg looked both ways up and down the street making sure that no one was coming. He did not care to get embroiled in an altercation with either press gang or the watch. He darted across the street and arrived at the spot where the guide was waiting in a small boat with another man. The other fellow sat at the oars. The guide indicated to Fogg to sit in the bow while he took the tiller. They shoved off and were on their way across the East River toward Breuckelen. There was a little fog on the river, which made their crossing a little more difficult as the guide was looking for a light on the east bank that would indicate the location of the shipyard. Once the guide signaled to the oarsman to halt and they sat very quietly while another boat passed very close by them. Fogg assumed that at this time of night it was smugglers or some other similar profession that was on the river. They resumed their journey and shortly they were in close to the east shore. The guide studied the shoreline for a moment and then signaled for the oarsman to row. He turned the boat north and within a few moments Fogg spotted the double hung lantern for which they were looking. Soon the pier was visible and a man appeared near the lanterns. He called out a word to the boat and the guide answered back, both satisfied that they were who they were supposed to be.

Fogg grabbed his kit and climbed up the ladder to the pier. The guide followed him up and the boat shoved off, disappearing into the fog. The guide and the man exchanged a few words and the guide turned to Fogg, gesturing that he should follow. They were in a complex of piers and the ship they were looking for was a couple of piers over. They had to cross a set of ways to get to it. Fogg could make out the vessel, a larger, sloop -rigged one. He could see that it had at least eight gun ports and a bow chaser. He had no doubts that there was also a stern chaser in the Captain's cabin. It was neat and clean and smelled of new wood. All of the rigging on the deck level was stowed neatly and the few people on deck acted like royal Navy as opposed to privateers. Fogg was introduced to the Captain who greeted him with a friendly grip.

"Welcome aboard, Mr. Fogg. We have a small but comfortable cabin for you below. We will be underway as soon as we gain a bit more light. I need to be in the South Bay just after daybreak, if possible. By the way, I am Captain Dunn and this ship belongs to Mr. Charles Nicoll. We call it the Lord Protector and we sail under letters of marque from the Royal Governor, the Assembly and the Admiralty. You might even say that we are a legitimate corsair."

"I thank you for taking me aboard, Captain. I assume that Mr. Hopkins explained my mission?" replied Fogg.

"Yes, Daddy Hopkins explained the urgency. Rest assured you are on the right ship for your needs. We will make the crossing in jig time, days ahead of that frigate that is setting in the New York harbor waiting for the correct wind and tide. If he didn't draw so much water, he could take the shortcut we will be taking. That is, providing that he had a good pilot. The channel changes constantly, not much, just enough to fool the unwary."

"I will leave you to your preparations then," remarked Fogg. One of the men on the quarterdeck indicated that Fogg should follow him and they went below. At the foot of the ladder was a short companionway that led to a cabin on the port side. The man opened the hatch and lit the lantern from the one he was carrying. Fogg observed that the cabin had a small desk built in at one end. There was a tied up hammock, and a chair with a back. In one corner was a small built-in cabinet to hold his kit. The overhead was just high enough for him to stand erect once he had entered. All in all, it was much better than he had expected considering the business of the ship. Fogg thanked the sailor and commenced to unpack his gear. He looked around the cabin and found a small space between the overhead and one of the ship's cross timbers. He took his packet with the report and forced it up into the space. With the lantern placed on its proper hanger, the space was not visible due to being in the shadows caused by the timber. Years of experience had taught him to trust no one. The Captain could be trusted due to his obligation, but that did not vouch for the crew.

*    *    *

Their passage down the East River and into the Great South Bay was uneventful. Once into the Bay, they made good time. Their schedule included a stop at one of the small settlements that dotted the bay. They picked up one of the ship's officers and an additional cargo of kegs. Fogg watched as all came aboard, the kegs being stored in the midship hold. The officer they picked up was the first officer who had been visiting his wife and family. He was young for a first officer, but seemed like a knowledgeable fellow. He was friendly but not overly talkative or pushy.

They cleared the Great South Bay at a place called Captree and were into the Atlantic. They beat up along the outer banks of the Island that formed the Great South Bay and by evening were well into the first part of the crossing. Fogg looked forward to the trip as he had crossed on the southern route from the Azores. The entire crossing was uneventful with the exception of one incident. It was early morning at the beginning of sunrise and the day was promising to be another clear day. Fogg heard a lot of activity in the companionway and decided to go up on deck to find out what was happening. When he appeared in the ship's waist the Captain called to him to come up on the quarterdeck. Fogg quickly climbed the ladder and the Captain handed him his glass.

"Take a look there, Mr. Fogg, ..." pointing toward the starboard fore-quarter, "...about five points off the bowsprit." Fogg took the glass and aimed it toward the spot that the Captain had indicated. At first he did not see it and then it appeared again as the ship rose on the next wave. Fogg could make out the masts of a ship.

"What do you make it out to be Captain?"

"The lookout can see it clearer than we can down here. He calls it out as a Frenchman." Fogg held the glass up to his eye once more and, after looking for a moment, determined that it was coming toward them. He handed the glass back to the Captain and commented that it appeared to be headed in their direction. The Captain held the glass up to his eye and studied it for a moment.

"Damned if you are not right, Mr. Fogg. Lookout! What is that ships heading?" shouted the Captain into the rigging. It took a moment for the answer to come back from above.

"She's coming dead on to us, Captain, and she's put on more sail," shouted the lookout.

"Can you tell her cut?" shouted the Captain. Fogg could see the lookout, perched up in the top mast. He had a good-sized glass held around his neck by a lanyard. The group below waited.

"I make her to be an eighteen gun frigate and I can see her ensign. She's a Frenchie alright!" came the long awaited answer. The Captain thought for a moment, weighing the odds. Discretion being the better part of valor, he gave the order to come a quarter to port. As they made the turn, the lookout called down from above.

"Captain, there's two of them. The following one was hid by the lead one!"

The Captain brought his glass up again and exclaimed, "Damn me! Sailing Master cram on more sail. Bos'n, pipe the gun

308

crews, we might just as well be ready. Ever been in a sea battle, Mr. Fogg?"

"Once a very long time ago, Captain, a very long time ago," answered Fogg.

"Ever command a gun section?" Fogg indicated that he had and the Captain told him to take command of the forward gun. Fogg quickly went down to his cabin, grabbed his coat, his dirk and a brace of pocket pistols. Within minutes he was back on deck and at the forward gun. The gun was well serviced as the crew had everything in readiness. Now they waited.

The Captain's maneuver of going to port had proved providential in two ways. First, it had revealed the second ship and secondly, it had put the Lord Protector into a more favorable position in regards to the wind. The sloop, being the lighter and faster of the ships, had gained some distance. The elation of the crew changed when the lookout called down that the Frenchman had changed course and appeared to be running parallel to theirs. This meant that he was probably pulling a few points to port in hopes of closing the distance over a long run. Fogg calculated that they had all day to continue this race and from the appearance, the Yankee Captain was slowly but surely winning. His ship was better rigged to maneuver in adverse wind conditions and he was fresh from the yards, meaning that his hull was barnacle free and as slick as a baby's bottom. The Frenchmen had probably been to sea for some time and would not have that advantage. The Captain had the bos'n pipe down the gun crews. Fogg went back to the quarterdeck.

"Well, Mr. Fogg, looks like we have a long day on our hands. I wager that the Frenchman is attempting to pull closer by degrees as he runs almost parallel. He can't hope to come close enough to get a shot at us today. I would suspect that he is hoping that we attempt to reverse course and cut behind him when it gets dark. He will most likely have his consort drop back in case that's what we try. I would if I were him. What would you do, Mr. Fogg?"

"I would wait until dark and come ninety degrees from our present course with the intent of cutting directly in front of him. Extinguish all the lights on the ship and run silent and dark. If we happen to come too close we will have the advantage of crossing his bow and can rake his sails. If we do not come close we'll be many leagues from him come daylight. That is what I would do, Captain," replied Fogg.

"That, Mr. Fogg, is a brilliant piece of strategy. If the wind holds all day, like it should, we can accomplish it come dark. Bos'n pipe All Officers." Within minutes, all the officers were assembled in the waist of the ship. The Captain and Fogg went down to the deck level for the Captain to address them. This way they would not be so easily spied upon from the French ships, though the distance might have been too much. The Captain explained the plan and the need for utter darkness and quiet. All acknowledged and returned to their stations. Fogg admired the way this Captain ran his ship. The officers and crew had been drilled in all the necessary procedures to not only sail the ship in combat, but to also fight the ship. There was even a section trained to act as marines. This meant that just like regular warships, the sloop was equipped with fighting tops, platforms about three-quarters of the way up the masts, for the marines to fire onto the enemy deck from above. There was nothing to do now except wait out the day. With each turn of the glass, Fogg noticed that while the Frenchman dropped a little further behind, he was closing the gap between the line of their two courses.

The Captain had the cook serve the midday meal on deck as well as the evening meal. While the crews were stood down, they lingered in the vicinity of their action stations. The watches changed as normal in order to keep the action station helm watch fresh for the night run. The Captain had the sailing master reef in the topsails to cut their speed a little, so as to appear that they might just possibly make the run to pass to the rear of the French. Just before the light started to fade, the lookout reported that the second Frenchman was starting to drop back. Fogg was on the quarterdeck with the Captain when this happened.

"By the Almighty, we've got them, Mr. Fogg, we've got them!" exclaimed the Captain pacing up and down the quarterdeck.

As it grew darker they continued along their course. They continued to sail on in the dark, with no lights. The lead French had lit their stern lights and the lookout could catch glimpses of them, passing down the word through several sailors on the standing rigging so as to avoid shouting. There were no lights showing on the second Frenchman and this concerned the Captain as he could not be sure where the second ship lay. When the word was passed down that the lookout had spied a brief light from the second ship, probably a companionway hatch opened with out masking the light or perhaps a brief signal to the lead ship. Either way, it indicated that they expected or hoped that the Englishman would turn to cut behind them.

By ten o'clock it was pitch dark and the Captain passed the order to man the guns. Fogg went forward to his station and when he reached it ,he felt the ship make its turn ninety degrees to starboard. All was silent on the Protector with every eye watching out to starboard for a sign of the Frenchman as he would be coming on fast. Minutes crept by, then a quarter hour, then a half and still nothing. Fogg was still watching to starboard when one of the gun crew tapped him on the shoulder. Fogg turned and the man was pointing toward the stern of the ship. There in the distance, at what Fogg figured to be a half to three-quarters of a mile was the stern lights of the lead Frenchman steady on his original course. They all breathed a sigh of relief but maintained their silence. They sailed steadily on this course all night, only varying it by a few degrees to port to maintain their easterly heading. When daylight came, they were all alone in an ocean that had the appearance of clouding over for a rain storm. The Captain changed course to a more easterly one and they bore on for England. The remainder of the journey was quite uneventful. Despite some foul weather, they made Portsmouth in good time, a full five days short of the original estimate. Fogg thanked the Captain for his hospitality and entertainment. They shook hands and Fogg departed with the Captain's invitation to sail with them again sometime. Fogg inquired as to the location of the London stage and walked the distance to the depot. It appeared as if he had arrived at the right time as the next stage departed in less than one hour. He paid for a place inside the coach, went next door to the attached tavern and grabbed a quick meal. The horn for 'all aboard' sounded just as he finished. He went out to the coach and started to climb inside. He noticed that an elderly woman was attempting to climb up to the open air seats on the top. He stepped over to her and gently taking her by the arm, ushered her to the door of the coach.

"Take my seat, please. I'll ride on the top," Fogg told her. In spite of her protests he ushered her into the coach. He closed the door and started to climb up into the after top side seat. A young tough who had been standing there laid his hand on Fogg's arm.

"That's my seat, swell. Pick another least you want to pay extra for it." he growled at Fogg.

Fogg looked him in the eyes and retorted, "Lest you want to attempt to grow another hand, you best remove that one." The tough started to raise his other hand to strike Fogg. As he did, Fogg clapped his other hand over the top of the tough's and swung the arm that was grasped so that his hand locked onto the other man's arm. Fogg then simply bowed and locked up the man's wrist, elbow and shoulder all in one agonizing move. The tough went howling to his knees in the dirt of the roadway. Fogg whipped up his opposite knee, knocking the man under the chin. The poor fellow went out without realizing half that had happened to him. Fogg grabbed him by the collar and dragged him up against the wall of the stage depot, leaving him sitting there.  He then proceeded to climb up onto the seat.  The occupants of the stage all stared in wonderment.  The stage took off with a lurch on its eighty-something mile trip to London.

## Chapter 59

Fogg had the rear seat all to himself, as he had thrown off the probable other occupant. He checked his pocket pistols to make sure the priming was in place and then took the two holster pistols out of his bag and stuck them into the belt that supported his dirk. He guessed why the tough wanted the rear, outside coach seat. It was an old highwayman's trick that Fogg had seen many times. You put an accomplice on the coach, usually in the back where he could not be watched easily. People did not pay much attention, as it required them turning around. When the time came, he would pull up his scarf and no one would really remember what he looked like. When the coach was stopped, he would draw his pistols and cover everyone on top from behind them. Fogg settled in to wait for the holdup to happen. He figured it would not be very near Portsmouth as the highwaymen and their accomplice would most likely not be from there. It would, most likely, be closer to first stop of the stage.

They made the way station with no trouble. There was another tough looking young man there who looked over all of the passengers, especially Fogg. When he looked at Fogg, Fogg nodded his head a little and the fellow acknowledged it with a similar nod. With that, he walked over to where a horse was tied, mounted and rode off down the road in the direction the stage would take. As soon as they had changed horses and all were remounted, they proceeded on their journey. Fogg took a scarf out of his bag and wrapped it around his neck, leaving the front loop slightly slack. Sure enough, within a couple of miles of the relay station it happened. Two figures appeared in the roadway in front of the stage, one firing a pistol up in the air and calling, "Stand and deliver!" Fogg recognized the clothing of the one from the relay station. He had a pistol in each hand and was wearing a hunting sword. The other fellow, dressed all in black with a black hood completely covering his head, was obviously the boss.

"Welcome to the private roadway of Captain Lighting. All who travel it pay my toll," he announced. *What a buffoon this one is. He couldn't hold a candle to the original Captain Lighting. Hell he doesn't even sound Irish.*

"My able assistants will help lighten your load of valuables," waving toward Fogg, who had pulled the scarf up to cover his face. Some turned around to look and gasp.

"Nothing to fear folks, this will only take a minute. You there coachman, throw down your blunderbuss," called Fogg, as he pulled out the two bigger pistols. The coachman threw the gun down into the roadway. The two highwaymen had stepped over closer to the coach and Fogg jumped down off of his perch to the same side as they. He was standing back from the doors of the coach as he did not know what anyone inside would do. The one who seemed to be in charge barked at him to do his job.

"If you insist!" replied Fogg and shot him square in the left knee, knocking him completely over backwards and into the other one. The accomplice tried to gain his balance but before he could raise a pistol Fogg shot him in the same place. Dropping both pistols he drew the two pocket pistols and walked over to the two screaming and writhing would-be highwaymen on the ground, kicking away their pistols. Fogg pulled off his scarf and ordered the driver and coachman to get off the stage and help him with these two bandits. Everyone seemed stunned that Fogg, who at first appeared to be one of them, had indeed turned out to be the downfall of the pair.

"I have heard of this type of operation before. When I thought about it after we left, I decided that the man at the Portsmouth depot was a part of it. When we arrived at the relay I was twice as sure when this one," nudging the accomplice with his foot, "nodded back at me. He did not know who the other one was by sight, only by dress and action. Obviously the boss did not know him either," was Fogg's explanation. They bound up the bandits' wounds after they had searched them and trussed them up. The driver and coachman then put them into the boot and secured it. At the next relay, they left them with the caretaker. He sent his boy to fetch the local representative of the sheriff and they continued on their way. They arrived at the overnight stop just twenty minutes behind schedule. By this time tomorrow they would be in London and Fogg would have accomplished his mission.

The rest of the memories of the mission and journey slipped away. Fogg's mind came back to the present time and he let the newspaper, with all of the talk of war on the continent, slip to the floor. He picked up the letter that lay in his lap, cracked open the seal and unfolded the letter. He started to read the contents of the letter.

*"Dear Mr. Fogg,*

*Once more your King requires your services. Please attend me at your most earliest convenience at the usual place...."*

314

He did not need to read further.   The war clouds were forming around the Corsican and every Englishman was obligated to assist his country.  Some more obligated than others.

"Tantum exordium" —said the first Senator who stabbed Caesar.